Macmillan Professional Masters

MACMILLAN LAW MASTERS

Law Series Editor: Marise Cremona

Basic English Law, 2nd edition W. T. Major
Business Law Stephen Judge
Company Law, 2nd edition Janet Dine
Constitutional and Administrative Law, 2nd edition John Alder
Contract Law, 2nd edition Ewan McKendrick
Conveyancing, 2nd edition Priscilla Sarton
Criminal Law Marise Cremona
Employment Law Deborah J. Lockton
European Community Law Josephine Shaw
Family Law Kate Standley
Land Law, 2nd edition Kate Green
Landlord and Tenant Law, 2nd edition Margaret Wilkie and Godfrey Cole
Law of Trusts Patrick McLoughlin and Catherine Rendell
Legal Method Ian McLeod
Torts Alastair Mullis and Ken Oliphant

MACMILLAN BUSINESS MASTERS

Company Accounts Roger Oldcorn
Cost and Management Accounting Roger Hussey
Employee Relations Chris Brewster
Financial Management Geoffrey Knott
Management (third edition) Roger Oldcorn
Marketing Robert G. I. Maxwell
Operations Management Howard Barnett
Personnel Management (second edition) Margaret Attwood and
   Stuart Dimmock
Systems Analysis John Bingham and Garth Davies

Study Skills

Kate Williams

MACMILLAN

First published 1989 by
THE MACMILLAN PRESS LTD
Houndmills, Basingstoke, Hampshire RG21 2XS
and London
Companies and representatives
throughout the world

ISBN 0–333–48778–8

Printed in Malaysia

10 9   8   7   6
00 99 98 97 96

Contents

Foreword   vii
Acknowledgements   viii
Introduction   x

Part I   Finding Out

1 Reading   3
  1.1 How to tackle reading   4
  1.2 Reading techniques   5
  1.3 How writing is structured   7
  1.4 How writing is linked   12
  1.5 Key words   18
  1.6 How we read   25
2 Make Notes Make Sense   27
  2.1 Why make notes?   28
  2.2 Guidelines for note taking   30
  2.3 How to make branching notes   33
  2.4 Practical points for linear notes   41
  2.5 Taking notes from lectures   42
  2.6 What to do with notes   47
3 Library Research   50
  3.1 Periodicals   52
  3.2 Reference books and materials   53
  3.3 The dictionary   53
  3.4 The lending library: how books are organised   54
  3.5 How to find a book   57
  3.6 Surveying a book   60
  3.7 Keeping records   61
4 Fact and Interpretation   64
  4.1 Case Study 1: Pursuing an inquiry   64
  4.2 Case Study 2: But is it true?   80
5 Life Goes on   91
  5.1 Problems with studying   91
  5.2 Some suggestions   92
  5.3 Dos and don'ts   96

Part II   WRITING

6	**Putting Pen to Paper**	**101**
	6.1 Paragraphs	103
	6.2 Instructions	108
	6.3 Articles	110
	6.4 Letters	114
	6.5 Reports	117
7	**Essay Writing: Analysing the question and planning the answer**	**121**
	7.1 What is the question asking?	123
	7.2 How to analyse the question	124
	7.3 Types of question/Styles of answer	129
	7.4 Judgement essays	131
	7.5 Factual essays	136
8	**Writing the Essay**	**142**
	8.1 Paragraphs: structure	142
	8.2 Paragraphs: relevance	145
	8.3 Writing introductions	153
9	**Remembering**	**159**
	9.1 Case Study: Make up your mind	159
	9.2 Memorising	164
10	**Being Assessed**	**169**
	10.1 The assessment process	169
	10.2 The revision period	171
	10.3 Exams	173

Part III

11	**Reference Section**	**181**
	11.1 How to get the most from your dictionary	181
	11.2 How to check alphabetical order	183
	11.3 How to punctuate	184
	11.4 How to check your work	189
	11.5 How to interpret instructions in essays	192
	11.6 How to make up exam questions	198
	11.7 How to set out letters	200
	11.8 How to draw up a questionnaire	202
	11.9 How to carry out a survey	203
	11.10 How to draft a report	205
	11.11 How to fix an average	207
12	**Answers Section**	**209**

Index	**241**

Foreword

This book is the outcome of my realization that most students have sufficient knowledge to do well in their exams. When results are disappointing, it is because people have not made full use of that knowledge. There is a knack, or skill, to success in exams and the studies leading up to them; I have been teaching these 'study skills' for some years, and many students have contributed to my understanding of what makes study successful and enjoyable. To them, and especially to those who have allowed their work, often in an unvarnished form, to be included in this book, many thanks. Time and space are the other essential requirements for study and work at home, and for this I owe thanks to Nick, who kept first two, then three children at bay while I worked.

Acknowledgements

The author and publishers wish to thank the following who have kindly given permission for the use of copyright material.

The Associated Examining Board, The Institute of Chartered Secretaries and Administrators, University of London School Examinations Board and the University of Oxford Delegacy of Local Examinations for questions from past examination papers

Tony Buzan for Fig. 22 from *Use Your Head*, BBC Publications, 1982

Causeway Press for extracts from *Sociology: A New Approach* by M. Haralambos, 1986, 2nd edition

Child Poverty Action Group for an extract from *National Welfare Benefits Handbook*,1987

Conservative Central Office for extracts from the speech by Norman Fowler, Secretary of State for Social Services, to the Conservative Party Conference, October 1986

Daily Mail for an extract from their 3.6.87 issue

Daily Mirror for an extract from their 8.6.87 issue

Equal Opportunities Commission for material from *Women and Men in Britain*

Richard Freeman for an extract from *Mastering Study Skills*, Macmillan, 1982

The Controller of Her Majesty's Stationery Office for material from *Social Trends 17*, 1987 and *Social Trends 18*, 1988

Longman Group Ltd. for an extract from *The Making of the Welfare State* by R. J. Cootes, 1966, pp. 28–33

Macmillan Publishers Ltd. for extracts from *The Business of Communicating* by Nicki Stanton, *Pan Breakthrough*, 1986; *Employee Relations* by Chris Brewster; and *Personnel Management* by M. Attwood, *Professional Masters*, 1989

Methuen Childrens Books for an extract from '*An Old Sailor*' by A. A. Milne

National Examinations Board for Supervisory Studies for an extract from the syllabus for the Diploma in Supervisory Management

New Society for material from *New Society*, 23.1.87

The Observer for 'Great Bed Robbery' by Annabel Ferriman, *The Observer*, 1.2.87

Open University Educational Enterprises Ltd. for extracts from *Teaching Students to Learn* by G. Gibbs, Open University Press, 1981

Royal Society of Arts for an extract from R. S. A. syllabus '*Background to Business*'

Sussex Publications Ltd. for an extract from a discussion tape *Poverty and Welfare*, Sussex Tapes

Every effort has been made to trace all the copyright holders, but if any have been inadvertently overlooked the the publishers will be pleased to make the necessary arrangement at the first opportunity.

Introduction

If you are looking through this book, you must be studying, either on your own or at college. You are probably also thinking – perhaps rather glumly – about what's involved in taking on a course. It may be a good few years since you last studied and the course is probably very different to anything you did in the past.

The aim of this book is to help you to be good at studying so that you are successful and still have time for the rest of your life. The methods are intended to be practical. Everyone knows that you are supposed to 'answer the question' when you write an essay. But how? The chapters on essay writing give practical, step by step guidance.

That said, it is up to you to try out the suggestions. Studying is a skill, not a body of knowledge, and, like any other skill, you need to try out new techniques, practise them and then decide what works best for you. This means you have to take an active part in your learning.

The *Professional Master* series is designed for students working on their own. Each text is a complete guide to the subject with practical work which enables you to practise points made in the text and to assess learning without the presence of a teacher. *Professional Master* texts can stand on their own or be used as supplements to a college course. This book is designed as a companion to the course you are taking, whether your studies are vocational, such as BTEC, NEBSS, RSA; professional, such as accountancy or IPM; or academic, such as A level or GCSE. All courses demand similar study skills from you, the student. Some will place greater emphasis on certain areas; a high standard of essay writing is essential at 'A' level for example, whereas BTEC stresses project work and interdisciplinary case studies. How you use this book and which sections you find most useful depends on the demands of your course.

How to use this book

If you like, you can work your way through from Chapter 1. There's nothing wrong with that and you have to start somewhere. However, you may find it more useful to turn to a particular chapter or section when the need arises. Before you commit time to studying a chapter, be sure to overview it. Look at the headings and subheadings and look through it for the bits most relevant to you. For how to survey a book see Chapter 3 and to overview a chapter see Chapter 1.

As you look through the book, you will see that there are practical questions and tasks throughout the text. There are three kinds of question:

Self-checks

In these short questions you are asked to practise a skill to gain a practical understanding of a point made in the text. The material you need for the answer will usually be in this book, so you can do Self-checks immediately and compare your answer with my comments. Self-checks are an important part of any *Professional Master* book, but they are essential here where you are practising a skill, so:
- do try and discipline yourself to do them
- cover up the comments with a card while you are doing them so you are genuinely finding out for yourself
- don't worry if your answers do not tally exactly with mine. You may learn as much by thinking about the differences between the answers as by getting them 'right'.

Activities

These tasks usually take a little longer. You may be asked to go and do a task or find out information following on from a topic in the text. Again, the experience of doing is essential, so don't skip them. If you can't do the Activity straight away, try and make time in the next few days.

Reviews

These are at the end of a chapter or section. Their purpose is to help you to review the topic covered, and to practise, usually in a longer exercise, the approaches suggested. There will sometimes be several questions. This is so you can do one or two immediately, and then come back to the chapter at a later date to review it and practise approaches on different questions.

Your Course

Your first task is to find out as much as you can about the course you are taking. This means getting hold of a copy of the syllabus or 'course outline'. You can get this information from your tutor, the examination board or the local or college library. When you have the information read it carefully.

Here are three extracts from Course outlines to give an idea of what yours might look like.

Extract 1

9840 — ECONOMICS

AIM

. . . The aim of the syllabus is to give candidates an understanding of the basic principles of economics, together with an appreciation of the more important economic forces and institutions so that they have a broad awareness of the main economic issues which confront them and society.

OBJECTIVES

In the examinations candidates will be expected to show:

(a) knowledge and comprehension of basic economic concepts and relationships, and an ability to apply these to the analysis of economic problems:

(b) knowledge and comprehension of facts relating to economic systems and institutions, including economic problems and policies;

(c) ability to assess the relevance of economic material , to select the appropriate methods of analysis, to detect logical fallacies in arguments, and to check that conclusions drawn are consistent with given information;

(d) ability to organize and present material and arguments in a clear, concise, logical, and relevant way.

EXAMINATION STRUCTURE

Four papers are set, as follows:

9840/1 Essay Paper (3 hours, maximum mark 100)

9840/2 Multiple-choice Objective Test ($1\frac{3}{4}$ hours, maximum mark 100)

9840/3 Comprehension and Analysis Paper ($1\frac{1}{2}$ hours, 20 per cent of the total marks of the examination)

9840/0 Optional Special Paper (3 hours, maximum mark 75)

All Advanced Level candidates must take Papers 1, 2 and 3.

SYLLABUS

This syllabus incorporates the agreed Inter-Board Common Core in Advanced Level Economics.

In Paper 1, candidates must answer any five questions from a selection which includes questions on the principles of the subject and on economic institutions, problems and policies with special reference to the United Kingdom, including its membership of the European Communities, as detailed in the list of topics in sections 1–10 below.

Paper 2 consists of fifty mulitple-choice questions, each containing five alternative responses. Questions are set on the list of topics below, and approximately twice as many questions are set on each of the sections marked with an asterisk (*) as on each of the other sections.

Paper 3 consists of two compulsory questions, requiring interpretation and analysis, one presenting numerical data, the other a written passage.

Paper 0, the optional Special paper, is set on the whole syllabus for Papers 1 and 2. Candidates must answer any three questions.

All papers will presume familiarity with concepts such as: equilibrium, the marginal principle and maximization and minimization, opportunity cost, the distinction between the short run and the long run, economic efficiency and externalities.

List of Topics

1. **The Central Problem of Economic Societies**. Scarcity, choice and allocation of resources; production possibilities, the market mechanism and planning. Market failure. Private and public goods.

2. **Theory of Demand.*** Consumer behaviour; the derivation of individual and market demand curves; price, income and cross elasticities of demand. Total and marginal utility; income and substitution effects, indifference curves, consumers' surplus; joint demand; shifts in the demand schedule.

3. **Theory of Supply.*** The nature and behaviour of firms; the derivation of firm and industry supply curves; elasticity of supply. The short run; the law of variable proportions. The long run; economies and diseconomies of scale. Total, average and marginal costs. Producers' surplus.

(Extract from *syllabus A level Economics*, 1988, University of Oxford Delegacy of Local Examinations).

Extract 2

THE DIPLOMA IN SUPERVISORY MANAGEMENT

The Objectives

The objectives of the DIPLOMA COURSE are to make the Supervisor more effective by:

extending the practising supervisor's knowledge and skills of the principles and practice of Supervision in terms of:

(a) problem identification and analysis; problem solving and decision making techniques;

(b) handling change at the workplace

(c) analysing the various barriers to effective communication;
improving listening and communication skills;
introducing the Supervisor to a specialist technique, or
extending his knowledge and skills of a specialist technique
in a subject relative to his work (where appropriate two or
more techniques may be offered); increasing the Supervisor's
ability to apply his new knowledge and skills. . .

Outline of Course Content

Courses of study, which should aim to complement the student's
supervisory experience and training within the working environment,
may be developed by centres on a flexible basis. . . .

Emphasis should be placed on the need for Supervisors to recognise
and deal with change – however brought about – with the intention of
teaching the Supervisor how to analyse the problems arising and make
appropriate decisions.

Approximately 70% of the time available should be allocated to the
Practice of Supervisory Management. The balance being devoted to
the **Specialised Technique subject** which should of course relate to the
particular need of the supervisors attending the course and the kinds
of industrial or commercial activity in which they are engaged. The
aim of teaching such subjects (e.g. critical path analysis, organisation
and methods) is not to produce a practitioner in the particular subject
but to enable the student to understand the application of the technique chosen for study.

Assessing Procedure

An Assessor will be appointed by the Board to each Centre with
approval to run a Diploma course.
No formal written examinations at the end of the course are required
but each candidate will be interviewed by a panel. The Diploma will
be awarded by the Board on the recommendation of the panel which
will be based on

(a) the log book

(b) the Project report

(c) the course tutor's report

(d) performance at the interview

(e) a minimum attendance of 80%

(Extract from NEBSS schemes).

Extract 3

BACKGROUND TO BUSINESS *Stage III (Advanced)*

Aim . . .
. . . Within the context of a changing environment, Background to Business III has been developed, with the following aims:
(i) to broaden the individual's understanding of business activity;
(ii) to provide the knowledge and skills to enable the individual to become more effective in business. . . .

. . . Recommended Weighting
The number of hours recommended for the teaching of each of the five sections of the syllabus is as follows:

1. Business	31 hours
2. Technological Change	12 hours
3. Legal Aspects	6 hours
4. Economic 'Climate'	31 hours
5. Socio-Political Aspects	10 hours
	90 hours

Methods of Assessment
The methods of assessment are as follows:

One 3 hour examination which comprises:
Part I — a compulsory case study with 5–8 questions for 40% of
      the total marks   40
Part II — a choice of FOUR out of SIX structured questions
      for 15 marks each — 60% of the total marks   60
                                                100

Syllabus Topic	*Behavioural Objectives*
1. Business	At the end of each unit of work the student should be able to:
1.1 Planning	1.1.1 explain why goals or targets are necessary and the methods whereby these can be achieved to fulfil the objectives of the organization
	1.1.2 explain the difference between policy. . . strategy . . . and tactics . . .
	1.1.3 describe the place of forecasting in the planning process
	1.1.4 explain how the statement of plans is translated into budgets
1.2 Operations	1.2.1 explain the role of co-ordination as the bringing together of resources so that optimum results can be obtained to meet defined targets
	1.2.2 describe the relationships between the departments, both line and staff, within an organization
	1.2.3 explain with reference to the operational departments the importance of the concept of span of control in its various managerial situations

1.2.4 give examples to illustrate the influence of computerisa-
. tion on the operation and control of various departments
within organizations

1.2.5 give examples to explain how plans are implemented by
decision-making and the part played by human factors in
this process

1.3 Control
1.3.1 describe the general nature of formal (quantifiable) and
informal (subjective) controls in the fields of, for
example, finance, human resources and production

1.3.2 state the purpose of budgetary control and give examples
of the methods used

1.3.3 explain how resources are allocated to various areas of
activity within the organization (eg. advertising, research
and development, welfare and production)

1.3.4 describe how working capital is controlled through cash
flow, management of debtors (credit control), management of stocks

1.3.5 describe the main features of the balance sheet and show
its significance for the operation of the business

Recommended weighting 31 hours
(Extract from RSA Single Subject syllabuses)

Self-check

Study these three extracts and for each pick out:
 i) Examples of what a student needs to **know**
 ii) Examples of what a student needs to be able to **do** – where that's explicit.
See if you can add this where it's not.
iii) How this knowledge and these skills are assessed.

It's surprising how different syllabuses can be, isn't it? Some stipulate in
detail the knowledge to be gained (extract 1), and say nothing about the
skills needed to gain that knowledge and to demonstrate it in the exam.
Others stress the skills in which knowledge is demonstrated – as in
extract 3. Others, such as extract 2, give the barest outline of course
content and stress its practical nature and flexibility in responding to the
local industrial and commercial situation.

The methods of assessment vary too. The methods in these three
examples include;

Examinations which take the form of

– essays
– case studies
– analysis of data
– structured questions (short written answers)
– multiple choice objective test

Coursework which includes
- record of work
- project
Assessment by staff which includes
- tutor's repoort
- interview with a panel.

Look closely at your syllabus. Identify the *knowledge* you need to acquire, the *skills* you need to learn and how these are *assessed*.

The skills identified in the syllabus are usually only the tip of the iceberg. In most courses you will need to:

● **READ** a variety of material. How efficient are you?

Self-check

– How many questions do you have to answer in Paper 1 of Oxford A level Economics?
– What is the main point of the second paragraph of this introduction?
– What topics are covered under 'theory of Demand' in A level Economics?
– Why is this heading marked * ?

To find the answer to the third question you would have to read in detail. The others you should have found very quickly. You need to develop different ways of reading to suit your purpose. Methods for tackling the reading in your course are suggested in Chapter 1.

● **MAKE NOTES** Why do you make notes? And how do you make sense of them six months later? Chapter 2 considers these points and makes practical suggestions for notemaking.

● **WRITE** essays, case studies, assignments. Writing is a major part of any course, and Part 2 of the book is concerned with this, from lists through to planning and writing articles, letters, reports and, in detail, essays. Many of the practicalities of writing are dealt with in the reference section at the end of the book: layout of letters and reports, punctuation, using a dictionary, for example. These sections are designed for quick reference throughout your course.

● **RESEARCH A TOPIC** In many courses you are asked to carry out a piece of research or project work. You might want to interview people, use a questionnaire, do a survey and present your results, find your own material from the library.

Use the contents and index of this book to look up particular topics. The 'How To. . .' reference section gives guidelines for tackling these aspects of project work, and Chapter 3 gives step by step guidance on finding information in a library and plenty of practice.

- **MEMORIZE** things like formulae, quotations, case studies, diagrams, dates either for an exam or to make use of your knowledge in your work or studies. How good are you at memorizing? Can you improve? You may like to try some of the suggestions in Chapter 9.

- **TAKE EXAMS** and pass them! All your study skills are put to the test both in the run up to an exam and in the exam itself. You have to perform under the pressure to succeed and the pressure of time. Your reading, analysing, planning, writing and proof reading need to have become second nature by this time. Chapter 10 gives suggestions for dealing with exams and assessment.

LIFE GOES ON meanwhile! Most mature students have to fit their studies into a busy life with other commitments – home, family, job (or all three) and other interests and passtimes. You may even enjoy the odd night out! You need to be well organised to find time for everything and space to enjoy your studies. It is obviously an individual matter, but see if the suggestions in Chapter 5 work for you.

Finally
Books on study skills can make studying sound like a gruelling régime in preparation for some kind of intellectual marathon. That is not my intention. If you think something looks worth trying, try it. If it doesn't work, try another approach. What you bring to the course, your interest, experience and motivation, is more important to your success and enjoyment in studying than any technique. So enjoy it, and get started.

Part 1

Finding Out

1 Reading

You are probably quite an efficient reader most of the time. You can follow manufacturer's instructions well enough to stick kitchen units together, keep up with news items that interest you, and check quickly whether there is anything for you in a brochure before you throw it out. If you could apply these same skills to the reading you need to do in the course of your studies, you would be an efficient student too.

People often feel oppressed by the sheer volume of reading courses require and depressed at the snail's pace at which they get through it. Worse still is the feeling that they have no idea what was on the page they have just read.

The purpose of this chapter is to highlight the different ways you read and to suggest how you could use these techniques consciously to improve your reading in your studies.

Self-check

Pick up a newspaper and spend ten or fifteen minutes reading it. Read it more or less as you would normally, making sure you include the following:
  (i) Find an article that looks interesting and read it.
 (ii) Are there any jobs you could apply for?
(iii) Do you agree with the view expressed in the editorial?

How did you set about this?
(i) You probably skimmed a page or two, looking at the headlines and the first couple of lines of several articles before you made your choice – and then read it.
(ii) You didn't read every ad, did you? Your eye skips across and down the page looking for particular words which trigger your interest, and then you pay close attention for a moment or two: pay? area? responsibilities?
(iii) Did you find the editorial? This is where the paper expresses its view on matters. This is a different sort of reading again – you may find yourself agreeing, especially if this is the paper you usually read. If it's not, you may disagree, at least with part of the argument.

One thing is certain; knowing you only had fifteen minutes to do this in you did not sit down to read every word. You need to be just as economical with your time and effort in the reading you do in your studies, to reject books and articles that seem too advanced, basic or irrelevant and to choose books that suit your purpose and understanding now. Some practical points to look for in selecting books are suggested in Chapter 3, *Surveying a book*. This chapter is concerned with how to approach the reading you face now.

1.1 How to tackle reading

SQ3R is a shorthand for Survey, Question, Read, Recall, Review, the five steps in the reading process. It is a useful approach to most kinds of reading, whether a textbook, an overflowing in-tray, an article or a single passage or letter.

• **Survey** Always survey the text document critically — title, subtitle, author, date of publication, contents and index – to make sure you have taken in all the basic information. Do the chapters have summaries? If so, read them first. This is a vital first stage – don't skip it.

• **Question** You need to ask yourself questions about what you expect to find in a book to keep your reading active and to help you to concentrate. What do I want to find out from this? Has the author covered the areas she said she would? You should keep up this process of questioning while you read.

• **Read** Reading is the *third* not the first and last stage in active reading. The preliminaries are not a waste of time – you will find that you read more efficiently once you have pinpointed what you are going to read and why you are reading it. You need to vary the way you read and your reading speed.
    Scan others for a particular piece of information. You did this when you looked at the ads.
    Skim some bits for an overview. You did this when you looked at several articles before deciding which one looked most interesting.
    Identify which sections need to be read in detail. You would need to take in every detail of a job ad before deciding whether to apply.
Don't make notes while you are reading – you need to concentrate on understanding.

• **Recall** What was the text about? Can you answer the questions you set yourself at the outset? Make your notes now. Don't copy. Set out the main points as you remember them and check with the text if you are not sure. Chapter 2 gives guidance on note making.

• **Review** There are two parts to the review. First, look back over the text to make sure you can answer the questions you set yourself and haven't missed anything essential or distorted the information in the passage. A review can take the form of a quick re-run of the first four stages:

(i) Survey the whole, note the structure.
(ii) Question – remind yourself of your purpose in reading.
(iii) Read the text rapidly, skimming. Any points missed?
(iv) Recall – check your notes for gaps.

The second part of the review concerns what happens to your notes now. Do you put them away and forget about them? or review them soon, and periodically?

Self-check

Somewhere in this book you will find the answer to this question: 'How does the Dewey Decimal Library classifiction system work?' Use the SQ3R method for locating the information and reading the relevant sections. Make a written note of your answer.

How did you set about it?

Survey the book – use the contents and index for page references. Survey the pages. Read the diagram.

Question This is your purpose in reading. What do you want to find out? how much do you have to read?

Read How did you read? Scan? Skim? Detailed read? There's more on this below.

Recall Can you answer the question set? What are the main points or basic principles? Can you make brief notes or a sketch?

Review Look over the passage. Have you missed anything important? Are your notes complete? Will they make sense tomorrow? Compare your notes with the original. They will of course be different – if they're correct, that's fine.

1.2 **Reading techniques**

While you've been using this book, you will have used several different reading techniques. You vary the way you read according to why you are reading and the sort of information you are looking for. In the last Self Check you had a specific task. What reading methods did you use? You probably:

scanned the index for page references – your eye is looking for one entry only;

T

skimmed the pages – to find out how much you were going to have to read and to get an overview. This often means reading the first sentence of each paragraph to note which bits you will come back to for a second read.

read in detail the essential paragraphs – two in this case. This will be quick – you already know from your skim reading and the diagram what they are about. In fact, did you need to read in detail?

By now you should have a good sense of the variety of reading techniques you can use.

Scan to find a particular piece of information, or answer to a particular question, or when you are looking through a pile of papers to decide which one really has to be dealt with now. You run your eye down the page with one question in mind and pay no attention to anything else.

Skim to get an overview of the material you are planning to read. Read fast, to get the gist of the text and to spot relevant bits to come back to. Remember – asking yourself questions is an essential part of any reading, so read with a purpose when you skim. Ignore the detail and examples.

Read in detail only when you have to. Could you find the information by skim reading or scanning? Of course there are times when you have to read very closely, but this should be the last, not the first reading technique you use.

Read critically when you are reading material in which a view is expressed either explicitly, such as in a newspaper editorial, or implicitly, such as when various newspapers give different interpretations of the same opinion pools. What do you think?

Read for pleasure any way you like! You're not going to be examined on it, you don't have to remember it, so just enjoy it!

The following Activities and Self Checks illustrate the different reading methods you can use in your studies.

Reading Activity 1 Scanning

1. Scan the index of this book for a reference to Norman Fowler. On which page will you find an extract from his speech?
2. Turn to the appropriate page and scan the chart to find out how many boys were employed with part time day study in 1974 and 1984.

3. Scan the article on P. 182. Your sole purpose is to find out how many hospital beds have been lost in Merseyside since 1979.
4. Find the extract from the Oxford A level Economics syllabus. How many multiple choice questions are there on Paper 2?
5. How many words are you allowed to use in question (a) of the language paper on P. 175?

1.3 **How writing is structured**

To skim read effectively, you need to know where to look in a chapter, section or paragraph for the main idea. We start with paragraphs, because these are the units that make up longer passages.

Topic sentences
In your own writing, when you move on to a new idea, you start a new paragraph. In a personal letter, you probably have no difficulty knowing when this is – you've finished writing about the disastrous camping holiday and have moved on to the children's progess at school. The sentence in which the writer expresses this new or main idea is known as the 'topic sentence'.

The topic sentence is usually the first sentence in the paragraph. The author states the idea and explains, develops and illustrates it in the rest of the paragraph. The last sentence often directly picks up the idea in the topic sentence and shows how the rest of the paragraph has modified or developed it.

Self-check

Look back at the last two paragraphs. Do they follow this pattern? For each, pick out
 (i) the beginning: topic sentence
(ii) the middle: explanation, illustration
(iii) the end: linking back to the idea in the topic sentence

They do, don't they? In each case the topic sentence is the first, then comes the explanation, or illustration, and the last sentence returns to the idea in the topic sentence, not to repeat it, but to show how it has developed.

How to skim
When you skim read, look for the topic sentence of each paragraph. Since this usually comes first, read the first sentence of each paragraph.

Reading Activity 2

● Try this on the. following extract. Skim read the passage, once only, and answer the questions below it – look for the topic sentence and expect the topic sentence to be the first.

Selection The purpose of any selection interview is to choose the right person for the job in question or to select someone who shows potential for more senior posts. Interviews may not represent the ideal method of selecting staff. For one thing, you will not know whether you have selected wisely until long after the interview. The period you have to wait will depend on the job in question. The lower the level of the job, the quicker you will discover how good you were with your selection. Be clear what you are trying to achieve by the interview and how you intend to do it.

Interviewing requries many skills which only develop with practice. Be careful that you are not being subjective in your judgements; try to be *objective* wherever possible. An example may illustrate the point. If you interview a long-haired applicant, you may be put off by the length of his hair; you may associate long hair with untidiness, dirt or laziness. This is a subjective judgement – another interviewer may not be affected by hair length in the same way.

Subjective misjudgement is sometimes called the 'halo and horn' effect. This is how it works. We meet someone neatly dressed and well spoken and from this we assume that they are all things good; they will be reliable, honest, hard working, etc. We are blinded by their halo. Conversely, on meeting a roughly spoken scruffy individual we decide they will be unreliable, careless and lazy. We only see their horns. This problem needs to be overcome, since we could so easily overlook first-class candidates for vital posts because we have not been objective.

(*From Supervision: A Fresh Approach* by M. Savedra and J. Hawthorn. Macmillan Professional Masters, 1989.)

1. What is the purpose of a selection interview?
2. What mistakes might an inexperienced interviewer make?
3. Which paragraph explains the 'halo and horn' effect?

Now check your answers with mine in the Answers Section. Did you manage to answer the questions by reading only the first sentences, once?

Points to note:
1. Think and question more, read less; you'll read faster and make more sense of it as you go.
2. If you can't find an answer, or follow an argument or explanation, note the section and skim on. Come back later; by then you may have a clearer idea of what you need to know.

Reading Activity 3

• Read the passage below, and answer the question set as the heading as quickly as possible.

Who should undertake employee counselling?
The relationship between manager and subordinate often will not be amenable to the development of a counselling relationship. The manager may be concerned with his own status and thus unwilling to put himself into the subordinate's shoes. Also there may be a tendency to be protective of information which might be useful such as the employee's *real* prospects of promotion. The employee is likely to find it difficult to seek counselling from his boss. For example, disclosure of domestic problems may hamper promotion prospects.

Specialist personnel staff often take on a counselling role. They may experience fewer problems than line managers. Nevertheless the problems of trust and fear of confidentiality so far as employees are concerned will arise. For this reason, some organisations use specialist independent services staffed by professional counsellors. Even where this is done it is certain that both managers and personnel specialists will take on the role of counsellor from time to time. In order to carry this out effectively they must be trained.

We have stressed the need for professional individual counselling services, but sometimes non-professional helpers may play a very useful role. For example, in career planning, employees can assist each other to identify career and life goals and to plan ways of achieving these. In this way mutual support is possible. This has been found particularly helpful for female employees and members of ethnic minority groups who often fail to achieve their full potential through lack of confidence and skills and a tendency by employers and others to undervalue their abilities. A few employers encourage such counselling as part of equal opportunities programmes.

(From *Personnel Management* by M. Attwood, Macmillan Professional Masters, 1989.)

Is the answer:
 (i) managers?
(ii) personnel staff?
(iii) non professional staff, other workers?

Did you find the question you were supposed to answer? Always look at headings! Your answers are probably along these lines:
 (i) managers – no, in general
(ii) personnel staff – sometimes, but...
(iii) other workers – sometimes, especially...

The topic sentences give enough information for you to come away from the passage with a qualified yes/no answer to each question, but each one leaves something hanging, which is enough if you are simply overviewing the section, but if you want to pinpoint the reservation, you need to take a closer look at the passage.

Before you decide to read the passage in detail, try reading the first and last sentences only, and add this information to your preliminary answers. What do you get?

Who should undertake employee counselling?
(i) Managers – generally not – personal problems – promotion prospects
(ii) Personnel staff – sometimes, but need training
(iii) Non professional workers – sometimes useful, especially concerning equal opportunities

Here, a skim reading of the first sentences answered the questions you first set yourself, but raised others. These were answered when you read the last sentences.

Points to note
For a closer skim, try reading the first and last sentences of each paragraph. Don't let this get silly – if the paragraph is very short, or you can't see where the last sentence begins, it may be quicker to read it all. But it can be useful.

Some exceptions
1. *Journalistic writing*
The topic sentence containing the main idea is not always first. When the writer aims for a reaction from the reader – to interest, persuade, shock, involve – the topic sentence is often further into the text. This allows the writer to interest the reader in the subject with an arresting introduction

before the main point is put forward later in the first paragraph or not until the second. Sometimes the idea of the first paragraph is not stated explicitly at all – the reader is left to deduce the idea from the graphic presentation of some aspects of it. These styles are most often used in journalism and other writing which aims to entertain or persuade, but sometimes textbooks use it too

Reading Activity 4

Below are the first paragraphs of 'Computers Mean Business' by Jacquetta Megarry. As you read, ask yourself:
1. What is the purpose of the first paragraph?
   Is it successful in this?
   What is the main idea of this first paragraph?
   Is this idea contained in a topic sentence?
2. What is the main idea of the second paragraph?
   Is there a topic sentence? Which?

If the motor car industry had progressed at the same rate as computer technology since 1945, a Rolls Royce would now be as cheap as this book; more powerful than the world's fastest train; could go round the world 3000 times on a single tankful of petrol; and would be so small that you could park eight of them on this full stop.

Such profound and rapid change is not without its penalties. It has revolutionary implications for the nature and structure of industry and for our methods of conducting and organizing business – indeed, for the very fabric of our society – yet conventional methods of education and training cannot adapt fast enough to catch up with the computer revolution. For men and women who are actively involved in business, the need to get to grips with the world of computing is very urgent: the rewards of successful computerization can make the difference between a profitable future and extinction. For business students, an understanding of computer systems can make the difference between being able to choose a job and being unemployed.

(From *Computers Mean Business* by J. Megarry, Pan Breakthrough 1984 p.11)

I would say that the purpose of the first paragraph is to interest you sufficiently to read on; I did. There is clearly a main idea – that change in the computer world has been profound and rapid – but it is not stated here in so many words. This is left to the topic sentence of the second paragraph, which summarises what has gone before as well as introducing the main idea of this paragraph.

12

2. *Poor writing*

Badly organised writing is much more difficult to understand, because you don't know where to look for the main idea, and ideas are jumbled. You may become aware of this when you read your own or other students' essays but sometimes material you have to read in the course of your studies is poorly organised too. There are several activities in chapters 6 & 8 which ask you to reorganise or rewrite passages to make writing clearer and easier to understand.

1.4 How writing is linked

Markers

In speech and writing there are words which link ideas. They refer the reader back to a point already made or help you to anticipate what is coming next. It helps your understanding and the speed of your reading if you are aware of these 'markers' and use them.

Self-check

Turn back to the passage on P.9 (Who should undertake employee counselling?)
Paragraph 1: what word in the last sentence shows the reader that a general point (in the topic sentence) is being illustrated?
Paragraph 2: what does 'this' in the last sentence refer to?
Paragraph 3: why does the author use 'but' in the top sentence?

---

1. 'For example', 'such as', 'eg' are useful markers which show that what is coming next is an illustration of a point already made. Check that you have understood the point itself.
2. 'This' refers to the 'role of counsellor' which directly picks up the point in the topic sentence. If you are having difficulty in knowing what 'this', 'those,' 'it', 'they' refer to in a passage, try substituting the word or phrase these markers stand for. The passage should quickly make more sense.
3. Words like 'but' ('however', 'on the other hand', 'nevertheless') indicate that a contrasting idea is about to be put forward. So far the passage has discussed the need for specialist, trained personnel in counselling; next, in contrast, the role of the non-specialist is to be considered.

The three markers discussed here are the ones you encountered on your skim read. In your reading in the next week, make a point of noticing these linking words so your use of them becomes instinctive.

Skimming a chapter

The principles of skimming a paragraph apply equally to longer passages, sections or chapters.

- Look for the organisation of ideas and spot the topic sentence
- Use the structure of writing and note the markers.

All writing, whether long or short, has a beginning – where the main concerns or themes are outlined; a middle – where these are explained, arguments or points developed and examples discussed; and an end – where the writer shows how the points made in the middle relate to the ideas outlined in the beginning and (usually) modify them.

When you skim read a chapter, section or article, look for the main ideas in the same way as with a paragraph, and, in addition, use the conventions of chapter layout to help you.

How to skim a chapter

Remember *SQ3R*. Set yourself questions. What do you hope to get from your reading? Then:

1. Note the chapter headings and subheadings and layout of the pages. (Do you need to read the whole chapter?)

2. Look at the end of the chapter or document to see if there is a summary. If there is, read it *first*.

3. Are there any diagrams? If you understand them, they will help you understand the text more quickly.

4. Read carefully the first paragraph of the chapter (and of each section). It introduces the topics to be covered.

5. Read the first sentence of each paragraph. These will usually be the topic sentences.

6. Read the last paragraph of the section or last two or so of a chapter for the conclusion.

Remember *SQ3R*. Whatever reading strategy you use, reading is the **third** step of SQ3R. For your recall and review look back over what you have read and string together the topic sentences. This should give you a summary of the whole piece. If it is not clear, you know where to go back and look for more detail.

After this make a written note of what you have read. See Chapter 2 for how to make notes.

Self-check

Try out this method of skimming on a chapter or section of any non-fiction book. Try it with articles in newspapers and periodicals, where you have some knowledge of the subject and are looking for updating and interpretations.

Reading Activity 5

● Using this method, read the extract below and answer the questions set. They are typical of the sorts of questions you should ask yourself as you read. The paragraphs are numbered (1-10) for ease of reference and the questions correspond.

    1. i) What is the study about? Who carried it out? Where? When?
       ii) What is his definition of poverty?
      iii) What is this definition of poverty known as today?
      iv) Were his criteria for judging poverty generous?
    2. Who did Rowntree survey?
    3. What proportion lived in poverty?
    4. Was this representative of the country as a whole?
  5. & 6. Where would you look for details of what life in poverty was like at the time?
  7. & 8. What were the consequences of poverty?
    9. How many causes of 'primary poverty' were identified?
    10. Where do you look for causes of 'secondary poverty'?

2 Poverty in York 1899

1. One of the earliest systematic studies of poverty was conducted by Seebohm Rowntree in 1899 in the city of York. . . .

Rowntree calculated a minimum weekly sum of money which, in his opinion, was 'necessary to enable families to secure the necessities of a healthy life'. Those whose income fell below this sum were defined as poor. This concept of poverty is known as absolute or subsistence poverty. Rowntree admitted that it was 'on the side of stringency rather than extravagance' being 'the lowest standards which responsible experts can justify'. These experts included members of the British Medical Association who drew up a diet sheet which contained food with adequate nutritional value at the lowest possible cost. Presumably Rowntree expected the poor to be able to select and puchase cheap but highly nutritious food.

2.   Early in 1899, with the aid of an interviewer and a secretary, Rowntree began a house-to-house inquiry, extending to the whole working-class population of York. This involved 46,754 people, two-thirds of the total population. The keeping of servants was taken as the dividing line between the working classes and those of a higher social rank.

3.   Rowntree found 20,302 people living in a state of poverty. In other words, almost 28%, or two people in every seven, did not have enough food, fuel and clothing to keep them in good health. Since this was almost half of York's entire working class population, there could be no question but that the Victorian reformers had left a great deal of problems unsolved. Of those in poverty, about a third did not have enough money coming in each week to live a normal, healthy life even if they spent every penny wisely (Rowntree called this 'primary poverty'.) All the traditional Victorian 'remedies' like thrift were no use to these people. You could not be expected to save money when you did not have enough for basic essentials. The remaining two-thirds had enough income to give them the bare necessities, but they spent some portion of it unwisely. As a result, they were forced to go short on food or clothing, or both (Rowntree called this 'secondary poverty'.)

4. These figures were very close to those arrived at by Charles Booth. He found just over 30% in poverty in East London, working on roughly the same definition of poverty as Rowntree. Therefore it certainly seemed likely that almost a third of Britain's town dwellers were forced to go without some of the necessities of a civilised life. The terrible effect of this on the health and well-being of the people can be seen from the fact that a third of the men applying to join the army at this time were rejected as unfit. These conditions were not confined to the towns. A few years later, Rowntree found that agricultural labourers were even worse off.

5. What was it like living in poverty? Rowntree found that most of the families in this situation could afford nothing better than a damp, dark slum. Often one water tap supplied several houses and, in many cases, this was fixed to the wall of the W.C.! 'Midden privvies' were the general rule in the slums. In these the functions of lavatory and dustbin were combined in a brick-lined pit. Rowntree said: 'A large number of them are found inches deep in liquid filth, or so full of refuse as to reach above the cemented portions of the walls.' To make matters worse, they were often shared by several families.

6. Broken window panes were stuffed with rags or pasted over with brown paper. In the neighbourhood of these houses, the smell from dirt and bad air could be almost unbearable. This is a typical example of living conditions taken from a Sanitary Inspector's notebook: '2 rooms. In the lower one a brick floor is in holes. Fireplace without grate in bottom. Wooden floor of upper room has large holes admitting numbers of mice. Roof very defective, rain falling through on to the bed in wet weather.'

7. In these conditions, it was not surprising that one child out of every four born died before it was a year old and many of those that lived were stunted and deformed.

8. The diet of the poverty-stricken slum dwellers was often seriously deficient. Many families could afford no butcher's meat at all. Although it may have contained enough bulk to fight off the feeling

of hunger, it did not contain sufficient nourishment to keep the family in good health. Extras like clothing often had to be paid for by going short of food. One woman said: 'If there's anything extra to buy, such as a pair of boots for one of the children, me and the children goes without dinner.'

9.   Taking those whose basic incomes were insufficient, i.e. those in primary poverty, Rowntree found two main reasons for their plight. In a quarter of these cases, the chief wage-earner of the family was out of action or dead. He might be ill or disabled, too old to work or unemployed. However, in over half the families in this category, the breadwinner was in regular work. His wages were simply too low to meet his family's needs. Unskilled labourers earned roughly 18 to 21 shillings a week in York at this time, yet Rowntree estimated that at least 21s 8d was needed to keep a family with three children out of poverty. The belief that a man could always provide for his family if he was thrifty and willing to work hard was shown to be false. However hard he tried, he could not keep out of poverty if he was seriously underpaid.

10.   In the case of those whose incomes were sufficient but who failed to spend every penny wisely, i.e. those in secondary poverty, it was more difficult to give definite reasons for their poverty. Drink and gambling – in that order – were almost certainly the main causes. When father drank, the children often went supperless to bed. Rowntree deplored these vices, but suggested that men often took to drink and gambling not from weakness of character but because of the terrible conditions under which they lived. Extravagant house-keeping was another cause of unnecessary poverty. Housewives often spent unwisely through ignorance of what was the best value for money.

(From *The Making of the Welfare State* by R.J. Cootes, Longmans, London, 1966, pp.28-33.

Whole extract from *Sociology: A New Approach* by M. Haralambos, 2nd Edition, 1986, Causeway Books, P. 121-4.

You probably spent more time reading the questions than finding the answers! We'll return to the textbook introduction which needs detailed reading. The report of the study can be skim read from topic sentences. Your answers to questions 2-10 will be along these lines:

2. Who? The whole working class population of York.
3. Poverty? 28% or 2/7.
4. Representative? Yes. 30% in East London (Booth). (The last sentence rounds off this point – agricultural workers were even worse off.)

5. Details? In paragraph 5 words like 'damp, dark slum', 'liquid filth' stand out; paragraph 6 continues 'Broken window panes..' etc.
7. Consequences? 1:4 children died, many deformed; paragraph 8 continues: inadequate diet, poor health.
9. Two reasons for 'primary poverty' are given.
10. Reasons for 'secondary poverty' are given.

Self-check

From this skim read, you should have a pretty good idea of Rowntree's findings in his study of poverty. If you pick out the points from these topic sentences as a summary for your review, you will have useful notes. You probably also have a few unanswered questions

• Formulate these questions, and jot them down.

The points on which I feel I would like more information relate to the last two paragraphs;
– What did Rowntree mean by 'primary poverty'?
– What were the two main reasons he found?
– What is meant by 'secondary poverty'?
– What were the causes of it?

• Find the answers to your questions as quickly as possible. Then find the answers to mine.

A reading strategy
By now, the points made earlier about varying the way you read according to your purpose should be making more sense. You
– *skimmed* for an overview, to pick out main ideas and pinpoint bits to come back to,
– *scanned* for further references to primary and secondary poverty,
– *read in detail* the first paragraph, and these definitions when you located them.

Reading in detail
It is important in any reading to read actively; this applies as much to close reading as to skim reading. This means that you set yourself questions as you go, and notice the markers to help you anticipate what is coming next and to link with what you have already read. If you have decided to read in detail, it will be because you have looked over the passage or chapter, and know that there is a section which needs your

close attention. The first paragraph of the Rowntree extract is an example of this.

Self-check

Look back at the first paragraph of the Rowntree study. Underline (in pencil and erase later if this book is not yours) those words and phrases which you think provide the essential information on the background to the study.
Compare your version with mine in the Answers Section.

What you have now are the *key words* of the passage. Turn back to p.14. Check that these key words point to the answers to question 1.

i) The study is about poverty, carried out by <u>Rowntree</u>, in <u>York</u>, in 1899.
ii) Definition of <u>poverty</u>, a <u>minimum weekly sum</u> for 'a <u>healthy life</u>';
iii) known today as <u>absolute or subsistence</u> poverty;
iv) judged by <u>stringent standards</u>, 'the lowest standards which responsible experts can justify'.

1.5 Key words

These are words which are clear, unambiguous, and which, when you look back at them in several weeks' time, will enable you to recall the essence of the passage or chapter. They will be the basis for your notes, a permanent record of your reading.

Self-check

Look back at the rest of the Rowntree extract. Underline the key words in the text of the study. You will remember from your skim reading that the topic sentences contain the main idea, so look here first for your key words. In the next chapter you will be asked to make notes on this passage based on these key words.

Reading Activity 6

Below is an extract from 'Employee Relations' by Chris Brewster. Read it as if it had been set as coursework reading, and identify the key points and words on which you will base your notes.
Stop! Remember 'read' is the third, not the first step of *SQ3R*. **Survey** it, by skim reading the topic sentences. Set yourself a **question** to answer – the heading is useful here.
Read it carefully, and underline the key words which answer your question 'Why do people join unions?'

Recall: Notes on this will be considered in the next chapter.
Review: Have you answered the question you set yourself? Have you identified all the reasons?.

UK trade union membership in the 20th century

Year	Membership
1985	$10\frac{1}{2}$ million
1980	13 million
1975	12 million
1970	11 million
1960	10 million
1950	9 million
1940	$6\frac{1}{2}$ million
1930	5 million
1920	$8\frac{1}{2}$ million
1910	$2\frac{1}{2}$ million
1900	2 million

People will join trade unions for various reasons, some immediate and others more general. The immediate reasons might include the wish to influence a pay claim, a threat of redundancy, or some high-handed action by management. It is possible, of course, to respond to these situations by leaving employment. For most people, however, that is not a realistic option. They need a job and other jobs may not be easy to find. Furthermore most employees will have invested their time in the organisation they work for. Leaving will mean they lose seniority, their pensions may suffer, they will lose certain legal rights and so on. If leaving is not a realistic possibility, collective action through a trade union certainly is. There is much evidence that people join trade unions in increasing numbers when the economy is booming (to make sure they get their share) and in the initial stages of economic decline (for protection). But look at what happened between 1920 and 1930 in table 3: in the economic downturn of the Depression of the 1920s, membership declined even faster than jobs. This has happened too since 1980.

The more general reasons for joining a trade union will include the attitudes of colleagues at work, the influence of particular individuals, how 'acceptable' being a union member may be in a person's social group and how actively the unions are recruiting. Overall the extent of union membership is perhaps determined mostly by the attitude of government and the attitude of employers. If both are supportive, union membership will grow as it did in the late 1970s. If both are antagonistic, it will decline – as it did in the early 1980s.

Joining a trade union is easy. There are far fewer hurdles to overcome than there are in joining a golf club, for example. It is not true, as some cynical commentators suggest, that a union will take anyone who is 'warm and willing' (i.e. alive and wants to join), but unions will generally want their membership to be as large as possible within the areas they cover – and some unions claim to cover all areas. In most circumstances, a potential member will find that there is a union which is recognised by fellow workers, management and other unions as being appropriate to that particular job.

If the rules governing which union you join and restrictions on who can join are less severe than those of a golf club, we should also add that it's a lot cheaper! A few unions fix their subscriptions at a percentage of their members' salaries – the pilots' union, BALPA, does it and, pilots being as well paid as they are, that makes BALPA a wealthy union. Most unions, however, have subscriptions fixed at certain weekly or monthly sums, adjusted when the union's policy-makers agree to do so. These subscriptions are often no more than the price of a pint of beer. They are significantly lower in Britain than in the rest of Europe. This in turn means that the resources available to the unions are meagre: the services, particularly the professional services, that they can provide are limited; and the unions rely heavily on their lay officials, the unpaid representatives amongst the membership who act as shop stewards or branch officials as well as working at their paid job. We will discuss them in more detail shortly.

(From *Employee Relations* by Chris Brewster, Macmillan Professional Masters, 1989.)

The topic sentences you identified in your overview are a helpful guide to the structure of the passage and the content of each paragraph.

Paragraph 1 outlines 'various' reasons and discusses the 'immediate' reasons: what are they?
Paragraph 2 discusses 'general' reasons: what are they?
Paragraph 3 indicates how 'easy' it is to join.
Paragraph 4 is about how 'cheap' it is.

When you look for key words, be sparing – underline only those which are essential to give you a clear and unambiguous record of the points in the text.

When do you need to read in detail?
Only when you have to or want to. There are of course times when you need to read very closely, missing nothing. You need to understand every detail of an exam question, or a DHSS publication if you are trying to work out if you are entitled to a benefit, or the small print of an insurance or legal document. There are also times when you feel like reading straight through a chapter or article. These are times when your concentration is good, your motivation high and you are enjoying your reading.

Self-check

Turn to the Law question on P. 54 (Library research). Where is the actual question you have to answer?
What is the importance of the lengthy quotation?
How many views are outlined?
You should be able to answer these questions from your skim read.

The question set by the examiners is last. It makes it clear ('Do you agree with *either* of these views..') that the candidate is expected to write about two views and to make a judgement about them. The markers guide the reader to the two views; 'On the one hand... (view 1)' ... 'on the other... (view 2)..'
Now go back to the question and *read it in detail*. Read, think and read again to be sure you have understood exactly what the subject of this essay is and that you have understood the views you have been asked to comment on. (The vocabulary of this question is considered in 'How to Get the Most from your Dictionary', in the reference section.)

Reading Activity 7

Below is an extract from 'The National Welfare Benefits Handbook' by CPAG which outlines the entitlement of part time students to Supplementary Benefit. Read it carefully and decide whether Angela and David (see below) are entitled to draw benefit while they study.

If your course is part-time, the easiest way of qualifying for benefit is if you come within the '21-hour rule' (see below – note that even if your course is 21 hours or less, you will not qualify for benefit if you are classified as a 'student'). Failing that, you will have to convince the adjudication officer at the unemployment benefit office that you are able and willing to take a job. Always check that the DHSS office has sent your case to the unemployment benefit office for a final decision on your availability for work.

You may think your course is part time, but college and the DHSS say it is full time (see 'If your course is full time' above).

Studying whilst unemployed: the 21-hour rule

If you are unemployed and want to study part-time, you will be automatically treated as available for work and thus entitled to benefit if:[26]

☐ you are not classified as a 'student' (see p11 and below),

☐ the course lasts 21 hours or less a week, not counting meal breaks and unsupervised study, *and*

☐ you are prepared to give up the course immediately a suitable job comes up, *and* either

☐ for the three months immediately before the course you were getting supplementary, unemployment or sickness benefit or you were on a YTS course*, *or*

☐ in the last six months before the course you were unemployed or sick and getting the above benefits for a total of three months altogether, or you were on a YTS course*, for a total of three months, and sandwiched between these spells you were working full-time or earning too much to qualify for benefit.

* The three months on a YTS course will only count if they are after the date you first became eligible for benefit after leaving school/ college (see p10 for dates).

If your course is advanced, you will be counted as a student automatically. Advanced courses are those above A-level (see p9).

(From *National Welfare Benefits Handbook* by Child Poverty Action Group (CPAG) 1987. P.12)

Angela took 6 GCSEs in June, but didn't get all the grades she wanted. She left school after the exams and looked for a job over the summer, but without success. At the beginning of September she decided to enrol at college for a part time GCSE course to try and improve her grades in three subjects. Is she eligible for Supplementary Benefit while she studies?

David was made redundant fifteen months ago and since then he and his wife, Linda, have been applying for jobs without success. He has decided that he needs to improve his standard of education to improve his chances, so, when he saw a leaflet, 'Part time study for adults', he decided to enrol at college. Can he do this without losing benefit?

What advice would you give Angela and David? When you have decided, check your answers with mine in the Answers Section.

This is an example of where you need to read in detail. Be clear about your purpose in reading, stop, think, and read again.

Note: DHSS regulations are complex and change often, so the advice in this extract may be incomplete or out of date. If you would like up to date advice on various benefits, the CPAG Handbook, published each November, is an excellent guide. Use your library research skills to find a copy and your reading skills to find the relevant section.

Critical reading

The focus of this chapter has been on suggesting ways in which you can be more efficient in your reading. An essential skill, the essential skill, in reading is the ability to evaluate or make critical assessments of what you have read. This means being able to distinguish between fact and opinion and to make up your own mind on where you stand in relation to viewpoints you are presented with. It also means being aware of some of the techniques authors may use to persuade you to agree with them. You are most likely to come across such writing in newspapers and magazines. The articles below are example of this, but academic authors too have their points of view, and these often influence their writing.

Self-check

What is the point of view of the newspapers from which the extracts below are taken?

Extract 1

ROLL UP! Roll up! Get your miracle cure for the National Health Service. See the waiting lists vanish. Watch the nurses rush to fill the staff vacancies. The most modern and expensive treatment for all. It won't cost you more than a penny extra on your tax. It's painless. It's cheap. It has the added ingredient of compassion.

That is the Socialist spiel at this General Election. Larded with the vocabulary of caring and compassion, laced with horror stories about the NHS under the Tories, it is, indeed, the most cruel of all confidence tricks: That played on the sick by the political quack.

To be sure, the Health Service could be better. And it could be worse, as it was when the Tories took over from the Socialists eight years ago.

Forget the hucksters on the hustings. Subject the facts to cool and clinical examination.

Extract 2

The Tories claim they are building more hospitals than ever, treating more patients than ever, and spending more money than ever.

They boast of more doctors and nurses, and better pay and conditions. "We are particularly keen to attract experienced nurses back into the profession and to encourage others to take up nursing."

"We shall continue to look for new ways of helping doctors and nurses and improving health care."

They have consistently promised that the health service is secure with them.

Indeed only a few weeks ago; Mrs Thatcher insisted again: "The NHS is safe only in our hands." The facts show a very different story.

There is no mystery here! Extract 1 comes from the Daily Mail (3rd June 1987), campaigning for the re-election of the Conservative government, and extract 2 from the Daily Mirror (8th June 1987), supporting the Labour party. Notice the language of persuasion;

– overtly dismissive of opponents' views; 'watch the nurses rush...'

– the 'purple prose' by which the reader is drawn into the writer's point of view by emotional use of language; 'miracle cure', 'larded with', 'spiel', 'laced with', 'boast',.

– use of images; 'Roll up! Roll up!', suggesting fairground quackery.

– the appeal each makes to 'the facts' as if to an independent referee to settle the dispute. The use of fact in argument is considered in detail in the Case Studies in Chapter 4.

1.6 **How we read**

Most people think we read like this;

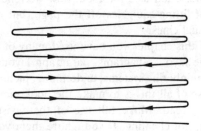

We don't. The eye can only take in information when it is still. Watch somebody, adult or child, reading. Their eyes jump along each line several times. A   slow   read   er   will   stop   many more   times   on   each   line   than an efficient reader. As a re sult   the   slow   reader   will get bored more quickly,   lose   concen   tra   tion   concen   tration   concen-tration,   reg? ress,   regress, and have to reread   several times to make any sense   of the   pass   age   ?   passage at all.

An efficient reader   will make fewer fixations,   take in more words at a time,   group words into phrases   that make sense maintain concentration   and read much better and faster.

Learn to read again
Below are two words in Tamil. Take note of them.

நீலம்   = blue   பச்சை   = green

Using this knowledge, what does the phrase below mean? A sketch is included to help you.

ஒரு நீல பந்து

Did you get it? I would not be altogether amazed if you did not. The phrase means 'a blue ball'. 'Blue' is repeated (without the ending) in the middle of the phrase and the sketch was intended to help. Although the words for 'green' and 'ball' have similarities, these are no more striking than those between 'tree' and 'treat'. It seems extraordinary that we learned to read by learning to interpret symbols, and that we expect our children to learn this way too. We even cover up the pictures to see if the child can 'really' read! How would you have done without the sketch of the ball? This exercise tell us a lot about how we read. Reading is not simply a matter of lifting squiggles off the page, but of interpreting a whole range of visual clues.

In the course of this chapter you have used many of these; headings, sub headings, page layout, diagrams, paragraph layout, print size. To this can be added numbering systems, underlining, pictures, typeface and so on. The purpose of all this is to make the book more attractive and therefore easier to read. Make full use of these visual aids; this is intelligent reading, not cheating. If you ignore them you make reading very much harder for yourself. You wouldn't read a newspaper like this – so why attempt it with your studies? It's not only slow, but inefficient. Adopt a flexible reading strategy: vary your style and pace, use visual clues to pick out the essential. Keep your time and concentration for when you really need it.

This chapter highlights the different reading techniques you use in your leisure reading and suggests how you can use them as you study. It is not, however, a rapid reading course. These can be helpful in particular circumstances, but simply being able to consume many hundreds or thousands of words per minute does not in itself make you a better reader. Woody Allen had this to say about rapid reading;

'I took a speed reading course, learning to read straight down the middle of the page, and I was able to go through *War and Peace* in 20 minutes. It's about Russia.' (Love and Death)

2 Make notes make sense

I made two sets of notes for this chapter. I made the first when I had finished drafting the last chapter, two weeks before I started work on this one. My notes looked like this:

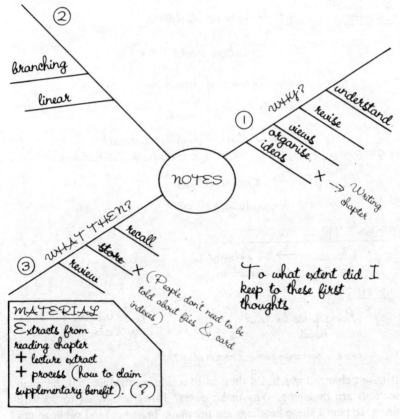

Fig. 3 *Make notes make sense. Chapter plan 1*

The second set of notes I made when I sat down to start writing. How has it changed?

Fig. 4 *Make notes make sense. Chapter plan 2*

It hasn't changed much. I'd thought of a title meanwhile, but the main sections are the same: **Why** make notes? **How?** and **What** to do with them. In plan 1 these headings are the main 'branches' and subheadings lead off them. In plan 2 these are the headings, and you can see that as I sat down to write, I was more concerned with detail – (eg: what material to use for activities?) The appearance of these notes on the page is different. Sometimes I use 'branching' notes (plan 1), sometimes linear (plan 2). Both styles of notemaking are considered in this chapter.

2.1 Why make notes?

'Now, – yes I know it's lunchtime – could you read Chapter 6 and make notes on it before the class next week? This gives a good outline, but you should do some reading around the subject as well. Go to the library and find . . .. Write up your notes from today's class and yes, thank you for reminding me, the first assignment is due in on the 10th . . .'

Does this sound at all familiar? If notemaking is set, it is often done in this incidental way. More often, tutors do not mention the need to make notes at all, and students are asked to 'read', 'prepare', 'write up', using their own judgement about how to set about it.

Self-check

How many tasks did this imaginary tutor set? What are they? Note them down as you would if you were a student in the class.

You need to identify the four tasks, note the deadline(s) and make out some order of priority to do them in. You would have to think about when you do them – find time in the library for the additional reading, time at home for reading the chapter and so on.

It all seems rather obvious, but several things can go wrong with this apparently simple process;
- you don't hear all the instructions; concentration has lapsed and dinner calls;
- you hear, but don't write the tasks down and only remember some of them;
- you write it down, but get details wrong;
- you note it all down diligently, but never look at the page again!

It may seem far fetched, but it happens, and often. It also illustrates some of the points to bear in mind when you take notes. You need to
- concentrate and listen for key points. This lecturer is rather disorganised, which doesn't help.
- write down key points even if you feel confident that you will remember them. In this example, students only have to remember a few items for a week, but people often expect their notes to make sense several weeks or months later.
- check that you have understood before you write.
- have some system for reviewing your notes.

Notes are useful:
(i) to help you make sense of what you read or hear. If you understand, you are more likely to remember.

(ii) as a permanent record of areas you have studied. You will probably find them useful for revision, whether this is immediate, for the next assignment, or longer term, for an exam.

(iii) to record a writer's or speaker's views. You can add your comments, other interpretations or detail later.

That said, you may have decided to do away with notes. If you have found that they don't help you to understand and that you never refer to them again, whatever your intentions, this may be a wise decision. If, on the other hand, you would like to make more use of notes, read on. The purpose of this chapter is to suggest guidelines and techniques which you can try out.

When to take notes

Remember *SQ3R*? Make notes as part of the *recall* and *review* stages of your reading, once you have understood the passage or chapter, and in a lecture, once you have understood a point.

2.2 **Guidelines for note taking**

There are no right and wrong methods of note taking. Since notes are only for your own use, you are the only person who has to feel satisfied with them. These guidelines are not a method; they are intended more as a checklist to consider when you assess a set of notes.

Notes should:
1. record your **source:**
   who the author, lecturer, participants are.
   where you gained the information; the book (title? page reference? which library?) article (publication and date?), venue and date (of a seminar). This information enables you to refer back later if you need to.
2. show **main ideas** clearly.
3. be **brief**. Don't try to copy down large chunks 'just in case'. Come back to it later, or ask.
4. show the **relationship** between main points and supporting points.
5. be **selective**. Avoid material that's off the point, lengthy illustrations, repetitions. If an illustration helps you understand, note it, briefly.
6. be **in your own words**. You will often use key words from the text, but be clear about the difference between this and copying out chunks of ready made phrases. This doesn't help understanding.
7. be well **spaced** on the page so you can add to them later.

Taking notes from your reading: Key words
As we saw in chapter 1 main ideas are indicated in keywords. When you have read and understood – and that means thought about the material and set questions to help your understanding – you are ready to make your notes.

Notemaking Activity 1

Turn back to the extract on 'Selection', on page 8. Make notes on it. Pick out the key words which indicate what the passage is about. Then pick out the supporting points. If you are concerned about identifying key words, go back to the passage when you have read my notes, and work backwards. When you have made your notes, read on.

You may have something like this:

('Supervision: A Fresh Approach'
by M. Savedra & J. Hawthorn)

SELECTION INTERVIEWS
  PURPOSE
    – choose right person for job
    – person w. potential
    – *what* trying to achieve?
    – *how*?

PROBLEMS
  – not always best method
    (time needed to know if choice good)

SKILLS
  – practice needed to interview
  – be objective

'Halo & horn' effect = subjective misjudgement

Fig. 5   *Notemaking Activity 1 Notes A.*

or this

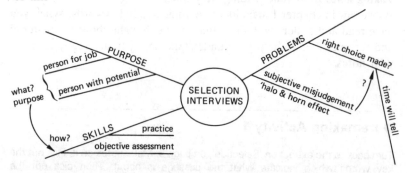

Fig. 6 *Notemaking Activity 1 Notes B.*
From 'Supervision: A Fresh Approach' by M. Savedra & J. Hawthorn, Macmillan
Professional Masters.

Which method of notemaking did you use? Whichever you used, try recasting your notes the other way. When you have done this, compare them under the headings of the 'Guidelines' above. As far as my notes are concerned, the comparison would look like this:

	Notes A	Notes B
1. Source?	Shown in both sets of notes.	
2. Main ideas clear?	Yes. Underlined. Four main headings	Yes. Three main sections
3. Brief?	A is about twice the length of B	
4. Minor points related to main ones?		Better shown here because the 'problems' mentioned in paras 1, 2, 3 are drawn together under one heading.
5. Selective?	Yes. Neither have too much detail. Do they both have enough?	
6. Own words?	In parts, Enough to show understanding?	Yes. The regrouping of 'problems' made me think more and so reword.
7. Enough space?	Some. How much do you need for a short passage?	Lots. By placing the subject in the middle of the page and spreading the 'branches' of ideas, space is automatically made.
8. Personal preferences; – attractive to look at? – easy to understand? – easy to remember?	?	?

This exercise illustrates the two methods of notemaking mentioned at the beginning of the chapter.

linear notes (Notes A)

branching notes (Notes B), sometimes referred to as 'sprays', 'spider' or 'patterned' notes.

Branching notes may not suit everyone all the time, but they do have certain advantages, and most people could profitably use them some of the time. Because branching notes may be new to you and look strange and inaccessible, the next two Activities give step by step guidance on how to make them.

2.3 How to make branching notes step by step

Notemaking Activity 2

Turn back to the extract 'Poverty in York 1899'. Let's suppose this is part of the reading set by the imaginary lecturer quoted at the beginning of the chapter. In the last chapter you read the passage – in several ways – and identified key words. At this point you are ready to make notes.

1. In the same way that you set yourself questions as you read, formulate questions so you can structure your recall and review of the passage, and write them down. Then turn to Fig. 7. This shows my questions or headings as the main 'branches'.
2. Try structuring your notes in this way. Write the subject, Rowntree's study of poverty, in the middle of a clean sheet of paper.
3. Add your questions or headings as the main branches of the topic. Allow plenty of space around each branch for detail to be added later. Now review the passage, using the key words you picked out before and add the main points to each of the headings or branches. When you have done this, turn to Fig. 8.

    You will see that I have noted some of the main points of the findings (for example that 28% or $\frac{2}{7}$ of the population were in poverty) but I haven't yet noted details such as Rowntree's definition of poverty. You will see Rowntree's distinction between 'primary' and 'secondary' poverty, but no definition or specific causes are given.
4. Now add detail from the passage, starting with the examples I've just given. When you have the detail you want, compare your notes with my completed notes, Fig. 9.

Think for a moment about the advantages of branching notes, and jot down your points. Here are some advantages you may have thought of;

- Notes are confined to one page, so it's impossible to ramble.
- You can make your notes in outline, all main points first, and then go back and add detail later without rewriting.
- You can record some sections in detail and leave others in outline, at least for the time being.
- Points are grouped together, which is a great help when it comes to writing on a topic.

34

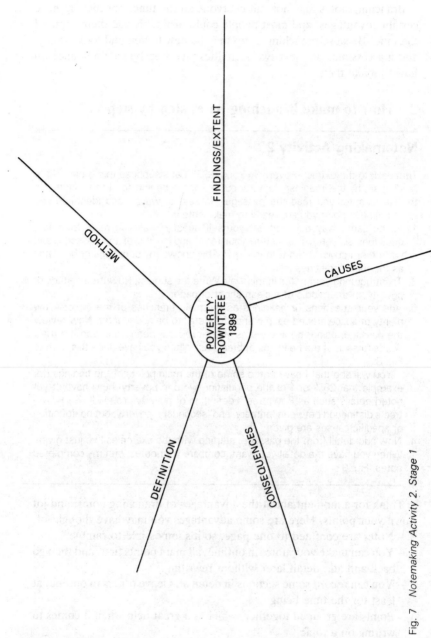

FINDINGS/EXTENT

METHOD

CAUSES

POVERTY.
ROWNTREE
1899

DEFINITION

CONSEQUENCES

Fig. 7 Notemaking Activity 2. Stage 1

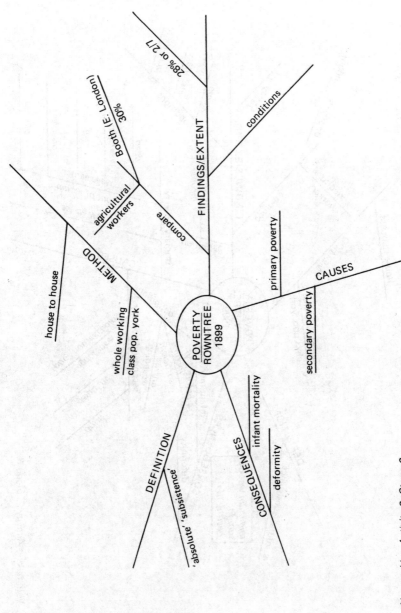

Fig. 8 Notemaking Activity 2. Stage 2

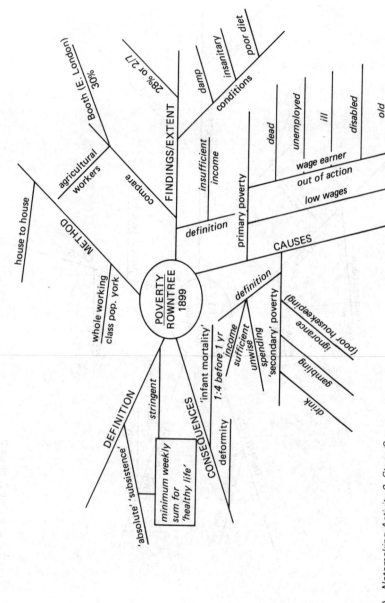

Fig. 9 Notemaking Activity 2. Stage 3

Notemaking Activity 3

This Activity uses branching notes on a longer piece of writing, such as a chapter. The extracts below are from the chapter on poverty from which the previous extract is taken. Each section has an introduction, reproduced below, followed by an account of a study or' view, such as Rowntree's study, and questions designed to help the reader to reflect on the issues raised.

• First, read the extract.

Remember, on your overview, set yourself questions to keep your reading purposeful. Try these:

1. What are the four main questions the chapter ('section') is concerned with?
2. How many subsections are there within the chapter?
3. What are the best headings to use for your note taking?

Section 6 Poverty

This section is concerned with four main questions: (1) What is poverty? (2) How is it measured? (3) What is the extent of poverty? and (4) What are the causes of poverty? These questions are closely related. For example, if two researchers use widely differing concepts or definitions of poverty they will produce very different figures on the extent of poverty. Just how different views on poverty can be is shown in the following extract.

1 Two views of poverty

During the early years of this century a group of workers are having their lunch break. The conversation moves around to poverty. . . .

2 Poverty in York 1899

One of the earliest systematic studies of poverty was conducted by Seebohm Rowntree in 1899 in the city of York. His view of poverty is similar to the one given by Jack in the previous extract. Rowntree calculated a minimum weekly sum of money which, in his opinion, was 'necessary to enable families to secure the necessities of a healthy life'. Those whose income fell below this sum were defined as poor. This concept of poverty is known as absolute or subsistence poverty. Rowntree admitted that it was 'on the side of stringency rather than extravagance' being 'the lowest standards which responsible experts can justify'. These experts included members of the British Medical Association who drew up a diet sheet which contained food with adequate nutritional value at the lowest possible cost. Presumably Rowntree expected the poor to be able to select and purchase cheap but highly nutritious food.

. . . . . .

3 Absolute vs relative poverty

Rowntree conducted two further studies of York, one in 1936 and one in 1950. They revealed a steady reduction in the extent of poverty. By 1950 only $1\frac{1}{2}$% of the population of York lived in poverty. It appeared that the days of the poor were numbered. However, Rowntree's research was based on a concept of absolute or subsistence poverty. A very different picture of the extent of poverty will result from research based on the idea of relative poverty. In terms of this view people are poor if they lack the resources to afford what is generally considered to be an acceptable standard of living and a reasonable style of life. The following extract begins with a definition of relative poverty by Peter Townsend. It then compares the results of Rowntree's 1950 study with those of a study by Abel-Smith and Townsend entitled *The Poor and the Poorest*. This was the first major study of poverty in the UK based on a concept of relative poverty. It claimed that in 1960, $7\frac{1}{2}$ million people, that is 14.2% of the population lived in poverty.

. . . . . .

4 The culture of poverty

There is a tendency for people who share similar circumstances and problems to develop a way of life which differs to some extent from that of the rest of society. In sociological terms they develop a subculture, that is certain norms, attitudes and values which are distinctive to them as a social group. A number of researchers have argued that the circumstances of poverty tend to produce a 'culture of poverty', that is a subculture shared by the poor. This idea was first introduced in the 1950s by the American anthropologist Oscar Lewis. It proved very influential forming the basis for the US government's 'war on poverty' during the 1960s. The following passage examines Lewis's ideas and their influence on the war on poverty.

. . . . . .

5 Poverty and class (1)

From a Marxist point of view poverty is the result of the so-called 'free-enterprise' capitalist system found in Western industrial society. From this viewpoint the poor are poor because the rich are rich. This state of affairs is due to the economic system which operates in the West and the class system which it produces (see Section 3, p. 64 for an outline of a Marxist view of social class). The rich and powerful owe their position to ownership of the forces of production. They own capital which they invest in private industry and, if the company is successful, are rewarded with much of the profit.

. . . . . .

6 Poverty and class (2)

It is not necessary to take a Marxist position in order to argue that the class system is the main cause of poverty. This is clear from the following extract which summarises the findings of an extensive survey conducted by Peter Townsend and published in 1979 under the title of *Poverty in the United Kingdom.*

> 'The chief conclusion of this report is that poverty is more extensive than is generally or officially believed, and has to be understood not only as an inevitable feature of severe social inequality but also as a particular consequence of actions by the rich to preserve and enhance their wealth and so deny it to others . . . The extremely unequal distribution of wealth is perhaps the single most notable feature of social conditions in the United Kingdom.'

. . . . . .

7 Poverty and the mass media

As a general rule the poor do not have a very good press. There is a tendency for the media to reinforce popular prejudices about the poor. This may well have important consequences as the following extract suggests.

(From *Sociology: A New Approach* by M. Haralambous 2nd edition 1986, Causeway Press, Section 6)

1. The authors state the concerns of the chapter in the first paragraph.
2. There are seven sections, or aspects to the topic.
3. It seems to me that you have several options over headings to use;
    i) to take the questions set at the beginning of the chapter;
    ii) to make notes on each of the 7 subsections in turn;
    iii) to identify main areas of debate and group ideas around them.

● Which approach will you take? Turn again to the authors' introductions, actively looking for headings for your notes. Write down possible headings.

---

i) The four questions seem good working headings – they were identified by the authors – but points raised under 'Culture of Poverty' (4) and 'Poverty and the Mass Media' (7) don't readily fit them. You need additional headings,

ii) This looks like hard work – more like summarizing than note taking, and you still have to identify themes from your shortened version. Notes written in this way are likely to be lengthy.

iii) This looks like a good idea. It makes you do some of your thinking first.

● Sketch out the basic structure for notes, using the headings suggested in (i) or (iii) above.
Use a whole side of paper, write the subject in the middle of the page and show the main branches or headings coming from the subject title.
   When you have done this, compare your version with Figs 10 and 11 in the Answers Section.

Your notes may resemble one of mine or be a combination of them or use different headings. There's no right or wrong here; you have to decide on headings that look useful to you. You may like to make a set of linear notes as an alternative or to compare with the branching notes. Be sure to leave plenty of space under each heading. It is harder to go back and add detail if you don't.

When you make notes in the course of your studies you usually have a particular purpose in mind; for instance, you are selecting points for a written assignment or revising a particular topic. This alone is enough to ensure that your notes will not look like anybody else's. With my two versions, the same points are noted, but grouped in different ways. Notes A takes the four questions set by the authors (as in (i) above) as the main branches or headings, and adds a fifth, 'Consequences'. Notes B follows the suggestion in (iii) above. Both versions give only the barest outline.

● Finally, complete your notes. If you are using my outlines, copy them, make any alterations you want to, and complete them, starting with the suggestions given on the dotted lines.

More Advantages of Branching Notes
You can structure your notes in several ways. This is particularly helpful in essay planning and revision.
- Notes can only occupy one side whether they cover a broad area (eg poverty) or narrow one (eg Rowntree's study).
- You have to think and link ideas, so you understand better.
- Notes have a visual pattern which often makes it easier to remember them.

2.4 **Linear notes**

Linear notes will always be many people's preferred method of making notes. The Guidelines on P. 30 apply equally to any style of notetaking. The points below are practical suggestions on how to make good linear notes.

Practical points for notemaking
1. Use lots of *headings* and *subheadings* to break up your notes into topics or sections. The headings correspond to the main 'branches' of branching notes.
2. Underline, use a *highlighter*, or different colours to draw attention to points.
3. *Indent* so that main headings are near the margin and minor points are set progressively further in.
4. Consider the various *numbering systems* you can use;
4.1 Numerals; 1, 2, 3, 4, 5.
4.2 Roman numerals;
4.2.1 large; I II III IV V
4.2.2 small; i) ii) iii) iv) v)
4.3 Letters;
4.3.1 capital; A B C D E
4.3.2 lower case; a) b) c) d) e)
    4.4 Decimal: the method used to number this list and to number the chapters and sections in this book. This system is not normally used in conjunction with other numbering systems. It is often used for long reports or studies, because cross referencing can be exact.

        When you use a numbering system, take care to be consistent, and use the same style of numbering for points of equal importance.
5. Write *one point* per line. Start a new line for each new point. This leaves some space for additions and makes your notes easier to read.
6. Use *abbreviations*. You will find you develop your own shorthand, but it's worth learning a few standard abbreviations too. In my notes on P. 212. I use these; cf, eg, →
Do you understand them?
Symbols can be useful too;
∴ therefore
∵ because
= is equal to, the same as
< less than
> more than

42

Styles of Notemaking

Notemaking Activity 4

The purpose of this Activity is to try out styles of notemaking, from the extract
'Why people join unions', (P. 19 Chapter 1).

(i) Re-read the extract.
(ii) Identify key words.
(iii) Make one set of branching notes on the passage and one set of linear notes.
When you have done this, compare your notes with mine in the Answers Section
(Figs 12 and 13.)
• Now take some time to assess for yourself the advantages and disadvantages of linear notes and branching notes and when you might want to use each.

2.5 **Taking notes from lectures**

Taking notes from lectures, discussions, conversations and meetings is
only different because the source is spoken not written. The guidelines
(P. 30) are the same, and you choose whichever combination of methods
suits you best.

Nevertheless, there are particular difficulties in taking notes from
lectures and this section considers what these are and how to deal with
them.

Self-check

Below are a number of statements about taking notes from lectures. Decide
whether each of these statements is true or false.
1. Lecturers (or seminar members) only say things once, so you only get one
   chance to note it correctly.
2. Lecturers give illustrations which are boring and irrelevant.
3. Lecturers give handouts at the end of the class, so you don't need to take
   notes.
4. You never know what's coming next, so you can't structure notes.
5. Once you've lost the thread of an argument, you've had it!
6. If you don't understand, try and write down as much as you can, so you can
   make sense of it later.
7. Take notes on what the lecturer says, not what the other students say.

---

1. Almost always *false*. Lecturers usually repeat points several times,
   first when introducing the topic, then often to illustrate it, and to

recap. In addition, lecturers often give a summary of main points at the beginning or end. It's surprising how often other seminar members repeat themselves too. Check this out. Listen carefully.

2. This could be true, but it is more often *false*. These apparent digressions serve several purposes;
   - to give you time to note down the main points;
   - to help you understand a point – in which case listen, don't write;
   - to give you a break between concentrated sections;
   - to keep you awake and/or amused!

3. *False*. If you know a lecturer gives handouts at the end of the class, discuss with the lecturer whether it would be helpful to have them at the beginning. This can help you:
   - understand, by gaining an overview;
   - concentrate, so you can identify main and minor points;
   - complete the notes your way. You may know some of the material already, but need to add detail to newer areas. The lecturer may keep handouts till the end to encourage you to take your own notes; in this case the handout acts as a checklist.

4. *True*. But try listening for the structure of the talk and you may find clues as to what to expect next. Speech depends more heavily than text on markers, and by being aware of them you can anticipate what is coming next, wait for a recap, pick out examples and so on. Some examples of markers were given on P. 12 (Chapter 1). Here are some others;
   - 'Firstly', 'I'll start with . . .', 'My next point is . . .', 'Finally' . . . These markers suggest some sort of list of items, and indicate where you are within the list.
   - Often a speaker rephrases a point; listen for words like 'in other words . . .', 'that is to say', This gives you the chance to work out what the point was if you missed it the first time.
   - 'So', 'therefore', 'thus', 'so we see', 'since'. These words tell you that the point you have just heard (or missed) has a consequence; again, you may be able to work backwards to the point itself.

5. If you lose the line of a complex argument or explanation you may have problems. But before you despair, try listening for markers or asking questions. This sounds obvious, and it's not always possible, but if you do it you can be sure that you are doing not only yourself, but the whole class a favour. It has already been stressed that formulating questions is an important part of making sense of what you are learning. In class you have the bonus of the lecturer answering them.

6. *False*. Except for formulae and specific references, writing is rarely a substitute for understanding. Keep listening – as in 4 and 5.

7. *False*. To ignore or discount the views and experiences of other students is a great waste. Some may have considerable experience of an area of work from which you can learn. You can clarify – and change – your own views through discussion with others. Don't be intimidated by your fellow students, though. Mature students often underrate their own experience and abilities and immediately assume that everyone else is cleverer, quicker or more articulate.

Try out these points about listening in your lectures and seminars, and even when you listen to the radio or TV. Listening to a tape is good practice – you can stop and replay it. The Activities here are a poor substitute for attentive listening.

Notemaking Activity 5

1. Listen to the weather forecast. What is the forecast for your area, Scotland and the South East? a) today? b) tomorrow?
2. Listen to the news on Radio 4 or watch a BBC or ITV news programme (or both) and make written notes.
   a) What are the headline news items?
   b) Are these all developed in greater detail in the programme? Add detail to the headlines you have noted.
   c) What news items are included in the programme which did not appear in the headlines?
   d) Are the closing news items identical to the opening ones?
   Did you leave enough space for the full story when you noted the headlines? With luck, the closing headlines will allow you to check points you missed.

Notemaking Activity 6

Below is a verbatim transcript of a taped discussion between two sociologists. Make notes on it as if it was a recording of a lecture you missed. Before you start, look back to the 'Guidelines' on P. 30 and the points about taking notes from lectures above.

Presenter:
  This discussion is between Professor Peter Townsend and David Bull, both of the Department of Social Administration at the University of Bristol. Their subject is explanations and trends of poverty in Britain. David Bull.
DB We shall try to approach this complex subject of poverty by taking briefly three approaches. First of all, looking at definitions and meanings; secondly, discussing a little about trends and thirdly,

going into explanations. Now, on the question of meanings and definitions students will always be inclined to go back into the late nineteenth century with the definition of Seebohm Rowntree and if you refer to Chapter 1 of Robert Holman's book you'll see a number of definitions that go back in that way. But Peter Townsend has said more than most about why we should not be satisfied in the later part of the twentieth century with the definition that Rowntree advanced almost a hundred years ago. Peter, do you want to say more about the inadequacies of Rowntree's definition for us today?

PT I think we should recognise that he had a very illuminated approach. He seized on a very good idea. There were nutritionists at work, and you must remember that in the late nineteenth century they hadn't yet discovered a lot of nutritional elements like vitamins but they had discovered the importance of calories and protein in the human diet and some of them were estimating how many calories an adult male and woman, er female, required. And he seized on the idea of translating the minimum requirement of calories and protein into market goods and then into cost. And this formed what he regarded as a scientific basis for the definition of poverty. But the problem was that he gave food and physical subsistence such domination in this definition of poverty – that you required an income to acquire the physical necessities of life – that he might have been treating human beings almost as Robinson Crusoes, as if they didn't belong to a society and I think we've inherited a rather grudging and a very bare approach which is not much beyond hunger or starvation as an interpretation of poverty. But I think we need to recognise that people live in a society, they're members of families, they are parents, they are brothers and sisters, they are neighbours, they are workmates, citizens with obligations to one another which they recognise as compelling them to buy things and I think if you move across from a basically physical approach to the definition of poverty to a more social one, that's really what my work and I think what a number of other people are writing about too.

DB Yes, I suppose the key adjectives that you used there for me were 'scientific', 'minimum' and 'physical'. We have to remember that Rowntree was a scientist and working as you say on the work of other scientists, notably nutritionists. 'Minimum'; he was trying to prove how much poverty there was and to shock the attitudes of the late Victorians, so that if his standards had been at all lax he would easily be jumped upon. So you can say even by those very minimum standards there was still a lot of poverty which was probably important at that time.

PT Yes, he had a great struggle, didn't he, at the time. It's very much an echo today. He and others were debating politically how much people could get out of poverty by their own efforts and how much they were poor for no reason or fault on their part.

DB Quite.

PT And we've still got that debate today of course.

DB Yes, and that's why it was so important that he had even by these very frugal standards which I've adopted, there is still so much poverty. But your third adjective that you used was 'physical'. Rowntree said, if I may quote, 'Nothing must be bought but that which is absolutely necessary for the maintenance of physical health'. And as you say, physical definitions are not good enough. We must have social definitions.

PT Let me give an illustration of that. If parents have to buy instruments, school instruments for their children at school, or they have to buy sports kits, or they have to fork out some money for a school outing, all these things they feel are necessary in order for their children to be treated the same as other children at school. And quite often we experience cases of parents and particularly mothers going without a midday meal in order to finance those things. Now people themselves feel these obligations to spend money on their children and that's I think an illustration of what we mean by moving across to a more social recognition of need. . . . . . .

(Extract from *Poverty and Welfare* SY12, speakers, Professor Peter Townsend and David Bull, one of a series of pre-recorded educational discussions on Sussex Tapes, reproduced with permission of Sussex Publications Ltd.)

● Before you look at my notes in the Answers Section (Fig. 14), give yours a critical look in the light of the points in the 'guidelines'.

1. Have you recorded your source? Who are the speakers? Where are they based?
2. What main topics will be discussed in the lecture? Under which of the headings does this extract come? Have you noted the main points of this section?
3. Are your notes brief? No more than one side, well spaced.
4. Are minor points shown in relation to the main points they support?
5. Have you been selective? Only essential points and illustrations that clarify the point for you.
6. Have you used your own words where possible?
7. Have you left space to add points later?

You may also like to look back to the true/false comments about lectures on P.42–4. This extract illustrates a number of these points; these gave a clear indication of the headings they were going to use, repeated and stressed points clearly, gave useful illustrations to help the listener. The style of their speech was informal, relaxed and slow – far slower than you read the passage. Intonations of speech help you in listening as paragraphs and punctuation do in writing. In the transcript you haven't much of either. Someone listening to this tape would have plenty of time to make short, clear notes.

2.6 What do you do with notes?

What do you really do with notes you make? Stop and think for a moment. Be honest!
What are the possibilities?
– Use them as a basis for a written assignment?
– Use them to check a subject before the next lecture or study period?
– Rewrite them?
– Use them for end of year revision?
– Wait till they get tatty and throw them away?
– Never look at them again?
Most people say they intend to use them for revision. Some studies have found that most students do not even look at them again. On the other hand, many students do use their notes at several points after they have made them. At which point along the spectrum do you come? Is this where you want to be?

These questions matter because if you don't refer to your notes again, they serve a completely different purpose to notes taken by somebody who checks over them regularly. The former takes notes to help understanding, and having understood, has no further use for them. If this describes you, advice about reviewing notes is pointless and even worrying – unless you would like to make more use of your notes and can't because you can't understand them three months later. This section looks at uses for notes after you have made them.

Review
The 'Review' stage of *SQ3R* is a reminder to do just this. Many writers on study skills urge regular reviews of notes and material. Tony Buzan shows in the form of a graph (below) the difference between recall of material when it is regularly reviewed and when it isn't.

Fig. 15 **Graph showing how properly spaced review can keep recall constantly high.**

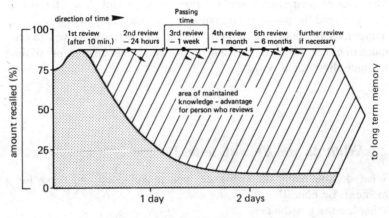

From *Use your Head* by Tony Buzan, BBC Publications, 1982.

Self-check

What is the relevance of this graph to you? Note the reviews Buzan suggests and comment on whether you think they are a) a good idea b) practicable.

1st review: after 10 minutes. A quick review of material covered to make sure you have understood. Try to identify bits you haven't.

2nd review: after 24 hours. Some students check over their notes to rewrite (always rewrite shorter), or pick out points with a highlighting pen; others don't. If you think this would help you – and it need not take long – think about finding time to do it.

3rd review: after one week. Ditto.

4th review: after one month. The volume of notes to review will be beginning to mount up. One approach is to rewrite, telescoping your original notes into subheadings, cutting detail and making links as you go. The notes on 'poverty' are an example of how a subject on which you made detailed notes (Rowntree's study) can be telescoped within a broader subject area. Again, think about scheduling this review. You may need to set the time and work involved against the prospect of revising a year's work for an end of year exam.

5th review: after 6 months. This may be the final run up to an exam. If you have reviewed regularly, much of the horror will be taken out of the final revision period. If you are familiar with the material to be memorized, you can concentrate on new angles and analysis.

You need to decide for yourself how to use your notes. As with styles of notetaking, try out the suggestions and work out a method that suits you.

3 Library Research

Before you start to work through this chapter, survey it. Find out what information it offers and look at the practical work it suggests. Ask yourself which sections look as if they will be immediately helpful to you and which ones you will skip, at least for the time being. Look at the diagrams. If you understand them, you can probably skip some of the text.

Finding out – your resources

In any course of study you will need to find out information. Often this will be practical, first hand information, particularly in project work. You may be referred to particular sources – a person, a book, a local firm – or you may be left very much on your own to decide how to set about your research. The reference section of this book offers practical advice on such things as setting out a letter or report correctly and how to formulate questions for an interview.

This chapter is concerned with how to make the best use of a library. You may want to use one to find books and magazines on your subject or only to find out the addresses of local firms for your project work. Whatever use you think you might make of a library, it is well worth spending time in the first weeks of your studies before work begins to pile up, getting to know the college library or local public library and how it works.

This chapter aims to:
- indicate what sorts of information you can expect to find in a library, and how a library works
- enable you to assess your skills in finding out information
- give you lots of practice, if you need it, in these research skills.

Self-check

What uses have you made of libraries in the past?
Take a few minutes to list them.

People go to libraries for all sorts of reasons. Your list may include some of these:

to choose books to read for pleasure
to take out books for children
to look at the job ads
to consult publications such as Which? before buying something
to borrow records or tapes
to look at the small ads or to advertise something
to use for private study
to look up information and use books in the course of your studies

The first and last of these are the uses most people would consider to be the main uses of a library but libraries offer a lot more.

Research activity 1

Find your way around the library
Go to your library for this activity, and answer these questions as you walk around it.

1. Has the library got a plan of its layout? If it has this should help with the other questions.
2. How many floors does the library take up? What's on each floor?
3. Find the reference section. Locate the dictionaries.
4. Is there a special collection of books in the library? If so, on what subject?
5. Is there a special display of books and/or pictures on at present?
6. Where are the current newspapers and periodicals kept?
7. Can you borrow records, tapes and software?
8. Can you use these in the library?
9. Does the library stock and/or display information on welfare rights, what's on locally and courses at local colleges?
10. Does the library stock games for adults (e.g. chess) and children (e.g. puzzles)?
11. Does the library subscribe to Prestel, Ceefax, or Oracle?
12. What kind of catalogue system does the library have; card, book or microfiche?
13. Can you get refreshments in the building?
14. What are the opening hours of the library?

The range of materials and services offered by a library is often surprising. I did not know that my local library stocked games for both adults and children and I was impressed by the comprehensive nature of the welfare rights and what's on information on display. The college library has a good range of software and tapes which can be used in study carrels. In both I was impressed by how friendly and helpful the library staff are. They clearly see their job as one of helping people not simply maintaining the stock.

In addition to other materials, all libraries will have periodicals (or magazines), a reference section, a lending library with fiction and non-fiction sections.

3.1 Periodicals

The term 'periodical' is used to cover all magazines, whether they are published weekly, monthly, quarterly or annually. Some cater for specialist interests; others for the general reader.

Research activity 2

How many periodicals does your library stock? Ask the librarian if you can see a list. Which ones do you think you might find interesting? Which ones might be useful?

Periodicals are useful in your studies and (if you choose the right ones) interesting. Several periodicals may carry articles on the same subject but give differing interpretations of events and issues. It is therefore helpful, when you are forming an opinion, to look at several periodicals. Periodicals are also useful for updating knowledge. Even the most recently published book will have been written at least a year earlier whereas periodicals can report on new developments week by week.

Research activity 3

Look at the periodicals in your library. To give your browsing a purpose, try and answer these questions as you go;
1. Does your library stock any specialist trade journals? Which? Are any relevant to your field of work or study?
2. Have a look at 'The Listener'. Use the contents page to find an article that looks interesting. If it is based on a radio broadcast, turn to the Radio Times to find out what is being broadcast at the same time this week.
3. Which periodicals might you turn to for comment on current social and political issues?

3.2 **Reference books and materials**

The library keeps a considerable stock of books and materials, often taking up a whole floor, in a reference section, so that they are always available for consultation. These include popular textbooks as well as handbooks and source material. This Activity is designed to take you to many of the standard reference sources.

Research activity 4

Try and answer these questions, using the reference section of the library. If you can't think where to look, I suggest sources in the Answers Section – but do try and find your own sources first if you can.
1. Which model of Ansaphone is recommended as the current 'Best Buy' in *Which?* magazine?
2. What train could you catch from London to Nottingham on a Tuesday morning, to arrive before 10.30?
3. How many ways of saying 'fool' (in English) can you find?
4. What qualifications would you need if you wanted to read Law at
   a) the Polytechnic of Central London
   b) University of Manchester?
5. From which languages and cultures do the following words originate: star; liberty; freedom; commuter; town; homosexual?
6. How has the use of private medical insurance changed since 1966?
7. How many people are employed by Boots Co PLC?
8. What symbols for correcting proofs do printers use to indicate i) a change to lower case letters ii) no new paragraph where one had been wrongly inserted?
9. What do these abbreviations, often found in textbooks mean: viz. ibid. sic?

Now check your sources and answers with mine in the Answers Section.

3.3 **The most useful reference book – the dictionary**

What do you use a dictionary for? To check the spelling of a word? To find out the meaning of a word? You probably already use a dictionary in your studies, at home, at work. The purpose of this section is to indicate a wider range of the dictionary's uses.

Which dictionary?

You need to have a good dictionary. The library will probably have the Oxford Dictionary in 12 volumes, or the Shorter Oxford Dictionary in two large volumes. Look up a word in these from time to time – they give lots of examples of usage, and show how the meanings of words have evolved over the centuries (see answer to Research Activity 4 Qu. 5). As a desk top companion, however, you should have one of these: The Concise Oxford Dictionary (or Pocket Oxford), Chambers or Cassells. Two dictionaries which are particularly useful if English is your second language are: Oxford Advanced Learner's Dictionary and Longman's Dictionary of Contemporary English.

Why use a dictionary?
Consider this essay title, from an 'A' level Law paper.
'On one view judges are seen as picking their way through dusty old volumes of law reports and loyally following the precedents without too much regard for the justice of the case. On another, they are seen as paying lip service to the system and "loyally" following all the precedents they agree with; those they do not agree with are distinguished on spurious grounds or just ignored.' (Smith and Bailey). Do you agree with either of these views of judicial precedent?
(Law A level, Oxford, May 86)
How can a dictionary help you to make sense of this question?

Self-check

Re-read the question, and use the dictionary to check the following:
1. any words whose meaning you are unclear of
2. any idiomatic expressions you used
3. any word whose pronunciation you are unsure of
4. a familiar word used in an unfamiliar way
5. a word which means different things depending on which part of speech it is
6. three words sharing the same Latin root.
For detailed comments on this exercise, see 'How to get the most from your dictionary' in the reference section.

3.4 The Lending Library

The lending library is what most of us first think of when we refer to 'libraries' – a place with books on every subject from hang gliding, to organization theory, to the history of reggae, with fiction and non-fiction sections. If you know how a library is organised, turn to Research Activity 5 on P. 57 to check your ability to find books quickly and easily. If not, read on.

How books are organized
Books are arranged systematically in a library.
Fiction is usually arranged in alphabetical order according to the author's surname. (For more on alphabetical order, see reference section). Some

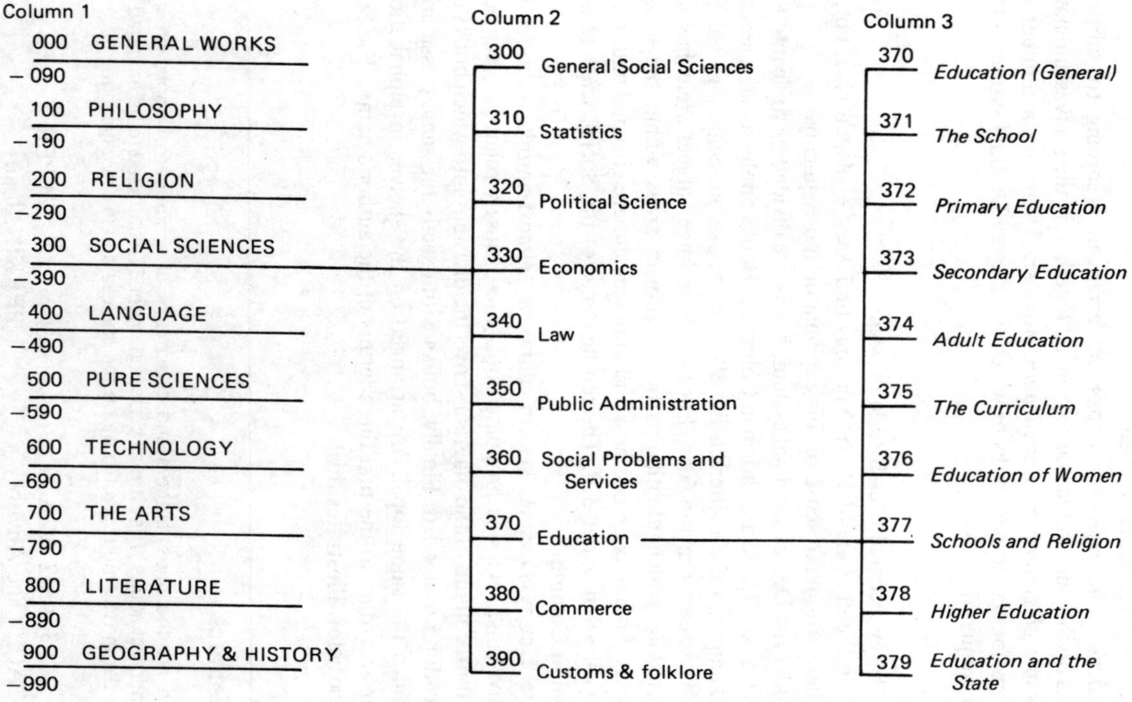

Column 1

000	GENERAL WORKS
–090	
100	PHILOSOPHY
–190	
200	RELIGION
–290	
300	SOCIAL SCIENCES
–390	
400	LANGUAGE
–490	
500	PURE SCIENCES
–590	
600	TECHNOLOGY
–690	
700	THE ARTS
–790	
800	LITERATURE
–890	
900	GEOGRAPHY & HISTORY
–990	

Column 2

300	General Social Sciences
310	Statistics
320	Political Science
330	Economics
340	Law
350	Public Administration
360	Social Problems and Services
370	Education
380	Commerce
390	Customs & folklore

Column 3

370	Education (General)
371	The School
372	Primary Education
373	Secondary Education
374	Adult Education
375	The Curriculum
376	Education of Women
377	Schools and Religion
378	Higher Education
379	Education and the State

Fig. 16 The Dewey Decimal System

libraries have separate sections for different types of fiction, with all the romance grouped together, for example. Others use different coloured labels on the spine of books to show their type. In others, you have to make the judgements yourself.

Non-fiction and *reference* books are arranged according to subject. Books on the same subject are arranged together on the shelves and have the same *classmark* or *classification number*. There are a number of systems for classifying books of which the Dewey Decimal system is the most frequently used.

The Dewey Decimal Classification system

Look at the diagram on P. 55. You may find it self explanatory. If not, it will help you make sense of this explanation more quickly.

Under the Dewey Decimal system, books are divided by topic into ten main classes. These are shown in Column 1. Books on the social sciences, for example, are classified in the 300s and books on technology will all have classmarks in the 600s. Each of these huge subject areas has ten subdivisions which identify particular subject areas within the broad category. So books on Business and Management are grouped under 650 and Education under 370. The ten headings of the Social Sciences are shown in Column 2.

The Dewey Decimal system allows an almost infinite number of subdivisions, each one grouping books more closely related by subject. The third column of the diagram shows the divisions into which books on Education are divided. Finally, books with exactly the same classmark, on much the same topic, are arranged on the shelves in alphabetical order according to the first three letters of the author's name. The Self Check below illustrates this.

Self-check

Below are the titles, authors and classmarks of a number of books on the education of adults. They are all classified under 374 but need to be arranged in the order in which they would be on the shelves and in the catalogue.

1.   374.942 ACA
ACACE (The Advisory
Council for Adult and
continuing Education)
*Continuing Education: from
policies to practice*

4.   374 PER
PERKIN, Joan
It's Never Too Late

2. 374.1 ROW ROWNTREE, Derek *Learn How to Study*	5. 374.942 BEL BELL, Judith and RODERICK, Gordon *Never Too Late to Learn:* *The complete guide to adult* *education*
3. 374.27 JEN JENKINS, Janet *Materials for Learning: How to* *teach adults at a distance*	6. 374 TIG TIGHT, Malcolm *Opportunities for Adult* *Education*

The correct order for these books is 4, 6, 2, 3, 1, 5. Assuming the books have been put back in their correct positions, this is the order they would be in on the shelf.

3.5 How to find a book

All libraries keep the details of their books in catalogues. These may be in a card index, on microfiche or computer, or sometimes in a loose leaf file or bound volume. Ask the librarian how to look for a book the first time you use the library.

In many areas libraries are in the process of introducing a fully computerized system for cataloguing their books. In these libraries you can find a book if you know the author, the title or even the publisher's ISBN reference number. You can also call up all the titles on a particular subject by using the subject classification number. The computer may also show the branch at which a particular book is held.

In other areas you will need to use the subject index and card catalogues to find books. Libraries do not all have identical systems, but they will normally have:

  i) Subject Index
 ii) Author Catalogue
iii) Classified or Subject Catalogue

Research activity 5

To check your library skills, set yourself the task of finding two books in the library. The flowchart on P. 58 gives step by step guidance on how to do this. *Search 1*: Look for a book, perhaps from a reading list. Make sure you know the author and title.

58

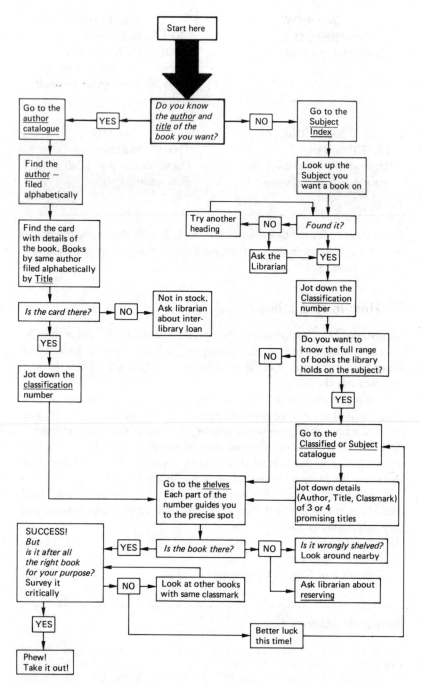

Fig. 17 *How to Find a Book*

Search 2: Think of a subject – any you would like to know more about. Follow the procedures in the flowchart to find it.

If you found both books easily, you are a competent library user. Skip the rest of this section and turn to 'Surveying a book' on P. 60. Otherwise, read on.

If you had difficulty finding the first book, check that you used the alphabetical index correctly. Refer to 'How to Check Alphabetical Order' in the reference section.

If you had difficulty finding a book on a subject area, look up a different heading in the subject index. Ask the librarian if you need help.

Thinking of headings
Try to be precise about the subject you want to look up. You may need to try a number of different headings. Check:

Is the subject a small part of a larger whole?

Is the subject too broad? Can I be more specific about the aspect I am interested in?

Is there a more correct term for the subject?

The ability to think of headings accurately and quickly is essential if you are ever in the position to use a phone link with a database. This service is not at present available to the general public, but it may be in the future.

Research activity 6

What headings would you look up if you wanted to find answers to the following questions;
1. How are computers used in stock control?
2. What support services are available to alcoholics?
3. What is the law on the closed shop?
4. What practical advice on healthy eating can I find?

Jot down your answers then check them with mine in the Answers Section.

Once you know the classification number of the subject you want information on, you can then find out what books the library has on the subject from the *classified or subject catalogue*. Look up the same number or heading. Note down three or four books on the subject (if you have the choice) and go to the shelves and see if they are there. You can, of course, go straight to the shelves, but if you do this, you will only see the books no one else has taken out.

Research activity 7

How many books does your library stock on Word Processing?
How many of these books are on the shelves?

Follow the steps in the flowchart on P. 58. Word Processing will be at 651 or thereabouts. There are probably far fewer books on the shelves. It's a popular subject!

3.6 Surveying a book – to read or not to read?

By far the most important skill in choosing a book is deciding how useful a book is going to be to you and to have the confidence to reject books which are not appropriate to you or your present purpose. If you have been given a reading list, this is a useful starting point; often a tutor includes alternatives and texts at several degrees of complexity, so students can exercise choice over what they read. To do this you need to have a sense of a book's level and relevance before you start to read it. So learn to select and reject books on the basis of a critical survey.

First – the general survey

Title: Obvious but necessary. Is the book on the subject you want or an aspect of it?

Subtitle: This often indicates the level of difficulty or style of approach to the subject e.g. 'a new approach', 'a student's guide', 'a handbook of'. Have a look at the titles and subtitles of the books listed in the Self Check on P. 56

Author: Can you trust the author? There is often information about the author's qualifications, life or experience on the title page or back cover.

Date of publication: This is given on the back of the title page. With some books (e.g. textbooks) it is important to know how up to date a book is. New does not mean good of course. A book may have several editions, each one including changes that update it.

Blurb: This is the write-up the publisher gives a book, printed on the back. View it critically – it is designed to sell the book, but it can give an idea of the style and purpose of a book.

Publisher A publisher may have a good reputation in a particular area. If it is published in the USA this may tell you something about the book's particular approach.

Self-check

• Check out these details on a general survey of this book.
Then make a closer survey of:

Contents: The chapter headings give an outline of the areas the book covers. Look to see if there is a detailed breakdown of the content of each chapter, with page references. Which of these topics do *not* have a chapter of their own: revision, mnemonics, remembering, writing letters?

Preface: This is written by the author and often explains the thinking behind writing the book.

Index: To locate a particular topic, scan the index at the back of the book. It should give you the page reference of every time the topic is discussed in the text. On which page(s) will you find information on: letter layout, writing instructions, O level grades of school leavers, writing introductions to essays?

Research activity 8

Select five books on a subject of your choice, perhaps from a reading list. On the basis of a critical survey, reject three of them, leaving you with the two most appropriate and helpful texts.

3.7 Keeping records

A useful way of keeping a record of the books and other publications you consult, is to make out source cards. This enables you to make a note of what you found useful and to find the book again.

On the front note down the details from the catalogue card;

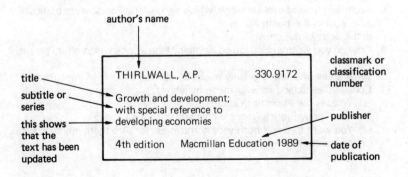

Fig. 18   *Source card.*

On the back make a note of what you found useful in the book e.g.
'good current figures on debt aid in chapter 13, esp. P. 307–312'.

Review

The purpose of this chapter is to help you find books and materials you need for
your studies – or interest – quickly and painlessly, so the library becomes a
resource for you, not a daunting hall of volumes. So the Review of this chapter
takes the form of a practical exercise in information retrieval. Refer back to the
flowchart on P. 58, if you need to. There are twelve questions. Pick three or four
to start with. You may want to come back and try some of the others at a later
date. Or you may feel you want more practice now. Use your judgement about
the best way to use the exercise.

For each question make a note of the following:

Answer: classmark:
Source: (Author and title)   page reference:
                                     How I found the book:

1. How would you set about raising capital if you wanted to set up a small
   business? Look for a book which offers practical advice.
2. What is 'Proportional Representation'?
3. Is there a book by John Bingham which gives practical advice on the
   preparation and layout of business documents using a computer software
   package?
4. What is the definition of the legal term 'mens rea'?
5. What should you do about stuttering in young children?
6. What is the title of a sociological study by Young and Willmott about the
   family in East London? When was it published?
7. Does the library have a book on economics by Samuelson? Does it have
   anything on progressive taxation?
   If the library does not have this book see if another economics textbook
   deals with the topic.
8. According to medieval astrology, which signs of the Zodiac were particularly
   influential in the treatment of
   a) the head b) the chest?
9. How do you write a good job description? Find a book which offers practical
   advice.
10. What areas of a firm's activity might be studied by O & M consultants?
11. Consult Ceefax and answer these questions:
    (i) What is the Newsflash about?
    (ii) How many French francs would you get for £1 today?
    (iii) You want to travel from your home in Exeter. Are there any roadworks
        on the motorway on your route?

12. Consult Oracle and answer these questions:
    (i) What time is the next British Airways flight from Los Angeles due at Heathrow?
    (ii) Use the Regional index to find 'Restaurants' in your area. Choose one to which you might like to take these American friends.

4 Fact and Interpretation

This chapter takes the form of two Case Studies. In the course of these you will be asked to establish facts, work out explanations and interpretations, and draw conclusions. The purpose of these activities is threefold: firstly, to encourage critical thinking, so that, by asking questions and looking for answers you can form your own opinions; secondly, by presenting information in a variety of forms, to give you experience in looking for information in charts, diagrams, graphs and tables as well as from text; and thirdly, to offer a practical introduction to a method of inquiry from source material increasingly required on a number of courses.

The Case Studies are:

1. **Pursuing an inquiry**; an introduction to understanding and interpreting data. The research question for this enquiry is: *How far has equality between the sexes in education and in work been achieved?*
2. **But is it true**? An inquiry into the 'facts' behind political debate. The context for this is the debate concerning the state of the NHS.

4.1 Case Study 1 Pursuing an inquiry

Research question: *How far has equality between the sexes in education and in work been achieved?*

In order to approach the fact finding necessary to answer a question of this sort, you need to ask additional specific questions. How do boys and girls do at school? What proportions of each sex go into further and higher education? What do they study when they get there? What jobs do men and women go into? How do their earnings compare? and so forth. These are specific factual questions to which it should be possible to find specific, factual answers. Your answers to these questions will be the material you need for your answer to the broad research question.

In this case study, you are asked to show your understanding of the issues raised in several ways. You are asked to answer one 'Find Out' question, for each chart or table, seven in all. In addition, there are activities on each one to enable you to check your understanding of detail. In the same way that you set yourself questions as you read text – remember *SQ3R* – set yourself questions to sharpen your focus as you look for information in a chart or diagram. Finally, at the end of the case study, you are asked to write a report in response to the overall research question (above), to bring all your findings together and draw conclusions. You can come back to this later – but it should make an interesting study.

Find out question 1:
Are opportunities open to girl school leavers more or less restricted in 1984 than in 1974?

Fig. 19 **Educational and economic activity of 16-year-olds. Great Britain, January 1974 and January 1984.**

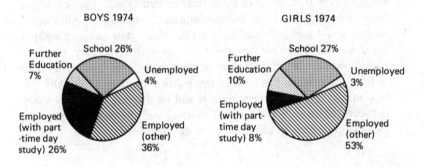

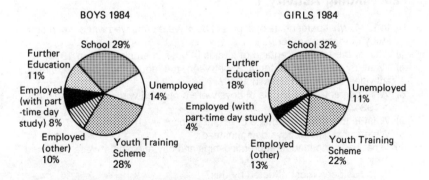

Source: DES statistical bulletin 5/85, February 1985
From *Women and Men in Britain, a statistical profile*, Equal Opportunities Commission, HMSO 1986

About the data

1. *The presentation*. This is a *pie chart* so called because the various parts are shown as slices of cake, or pie. The whole always adds up to 100%. Pie charts have an immediate visual impact, so the main features stand out at a glance even if you forget the exact figures – which should always be given. Pie charts are a good way of showing proportion (how a whole divides up) and how proportions change in relation to each other. Two pie charts side by side show trends and changes clearly. They do not, of course, show the size of the whole, here the total number of 16 year olds, and so cannot be used in discussions about the size of the 'cake'.

2. *The source* of data should always be given. This is so that you can check it out if you want to, and you can make up your own mind about how objective – or biased – it is likely to be. In this example, the source is figures given in the DES Statistical Bulletin 5/85, February 1985, and the translation of these rows of figures into a pie chart has been done by the Equal Opportunities Commission. All charts, diagrams and tables should have a title which states exactly what is being shown. This title has been chosen with some care to cover education, training, employment and unemployment. Notice the date of both the original figures and the publication itself. This tells you how up to date your information is and by noticing any discrepancy between the date of the original findings and the diagram, you can pick out rejiggings of old data – not the case here.

Fact-Finding Activity 1

1i) In 1974, what percentage of a) girls b) boys were employed without part time study ('Employed other')?

ii) What is the total percentage of a) girls b) boys in employment in 1974?

iii) What is the major difference between the educational and economic activities of girls and boys in 1974?

2i) What percentage of a) girls b) boys were employed without part time study in 1984?

ii) What is the total percentage of a) girls b) boys in employment in 1984?

iii) What are a) girls b) boys doing instead?

3i) What has happened to apprenticeships and day release between 1974 and 1984?

ii) Who has been most affected by this?

● Check your answers with mine in the Answers Section then write your answer to Find Out question 1, before you read my comments below

The patterns of educational and economic activities of boys and girls have become much closer in the ten years to 1984. Why this is, and whether this represents a broadening of options for girls depends on the interpretations you put on these changes. Employment was an option for few young people in 1984; unemployment among boys was higher than for girls. The high take up of education options among girls (half the age group staying on at school or college) could be seen as a constructive response to unemployment and an encouraging sign of young women planning a future career. It could, however, suggest that young women found the alternatives of unemployment and the YTS scheme particularly unattractive. So are the opportunities open to girl school leavers more or less restricted than in 1974? Certainly fewer go into dead end jobs, . . . what is your view?

This activity shows that you can draw very different conclusions from the same basic facts. Data does not give answers; it simply presents information. The next stage of the inquiry is to consider the qualifications gained by school leavers.

Find out Question 2
Are girls better or worse qualified than boys when they leave school?

Table 1: School leavers – highest qualification: by sex, 1975/76 and 1985/86

United Kingdom	Boys		Girls	
	1975/ 76	1985/ 86	1975/ 76	1985/ 86
Percentage with:				
2 or more 'A' levels/3 or more 'H' grades	14.3	14.9	12.1	14.2
1 'A' level/1 or 2 'H' grades	3.5	3.6	4.0	4.3
5 or more 'O' levels/ A–C grades*	7.2	10.0	9.4	11.9
1–4 'O' levels/ A–C grades*	23.9	24.4	27.0	28.7
1 or more 'O' levels:				
D or E grades, or CSE grades 2–5	29.9	34.0	28.4	30.9
No GCE/SCE or CSE grades	21.2	13.2	19.1	10.0
Total school leavers (= 100%) (thousands)	423	444	400	427

United Kingdom — Percentages and thousands

*Includes CSE grade 1.
Source: Department of Education and Science. From *Social Trends* 18, 1988, published by Government Statistical Service HMSO.

About the data

This is a table, the basic method for presenting statistical information. Note the source (DES), the publication from which it is taken (Social Trends 18), who publishes this (the Government), and the title. Tables are not particularly attractive to look at, but they usually contain more information than can be shown on most charts. You need to look carefully at the figures. To keep yourself alert, try asking yourself simple questions;

Does the table show percentages (all the figures in a column add up to 100%) or numbers? The main table here shows percentages, and total numbers are shown in thousands at the bottom. With percentages, when there is an increase in one part, there must be a decrease somewhere else. Where? and why? is this figure up or down on the last? (Compare 1976 and 1986)

Fact Finding Activity 2

1) What percentage of a) girls b) boys left school with no GCE or CSE grades in i) 1976 (ii) 1986?
2) What percentage of a) girls b) boys left school with two or more 'A' levels (or 3 Highers) in i) 1976 ii) 1986?
3) What proportion of a) girls b) boys left school with at least one 'O' level grade A–C (or equivalent) in i) 1986 ii) 1976?

● Check your answers with mine in the Answers Section then write your answer to Find Out question 2, before you read my comments below.

This question cannot be accurately answered by giving a blanket 'better' or 'worse' verdict on the performance of girls and boys. Both sexes have improved their results in recent years and fewer girls than boys left school in 1986 with no qualifications. Girls did better than boys at 'O' level and there is less than a single percentage point between the proportion of girls and boys who pass two 'A' levels, the normal requirement for entry to Higher Education.

This question can also be answered in many ways. You can see how someone keen to prove a point can use data to support just about any point of view. You could, for example, use this data to argue that boys are cleverer or that girls are cleverer. How? You'd point to the better results at 'A' level achieved by boys to argue the first, and the better overall results, especially at 'O' level, achieved by girls to support the second. The moral of this is to be wary of value judgements arising from information you have not had the opportunity to check.

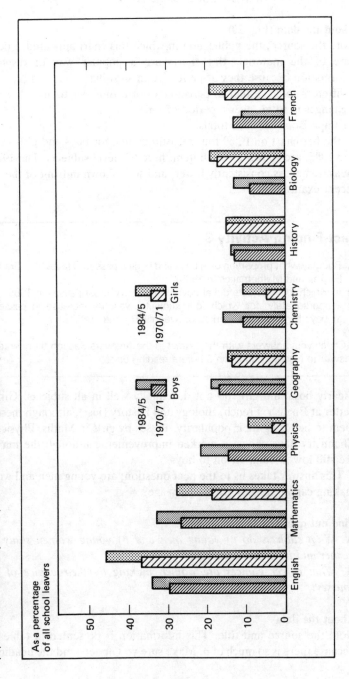

Fig. 20. **School leavers possessing an 'O' level pass grade A–C** (including grade 1 CSE, but excluding 'O' level passes on 'A' level papers) in selected subjects: by sex, 1970/71 and 1984/85, England and Wales.

Source: Department of Education and Science, from *Social Trends 17*, 1987 Edition, HMSO.

Find out question 3:
Do girls do as well as boys in all subjects?

About the data (Fig. 20)
Note the source, the publication in which this chart appeared, title and date of the material. Bar charts are a popular way of displaying information because they are effective in showing:
– different totals, either as percentages or as number totals
– changes in totals over a period of time
– comparisons between totals.
In the bar chart on P. 69 four measurements, for boys and girls in 1971 and 1985, are shown for each item, here 'O' level subjects. The 1970/71 measurement is consistently lower, and so is shown in front of the more recent exam results.

Fact-Finding Activity 3

1) Roughly what proportion of a) boys and b) girls passed O level/CSE Grade 1 in English and Mathematics in 1985?
2) In which four subjects did a) boys b) girls have most passes in 1985?
3) Proportionately, for which four subjects was the increase in passes for a) boys b) girls most marked between 1971 and 1985?

● Check your answers with the extract in the Answers Section then write your answer to Find Out question 3 before reading on.

Clearly boys and girls do not do equally well in all subjects. Girls do better at English, French, Biology and History (just), although these last seem to be losing their popularity. Passes by girls in Maths, Physics and Chemistry have shown a marked improvement, although the numbers are still low in comparison to boys.

This answer takes us to the next question; are young men and women making career choices at this early age?

Find out question 4:
A. *What subjects do a) young men and b) young women study in i) further and ii) higher education?*
B. *What career choices are women making by their choice of FHE courses?*

About the data
Note the source and title. This information is presented in table form because there is so much of it. Make sure you understand the headings or

Table 2. Students enrolling on further education courses by selected subjects, all modes, England and Wales, November 1984

Thousands

Subject	Non-Advanced[1]			Advanced[2]		
	Male	Female	% Female	Male	Female	% Female
Education	4.5	7.5	62.4	16.8	34.2	67.0
Medical, health and welfare	6.7	31.1	82.3	4.6	11.3	71.0
Engineering and technology	325.4	21.2	6.1	87.7	4.5	4.9
Agriculture	22.3	6.1	21.4	1.6	0.6	25.7
Science	21.0	12.5	37.4	33.6	15.8	32.0
Social, administrative and business studies	73.9	213.1	74.3	81.4	55.4	40.5
Professional and vocational subjects	49.7	121.1	70.9	12.8	9.7	43.0
Music, drama, art and design	22.3	33.5	59.9	13.3	17.7	57.1
GCE, CSE and CEE	135.7	181.7	57.2	—	—	—
Unspecified	105.4	217.0	67.3	—	—	—
All subjects	795.4	920.8	53.7	260.9	167.3	39.1

[1]Non-advanced = work below degree level at colleges or sometimes polytechnics
[2]Advanced = degree or degree equivalent work in colleges, polytechnics & universities.
Source: Department of Education and Science, *Statistics of Education*: *Further Education*, England, November 1984 Table F18; Wales; Welsh Office. From *Women and Men in Britain: A Statistical Profile* Equal Opportunities Commission, HMSO, 1986

terms used; (e.g. non advanced, advanced). Notice the layout of the figures; the numbers of male and female students taking the various subjects are given in thousands, and the percentage of women is given in a third column. Look for:
   (i) figures which stand out because they are very high or very low.
  (ii) contrasts between the two parts of the table; here marked differences in the take up between non-advanced and advanced.
 (iii) whether the point emerges more clearly from the percentage figures, or from the absolute number.

Fact-Finding Activity 4

i) How many males took a) non-advanced b) advanced Engineering and Technology courses in 1984? Roughly what proportion of the total number of men taking courses in all subjects do these figures represent?

ii) What are the equivalent figures for women?
iii) Which are the two most popular vocational (i.e. not GCE etc.) areas of study for women, in terms of numbers enrolling at a) non-advanced and b) advanced level?
iv) Which areas of a) non-advanced b) advanced study have the highest percentage of women enrolled?

• Check your answers with mine in the Answers Section then write your answer to Find Out questions 4 before reading the comments below.

---

1. This is the summary of the table given by the EOC:
   The total number of enrolments on further education courses in 1984 has continued to increase. Women's share of the enrolments has increased too–to 53.7% on non-advanced courses and 39.1% on advanced courses. In 1984 women predominated on arts, education and health and welfare courses and men on science, engineering and technology courses. The pattern of subject choice was broadly similar at both levels, except in social, administrative and business studies courses and in professional and vocational subjects, where women were in the majority on non-advanced, and men on advanced courses.
2. It is clear that career choices lead to very different patterns of Further and Higher Education in men and women – or vice versa. Large numbers of women are heading towards office work, particularly at a lower level and women form an overwhelming proportion of the intake to the 'caring' professions, Medical, Health and Welfare, and Education. Is this reflected in the jobs women actually go into?

Find Out Question 5:
Which occupations do most women enter?

About the data (Fig 21 opposite)
Note the source and the title. This is a horizontal bar chart, showing the percentage of women working full and part time in various occupations. This chart contains a lot of information – too much perhaps for it to be easy to interpret at a glance. While it is easy to see that some bars are considerably longer than others, some of the categories of occupation are not clear – you have to hunt for 'Education' for example. The information does not seem to be organised in any particular order. The grid stops at 80%, which is normal practice, but the message might be clearer if the 76% women in Catering cleaning etc jobs *looked* like three quarters of the total workforce.

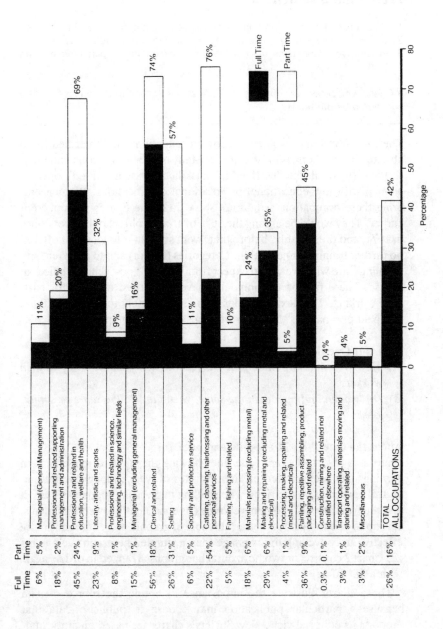

	Full Time	Part Time
Managerial (General Management)	6%	5%
Professional and related supporting management and administration	18%	2%
Professional and related in education, welfare and health	45%	24%
Literary, artistic and sports	23%	9%
Professional and related in science, engineering, technology and similar fields	8%	1%
Managerial (excluding general management)	15%	1%
Clerical and related	56%	18%
Selling	26%	31%
Security and protective service	6%	5%
Catering, cleaning, hairdressing and other personal services	22%	54%
Farming, fishing and related	5%	5%
Materials processing (excluding metal)	18%	6%
Making and repairing (excluding metal and electrical)	29%	6%
Processing, making, repairing and related (metal and electrical)	4%	1%
Painting, repetitive assembling, product packaging and related	36%	9%
Construction, mining and related not identified elsewhere	0.3%	0.1%
Transport operating, materials moving and storing and related	3%	1%
Miscellaneous	3%	2%
TOTAL ALL OCCUPATIONS	26%	16%

Fact-Finding Activity 5

1. What proportion of women in the population work a) full time b) part time?
2. Which five occupations have the highest percentage of women workers?
3. Which five occupations have the highest percentage of part time women workers?

• Check your answers with mine in the Answers Section then answer Find Out question 5 before reading on.

The concentration of women in certain occupations, and their near total absence from others, is most marked. Many of the occupations under (i), (iv) and (v) would be described as 'unskilled' or 'semi-skilled', open to women with low educational or vocational qualifications. Women entering these occupations would not show up in the figures we looked at earlier. They would be among the 50% of 16 year old school leavers who, in 1974, and presumably, before that, went straight into jobs that offered no further training or education. Categories (ii), (iii) and to an extent (iv) ('Selling') are what we would expect from women's post school choices of course. These five occupations also have the largest demand for part-time workers. The next questions come immediately to mind; are these low paid occupations? How do women's earnings compare with men's?

Find Out Questions 6:
A) *How well paid are these jobs with the highest proportion of women workers?*
B) *Do women and men earn the same when they do the same or similar jobs?*

About the data (Fig. 22 opposite and page 76)
Chart 1 is a sort of graph; the line showing the upward movement of earnings has been plotted on the two axes of 'year', along the bottom, and '£' vertically on the right. The shading in gives the graph a 3D effect and the front 'block', women's earnings, is consistently lower than men's. It is up to you to decide whether this sort of graphic presentation is more effective in conveying the message than a simple line graph such as Fig 23. Chart 2 consists of two horizontal bar graphs arranged in order, again with a 3D effect.

These charts illustrate the importance of noting the source of data because a particular publication may choose to publicise data that supports its editorial view. New Society's charts are based on authoritative Government sources – the New Earnings Survey, published by the Department of Employment. The compilers have been precise about

Fig. 22 **Chart 1: How Earnings have moved.**

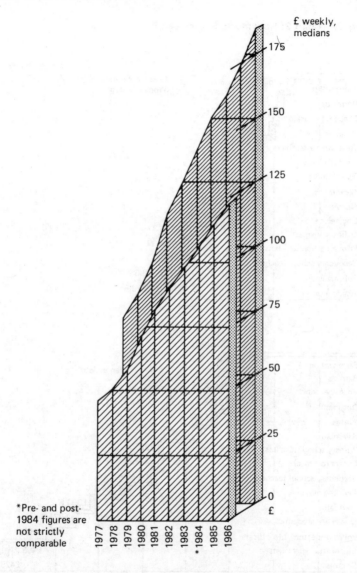

£ weekly, medians

175
150
125
100
75
50
25
0
£

*Pre- and post-1984 figures are not strictly comparable

1977 1978 1979 1980 1981 1982 1983 1984 1985 1986
*

Source: *New Earnings Survey*. From *New Society* (Database), 23 January 1987.

how they have calculated the figures for the average weekly earnings shown in both charts; 'median' in Chart 1, 'average' in Chart 2. For why this is important see 'How to Fix an Average' in the reference section.

76

Fig. 22 **Chart 2: How much do they earn?**

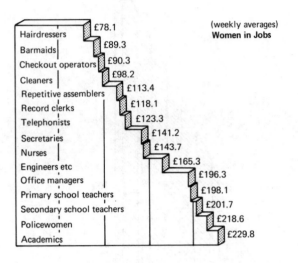

(weekly averages)
Women in Jobs

Hairdressers — £78.1
Barmaids — £89.3
Checkout operators — £90.3
Cleaners — £98.2
Repetitive assemblers — £113.4
Record clerks — £118.1
Telephonists — £123.3
Secretaries — £141.2
Nurses — £143.7
Engineers etc — £165.3
Office managers — £196.3
Primary school teachers — £198.1
Secondary school teachers — £201.7
Policewomen — £218.6
Academics — £229.8

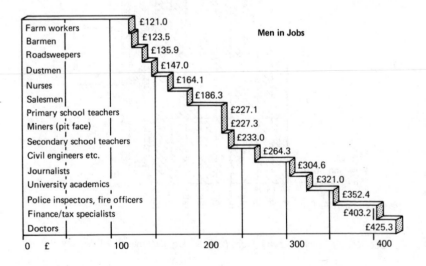

Men in Jobs

Farm workers — £121.0
Barmen — £123.5
Roadsweepers — £135.9
Dustmen — £147.0
Nurses — £164.1
Salesmen — £186.3
Primary school teachers — £227.1
Miners (pit face) — £227.3
Secondary school teachers — £233.0
Civil engineers etc. — £264.3
Journalists — £304.6
University academics — £321.0
Police inspectors, fire officers — £352.4
Finance/tax specialists — £403.2
Doctors — £425.3

0   £   100   200   300   400

Source: *New Earnings Survey*, 1986. From *New Society (Database)*, 23 January 1987.

Fact-Finding Activity 6

i) What are the five least well paid occupations for women shown in Chart 2? What is the relationship between these jobs and the five employing most women shown in Fig 21?

ii) How do the earnings of men and women in the same occupations compare? Complete this chart:

Occupation	Men	Women	Difference
Bar Staff			
Nurses			
Primary teacher			
Secondary teacher			
Academics			

iii) From your reading of Chart 1, during which year(s) were the earnings of men and women closest? What has happened to earnings since then?

• Check your answers with mine in the Answers Section then write short answers to Find Out questions 6 A and B before reading my comments.

A. The short answer to this is that the jobs with the highest proportion of women are the worst paid; they are also the jobs with the highest proportion of part time women workers, as shown in Fig 21.

B. Even when men and women do the same or similar jobs, men earn substantially more. Below is the commentary by New Society on these charts. It picks out some points you will have noticed, and adds some new information.

In 1986, for the first time, the average man broke through the £200 a week pay barrier. Last April, for a full week's work, he earned £207.50, and his pay was still going up—in manufacturing last autumn, at a rate of 7.75 per cent a year.

His female counterpart, however, lags behind. The average female wage in April was just £137.50 a week—66.3 per cent of the male average wage. Female manual workers do even worse, earning 61.6 per cent of the male wage.

To some extent, the discrepancy reflects the longer hours worked by men. The average manual male worker makes £25.10 a week in overtime, compared with just £5.10 for the average female. He is also likely to benefit from extra money for productivity (£13.10 for manual men, but just £9.00 for women) and for shift working (£3.40 compared with £2.30 for women).

In part, this reflects the fact that certain highly paid occupations are virtually confined to men. In compiling the *New Earnings Survey*, the statisticians failed to come up with enough female doctors or journalists to calculate an average. Meanwhile, low-paid occupations, such as hairdressing, are dominated by women.

However, even when men and women are in the same occupation, they can be getting very different pay. A male primary teacher gets £227.10 a week, on average; a woman £198.10. Although rates for the two sexes are the same in teaching, males tend to fill posts higher up the pay scales, or to have longer service, thus accumulating more increments.

Find out question 7:
How have men and women been affected by unemployment?
The last question in this inquiry into opportunities open to women must be concerned with what impact unemployment has had on both sexes.

About the data (Fig. 23 opposite)
Note the source; note the title. This is a line graph. Graphs are effective in showing
– the changes or movement in a measurement over a period of time
– the changes in several measurements over a period of time so comparisons can be made
They convey essential trends at a glance, such as the fluctuations in a hospital patient's temperature. Graphs are drawn by joining dots carefully placed in relation to the vertical and horizontal axes. Here the employment situation in 1971 is taken as the baseline, the 100%, and the ups and downs recorded since show changes in relation to this baseline. It is important to realise this; if you didn't, you could get the impression that, for example, there are many more part time women workers and self employed people than full time employees. This is not so. The graph shows the changes in the proportionate sizes of these groups relative to the situation in 1971.

Fact-Finding Activity 7

i) When did a noticeable fall in full time employment for both men and women occur?
ii) Briefly describe the trend in self employment before and after 1979.
iii) What is the trend in employment for women?

• Check your answers with mine in the Answers Section then write your answer to Find Out question 7 before reading on.

Unemployment has had quite different effects on men and women. Full time employment for both dropped after 1979, but since then women

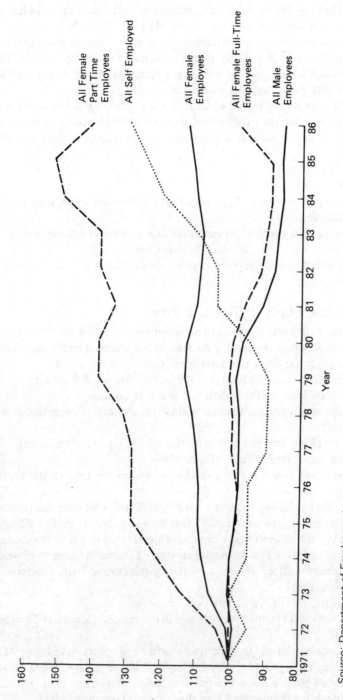

Fig. 23 **Employment trends: Great Britain 1971–86 (1971 = 100).**

Source: Department of Employment.
From *Women and Men in Britain: A Statistical Profile*, EOC, HMSO 1987.

have offset this fall by a dramatic increase in part time work – which, as we have already seen, tends to be poorly paid. There has also been a marked increase in self employment, presumably because many of those who lost their jobs, especially men, have turned to self employment. The increase in full time jobs for women is not shared with men; the number of men with jobs continues to decline.

This brings us to the end of Case Study 1. I hope you enjoyed it and learnt quite a lot (as I did) about patterns of employment of men and women. You are now in a position to write a longer piece on your findings.

Report
Write a report in which you present your findings and conclusions on the research question:

> *How far has equality between men and women in education and in work been achieved?*

Advice about writing reports is given in chapter 6 and the reference section.

4.2   Case Study 2: But is it true?

This case study takes the form of an inquiry into some of the facts behind the political debate concerning the state of the National Health Service, a subject never far from the news headlines;

'Consultants unite to fight ward closures' (Surrey Advertiser)

'Hospitals lose 40,000 beds in six years' (Guardian)

'Health cuts fury: fear that axe will fall on services' (Epsom and Ewell Herald)

'NHS waiting lists rise to highest for two years.' (Independent)

'Truth about those "cuts" (Daily Mail)

Politicians are ever keen to give their views on the state of the health service:

'The NHS is falling to pieces. Health authorities all over the country are on the verge of bankruptcy'. (Michael Meacher, Guardian 12/3/87)

'The fact is that more resources are being devoted to health than at any time in the history of the health service – £11 million more than when we came to office.' (Normal Fowler, Conservative Party Conference October 1986)

Perhaps the most famous pronouncement is:

'The National Health Service is safe in our hands.' (Margaret Thatcher 1983)

The problem for us, the listeners, readers and voters, is to know what to believe. The extracts on P. 24, Chapter 1 illustrate how 'the facts' are cited by all parties when the political temperature runs high. Do 'the facts' speak for themselves? Can they all be telling the truth?

This Case Study takes as its starting point two documents; an extract from Norman Fowler's speech to the Conservative Party conference 1986, and a newspaper article from the Observer. You will be asked to identify the facts alleged in these documents, and then to account for them – or disprove them – by referring to the data in the Case Study.

Document 1

Extracts from the speech by the Rt Hon Norman Fowler, Secretary of State for Social Services to the Conservative Party Conference 8th October 1986

You know, Madam Chairman, at times I have difficulty in recognising some of the descriptions of the National Health Service used by our opponents. They say it is in decline, run down, being cut. Yet what are the facts?

. . . the fact is that we are providing more and better patient care than at any stage in the history of the health service – $4\frac{1}{2}$ million more patient cases are being treated today than when we came to office.

And I say to you, against that background it is grotesque to claim that the health service in this country is in decline. It is selling the health service short. It is selling short the success of health service staff. It is selling short the achievement of this Government.

But of course when confronted with the facts our critics say that they are just "statistics".

When they hear that in England last year we treated nearly 1 million more in-patient cases than in 1978, they dismiss that as "statistics".

When they hear that we treated 400,000 more day cases, they dismiss it as "statistics".

When they hear that we provided for over $3\frac{1}{4}$ million more outpatient attendances, they dismiss it as "statistics".

What they forget is that each and every one of those $4\frac{1}{2}$ million statistics is a personal story – a story of care; of dedicated staff working night and day; of patients' pain relieved and hope renewed.

They are the real figures of health care in this country. They show that health care has developed. Above all, they show that the National Health Service today – under this Government – is bringing more help to more people than ever before. . .

You know, ladies and gentlemen, we have been here together before – you and I – with cries of "crisis" ringing in the air. But our policies have now been tested. The public can now judge who was right and who was wrong. . . .

Perhaps no issue is of more concern to the public than waiting lists. The last Labour Government left record waiting lists of three-quarters of a million people. We have reduced the number.

Document 2

THE OBSERVER, SUNDAY 1 FEBRUARY 1987

Great bed robbery

PATIENTS are being discharged from hospital dangerously early because of the huge reduction in beds since the Conservatives came to power, according to a study to be published tomorrow.

More than 36,000 beds—10 per cent of the total— have been cut since 1979, putting pressure on doctors to delay admissions and hasten discharges.

Even in geriatrics, a speciality regarded as top priority by the Government, the number of hospital beds has remained static at 57,000, although the number of people over 75 has increased by 20 per cent since 1979.

These figures are revealed in a Labour Party analysis of Government statistics for 1979–85, to be released tomorrow.

Specialists in geriatrics, gynaecology and general surgery last week condemned the bed reductions, saying the trend had gone too far and should be reversed.

Although some of the effects had been mitigated by faster turnover of patients and day procedures, in some places patient stays had been reduced to a bare minimum and the loss of beds was increasing waiting lists, they said.

Dr Jacqueline Morris, deputy secretary of the British Geriatric Society and consultant at the Royal Free Hospital, north London, said it was leading to 'dangerously early discharges.

'Half of the old people admitted to hospital go into acute medical beds and half into geriatric beds' she said. 'The cut in the number of acute beds across the country and the failure to increase the number of geriatric beds has, in fact, meant a cut in the service.

'Patients are being discharged precipitously and community services have not increased enough to cope with them. Patients are also having to wait too long to be admitted.

'I have been trying to admit one patient with bronchial pneumonia and rheumatoid arthritis for two weeks and finally managed to get her in last Thursday. That sort of thing is terribly risky. Others are waiting in corridors until a bed is available.'

Despite claims by the four Thames health regions that they are the worst-hit areas, the analysis reveals that Merseyside has suffered the largest cuts, losing 3,518 beds, 16 per cent of its total.

Mr Donald Menzies, consultant at the Women's Hospital, Liverpool, and chairman of the medical executive committee of the district's central and southern sector, said: 'The problem is that this Government is more concerned with business standards than with professional standards. What is efficient financially is not necessarily efficient medically. Medical efficiency requires time and that has been cut down and down.

'In my department, the number of consultants has been reduced from four to three but we have nevertheless increased the throughput of patients by 30 per cent.

'This has led to an increasing number of complaints. Patients feel less satisfied. It has also led to increasing fatigue among the consultants. That has occurred throughout the district.

'Patients are staying in hospital for shorter times. For Caesarean sections, they used to stay in hospital for a fortnight and now it is eight days. For hysterectomies, it used to be three weeks, now it is also eight days. But you get patients being readmitted because of complications.'

The analysis of bed reductions, carried out by the Shadow Social Services Secretary, Mr Michael Meacher, follows closely on another Labour survey, showing how many days last year hospitals had to refuse non-urgent admissions because they were full. 'One is the product of the other,' Mr Meacher said.

'Patients are not only waiting ever longer for urgent operations but they are being turned out of hospital to make room for others needing treatment, often before they are ready to look after themselves.

'In turn this means more patients are having to be readmitted to hospital, causing distress, extra cost to the NHS, and further bed shortages. The only people who gain from this vicious circle are the Government—they use the faster throughput to claim more people are being treated.'

ANNABEL FERRIMAN
■ Health Correspondent

WHERE THE CUTS HURT

REGION	BEDS CUT	% CUT
Mersey	3,518	16
NW Thames	4,088	15
SW Thames	4,033	14
SE Thames	4,211	14
Yorkshire	3,152	11
S. Western	2,524	10
NE Thames	2,608	9
W. Midlands	3,157	9
Oxford	1,235	9
Wessex	1,368	7
Trent	2,321	7
N. Western	1,790	6
Northern	1,533	6
E. Anglia	560	4
TOTAL	36,098	

Table 3. National Health Service hospital summary: all specialities

United Kingdom	1971	1976	1978	1979	1981	1983	1984	1985	1986
All in-patients									
Discharges and deaths[1] (thousands)	6,437	6,525	6,686	6,710	7,179	7,461	7,666	7,884	7,955
Average number of beds available daily[2] (thousands)	526	484	—	461	450	440	429	421	409
Maternities	19	16	16	16	15	14	14	13	13
Other patients	417	378	364	358	350	340	333	327	316
Total–average number of beds occupied daily	436	394	380	374	366	354	347	341	329
Patients treated per bed available (number)	12.3[5]	13.6	—[3]	—[3]	16.0	17.0	17.8	18.7	19.5
Average length of stay (days)									
Medical patients	14.7[6]	12.1	11.4	11.2	10.2	9.5	9.1	8.7	8.5
Surgical patients	9.1[6]	8.6	8.2	8.1	7.6	7.2	6.9	6.7	6.5
Maternities	7.0[6]	6.7	6.4	6.0	5.6	5.1	4.9	4.7	4.5
Percentage of live births in hospital[4]	89.8	97.6	—[3]	—[3]	98.9	99.0	99.0	99.1	99.1

Private in-patients[5] (thousands)								
Discharges and deaths	115	95	93	92	98	84	79	71
Average number of beds occupied daily	2	2	2	2	1	1	1	1
New out-patients[6] (thousands)								
Accidents and emergency	9,358	10,463	10,943	11,030	11,342	11,932	12,279	12,492
Other out-patients	9,572	9,170	9,394	9,426	9,816	10,119	10,376	10,604
Average attendances per new patient (numbers)								
Accidents and emergency	1.6	1.6	1.4	1.4	1.4	1.4	1.4	1.3
Other out-patients	4.2	4.0	4.3	4.3	4.4	4.3	4.3	4.3
Day case attendances (thousands)	..	565[6]	667	708	863	979	1,081	1,166

(continued)

..	..
12,682	10,705
1.3	4.3
1,286	

1. 'Discharges and deaths' are the terms used to cover all patients who leave hospital.
2. Staffed beds only.
3. This information was not given in *Social Trends* 12, 1982.
4. Great Britain only.
5. England and Wales only.
6. The 1971 and 1976 figures for out-patients in Scotland include ancillary departments.

Source: Department of Health and Social Security; Scottish Health Service, Common Services Agency; Welsh Office; Department of Health and Social Services, Northern Ireland. From *Social Trends 18*, 1988, with data for 1978 and 1979 added from *Social Trends 12*, 1982.

Fact-Finding Activity 8

For each of these documents:
1. Make a list of the 'facts' (avoiding individual case histories) on which each relies.
2. Describe briefly the view of the state of the NHS taken by each.

When you have done this, compare your findings with mine in the Answers Section.

In the face of these conflicting statements you need to do some fact finding yourself. In the last activity of this case study you will be asked to comment on the use of facts contained in the data below in relation to these two interpretations.

Find out question 1:
Are Norman Fowler's claims about the increase in the numbers of patients treated justified?

About the data (Table 3)
This table, a 'summary' of hospital services year by year from 1971, records an enormous amount of information. In his speech, Norman Fowler compares numbers of patients treated in 1985 with those treated in 1978, the year before the Conservative Party came into power. There are some gaps in the data in this table. For an intelligent guess at missing figures, you can plot a graph (e.g. 'Year' on one axis and 'Average number of beds available daily' on the other), using either graph paper or a computing package. This exercise would also illustrate the use of graphs for projecting.

Fact-Finding Activity 9

1(i) How many in-patients were treated in a) 1978 b) 1985? See * on the table.
(ii) How many more in-patients were treated in 1985 than in 1978?
2(i) How many day cases were treated in a) 1978 b) 1985?
(ii) How many more day cases were treated in 1985 than in 1978?
3(i) How many out-patients were treated in a) 1978 b) 1985?
(ii) How many more out-patients were treated in 1985 than in 1978?

• Check your answers with mine in the Answers Section, then write a short answer to Find Out question 1 before reading my comments below.

In general Norman Fowler's figures seem well founded in fact. More patients were treated in 1985 than in 1978, over a million more, and the figure for day cases is even higher than the 400,000 he cites. However, his figure for the increase in outpatient attendances ($3\frac{1}{4}$ million) is higher than the $2\frac{1}{2}$ million indicated here. In view of these findings, we need to check out the Observer's facts with care.

Find out question 2:
Are the claims made by the Observer equally well founded in fact?
Points 1.2. and 4. from P. 219 of the Answers Section can be checked in Table 3 pages 84–5. Note that the Observer makes the comparison between 1985 and 1979. Point 3 (the increase in the elderly population), is also part of this question and can be checked from Fig 24. I suggest you tackle Find Out question 2 when you have worked your way through activities 10 and 11. The debate about the length of waiting lists, raised by Norman Fowler (Point 2) and the Observer (Point 5) will be considered in Find Out question 3.

Fact-Finding Activity 10

Point 1 On average, how many beds were there in a) 1979 b) 1985? Is this an increase or decrease? by how many? Try working this out as a percentage.
Point 2 What was the average length of stay for hospital in-patients in a) 1979 b) 1985? By roughly what proportion has this dropped?
Point 4 The increase in day care has already been established.

Check your answers to 1 and 2 with mine in the Answers Section.

This brings us to Point 3 from the Observer article: 'the number of people over 75 has increased by 20% since 1979'. Has it?

About the data (Fig 24)
This graph shows the upward trend in the size of the elderly population at a glance; this is its main purpose and message. It is harder, however, to work out the figures for each section in a graph that shows 'layers'. Remember to subtract the previous layer(s) when you are working out numbers for sections higher up the graph.

Fig. 24   **Elderly people: by age group, England and Wales.**

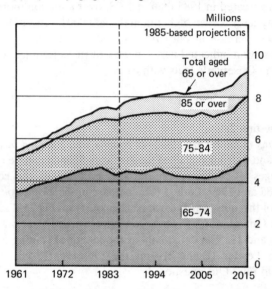

Source: Office of Population Censuses and Surveys; Government Actuary's Department. From *Social Trends 17*, 1987.

Fact-Finding Activity 11

1. By roughly how much has the 'young elderly', aged 65–74 increased between 1961 and 1985?
2. By how much has the over 75 age group increased in this time?
3. What is the trend for the future?

● Check your answers with mine in the Answers Section then write your answer to Find Out question 2 *Are the claims made by the Observer equally well founded in fact?* Because there are several parts to the question, you need to think for a moment about the order in which you take your points. A plan for a short piece does not have to be written, but it does have to be clear.

The Observer's figures also seem to be well based in fact. Their figure for the reduction in the number of beds is 36,000; the evidence in Table 3 is that this may be an underestimate. Patients are not staying in hospital as long as in 1979; there has been a steady decline in the length of stay in all categories of patient. The population of frail elderly over 75 is increasing sharply. From the chart here it is difficult to say whether the figure of 20% is accurate, but the trend is clear.

Find Out question 3:
Norman Fowler claims to have reduced the number of people on the

Table 4. Hospital in-patient waiting lists[1]: by speciality, United Kingdom.

Thousands

	1976	1979	1981	1984	1985	1986
Speciality						
General surgery[2]	200.5	208.9	169.1	183.3	174.0	180.3
Orthopaedics	109.8	153.6	145.1	165.4	154.1	160.5
Ear, nose or throat	121.7	130.9	115.4	128.8	128.7	132.2
Gynaecology	91.8	121.7	105.6	107.4	107.1	106.6
Oral surgery	26.5	33.6	35.5	55.3	55.1	56.3
Plastic surgery	44.7	51.8	49.2	50.4	46.0	46.1
Ophthalmology	41.2	50.6	43.4	53.4	55.2	64.6
Urology[3]	22.0	30.6	29.1	39.2	38.9	42.7
Other	42.5	46.7	44.2	44.6	43.4	41.3
All specialities	700.8	828.4	736.6	827.9	802.6	830.6

1. Waiting lists of NHS hospitals only as at 30 September each year.
2. Includes the Northern Ireland figures for 'urology'.
3. Great Britain only.
Source: Department of Health and Social Security. From *Social Trends 18*, 1988, including figures for 1979 from *Social Trends 1986*.

waiting lists since 1979. The Observer describes 'increasing' waiting lists. Are both true?

About the data (Table 4)
Notice the date on which these figures are compiled each year. This is relevant to Activity 12 question 3.

Fact-Finding Activity 12

1. Compare the total number of people waiting for in-patient treatment in 1985 with a) 1979 b) 1981. Are there more or fewer on the waiting lists in 1985?
2. For how many specialities would you have to wait longer for in-patient treatment in 1985 than in a) 1979 b) 1981?
3. Norman Fowler based most of the points in his speech on 1985 figures. If he had known the 1986 figures when he spoke that October, why might he still have preferred the 1985 figures?

● Check your answers with mine in the Answers Section then write your answer to Find Out question 3 before reading my comments below.

Both Norman Fowler's and the Observer's claims are true. It all depends on which years you make your comparisons with. It is true that the lists were longer in 1979 than in 1985 but not 1986. It is also true that the lists in 1985 and 1986 were longer than in 1981. Politicians choose their comparisons with care!

Review

You can now go back to the starting point – the research question:

But is it true?

- Write a short critical piece of between one and two sides to answer this question. Comment on how and why facts have been used to support conflicting interpretations. Use examples from the Case Study to support your points.

But is it true? Some conclusions

We now have a strange, but, with statistics, common situation. Two authors present truthful information, based on the same figures but each draws radically different conclusions from them. Norman Fowler presents a positive, optimistic picture of the benefits the NHS is bringing to the nation under his government; the Observer, meanwhile, paints a picture of hardship, increasing needs, cuts and deteriorating standards of patient care.

The answer to 'But which is true?' is that both are factually correct. The figures from the government's own sources – Social Trends – show this. Whether this makes a statement 'true' or not is another matter – one for you to judge. You look at the figures and ask questions; Norman Fowler is correct to assert that there are 'more' patients being treated than ever before, but his assertion that this care is 'better' has no more validity than your opinion or mine. Here he is in the realm of judgements about the quality of care of patients. To make up your own mind, you have to bring to the facts a questioning approach, a readiness to consider various explanations, and your own values and experience.

This tendency for facts to be manipulated to support a viewpoint is what led Disraeli to utter his much quoted phrase 'Lies, damned lies and statistics', and Jim Hacker (in 'Yes, Prime Minister') to complain, 'Your statistics are facts. My statistics are just statistics.' This case study is an illustration of just this.

5 Life goes on

5.1 Problems with Studying

What are the main difficulties you have found with studying so far? Jot down two or three points, then read on.

I asked some students aged 18–47 this question. Their replies included the following:
- My essays don't look like much but I start again and again and throw them in the bin. It's as if there is a block between my brain and my hand.
- I put off starting until it's too late.
- I get bored just sitting there but I don't feel I can leave it.
- There's much more to do between classes than I thought. I hadn't really thought about that, just getting to the classes.
- Not having anywhere quiet to work.
- I know I don't use my time well. If a class finishes at 11, I have coffee and get chatting, then it doesn't seem worth starting until after lunch.
- The day goes by and I've done nothing.
- I watch all sorts of rubbish on TV instead of getting down to it.
- I work late at MacDonalds three nights a week and Saturdays. I have to. I'm too tired to study and I know I miss classes.
- My wife looks after the kids all week and now I'm sneaking off upstairs to study at weekends too. I feel bad about that.
- I get fed up and go out.
- Time is a big problem. I was busy before, but there's no slack now.
- I never go out but I still can't study.
- I love the reading and the classes but I do anything to put off writing essays.
- It's difficult with my husband. He was studying himself until recently, but I don't think he wants me to.
- I play a lot of sports and train most evenings. I've got behind with the work.
- There are a lot of bits and pieces to do; read this, write that. I often find I've missed out something.

My own list of problems I have encountered writing this book runs like this: – finding time;
- – losing the thread between one work session and the next;
- – interruptions;
- – finding it difficult to work at certain times of day.

5.2 **Some Suggestions**

While problems don't stop being problems just because you have identified them, I have established some ground rules which may be of interest to you as you work out your own study schedule.

(i) *Finding time* is my major problem. I have a part time job and three young children but I know that I was no better (in fact rather worse) when I was younger and had lots of time. So it's a question of using time, not just having it. I work to a schedule: $1\frac{1}{2}$ hours 'start up' time on Fridays, to review stuff and plan what to do next. Saturday is my main writing day. I get up early on Sunday mornings to work and usually find a session in the week by swapping children with a friend.

(ii) *Losing the thread between sessions*. There is no easy answer to this. The Friday 'start up' session helps. I write lists of things to do and leave notes for myself. It helps to identify what can be done in short bursts and what is best left for a longer stretch.

(iii) *Interruptions* are irritating especially when you've just got going, and it's something the home student/worker is prone to because our work times are other people's leisure times. I have learnt to be firm about counting myself out of activities, and saying 'Not now, tomorrow' if a work session is threatened. If you know a work session will be cut short, think of it as a planned break and enjoy it. Short interruptions – hanging out the washing – can be positively helpful to break up a long study session, as long as you are disciplined about going straight back to work.

(iv) *Finding it difficult to work at certain times of day* is a major source of regret. I always feel sleepy around 2.00pm when I work at home, so I don't try to work then. I either give in, or do something active. I do sometimes use the evenings for marking, checking or routine paper shuffling, but I do not count on it. I have learnt that there's no point trying to work when I really don't feel like it. This has its compensations; it leaves some time for other things. It is, of course, a highly individual matter. A friend doing an OU course aims to do all his work in the evenings to leave the weekends free for family activities.

Self Check

Look back at the list of problems with studying on P. 91 and add your own to it. Try and group these problems, and think of ways of dealing with them. Compare your groupings and comments with mine.

It seems to me that most of the problems are to do with:

1. Realising the **implications** of returning to study and its *impact* on other aspects of life. This is the most difficult problem to address because it involves other people and other commitments. You need to give thought to it early in your course. Talk to the people you live with about what you are doing and why and discuss realistically what your needs are and the impact on them. The family may have to do more chores, partner take a greater part in running the household, flat mates be quieter at times. But they have needs too, and you must strike a balance.

   You must also make decisions; if your circumstances simply won't allow you to study this year, plan for the future. How essential is the MacDonalds job? This student's answer was 'absolutely'. He dropped a subject and one evening and so made time for the rest; it was not an easy decision.

2. **Personal organisation**

   Make lists of everything you have to do and tick them off as you go. I sometimes cheat a bit by putting down things I have just done and ticking them off – for encouragement.

   Keep a diary to make a note of all your work, home and study commitments and deadlines. Remember to refer to it.

   Organise your papers. Give some thought to practicalities. How many folders will you need? Do you need to carry all your papers around or will you have a system for transferring work to a current folder? If you don't use your diary for this, use a notebook to keep track of work set and deadlines. Would you have any use for cards for recording your reading (see chapter 1) or for revising (chapter 10)? Work out a system early in your course, and develop it as you go along.

3. **Practice** with reading and writing. You will get better at it. The purpose of this book is to help with this; what to read? how much? how much detail? Try some of the short exercises in the writing chapters. They may be different to the tasks you are set, but it's practice and confidence that counts. Do talk to your tutor. Tutors are usually very sympathetic to people returning to study, and have probably experienced similar problems to you in the past if not at

present. Don't wait until you fall behind in your work; discuss specific problems as soon as they arise.

4. **Getting down to it**. Don't try and flog yourself. Plan a schedule which allows you time for the things you value most whether this is a TV programme, sport, socialising or relaxing at home. But do work at work times. Set yourself realistic targets for a work session and when you have finished reward yourself.

5. **Finding time** for study underlies many of the problems on the first page. If this is a problem for you, you may like to try a time planning exercise. On P. 95 is a blank time planning sheet with a slot for every hour of the week, from 6.00am to midnight. I'm not going to suggest that you account for every minute of that time but use it as a basis for thinking about *how* you really do use your time; which, of the various things you regularly do, is absolutely essential to you, your commitments and your wellbeing; where you could find extra time for study if and when you need to, with the minimum disruption to the rest of your life.

Self-Check

Decide which of these you would like to investigate, and complete the chart accordingly.
How do you really use your time? At the end of each day, for a week, review the day and record, honestly, what you did, when and for how long. Record the time you got up, travelled to and from work or college, classes you (really) went to, time spent cooking, eating, time with the family, out, doing chores, studying, doing nothing much, sport, watching TV etc.

Review your sheet. Does anything come as a surprise?

What is absolutely essential? If you can make some major changes to find more time for study, well and good – as long as you are comfortable with what you propose and are not overambitious. Most people cannot make major changes, so look for minor ones;
– look closely at 'watching TV'. Which programme do you really want to watch? Switch off the TV afterwards.
– you may find 5–8pm a time you could use better. One student does her homework with her children at this time. Another found he could go out at 8 having done three hours work by using this slot.
– can you get up early to study one day a week?
– can you shift some chores to the evening and free some time in the day?

	MONDAY	TUESDAY	WEDNESDAY	THURSDAY	FRIDAY	SATURDAY	SUNDAY
AM 6							
7							
8							
9							
10							
11							
12							
PM 1							
2							
3							
4							
5							
6							
7							
8							
9							
10							
11							
12							

Fig. 25 Time Planning Chart

– can you find a long stretch somewhere?

– try and find a time when you could work if you had to, but don't need to use every week. This is useful when you have to catch up after a busy weekend or if the children are ill.

A problem one student had was that she had allowed too much time for study, had cut out several activities she valued, made herself miserable, got terribly bored and her studies suffered. She used this exercise to structure her time, set herself specific tasks and when she completed them, she went out!

Planning study time

When you have identified a slot to use for studying, allocate a particular task to it. Rather than write 'Studying' note, or think, 'Read Ch 6' or 'think about essay' at particular times. When you have done this, look at it from time to time. Unless you find it helpful, don't treat it as a timetable; that is far too inflexible, and doesn't allow for the unexpected – an invitation, a rush at work, illness.

5.3 Dos and Don'ts

This chapter ends with a list of dos and don'ts, tips from students and tutors. Some repeat points made earlier, others are new. Read critically – identify ideas you think could be worth trying; be clear about which are irrelevant to you.

DO

– Talk to other members of your household about your plans to study.
– Find somewhere you can settle to work quickly. If you have not got a room of your own try keeping your things in a box or on a shelf so you can get them out quickly or use a library.
– Find out which times of day you work best and plan to work at these times as much as possible.
– Write lists of things to do, and tick them off when you have done them.
– Keep a diary of all fixtures.
– Allow free times in the week and free weeks in your long term schedule, so you are not thrown by the odd interruption, illness or holidays.
– Give up if you get fed up. Come back to it when you are feeling fresh.
– Plan and take short breaks to break up a long work session.
– Stop while you're winning. If you've done a task well and quickly, reward yourself with a break/trip out, rather than pressing on. Enjoy your studies.

DON'T
– make yourself miserable by cutting out all your leisure activities.
– expect to do nothing between one class and the next. Ask your tutor what a reasonable minimum of private study is. Start with this and increase it if you find it necessary.
– be overambitious about how much studying you are going to do in a week.
– try to study for great tracts of time without a break. Plan to break for five minutes or so every 45 minutes to an hour – stretch your legs, make a hot drink – and come back!
– set yourself an amount of time to study. Set yourself a task to do. Stop afterwards.
– work when you can't. Work at times when you work best.
– worry about following advice about approved ways of studying.

Do whatever works for you, and look for advice when you are not satisfied with your own work methods.

Part 2

Writing

6 Putting Pen to Paper

It is often the prospect of writing that causes the greatest dread in students – particularly when the only writing they have done in the past few years is the weekly shopping list and such like. As with any neglected skill, with practice you will regain confidence in your ability to write. But before you can write, you need to be able to organise your ideas. The aim of this chapter is to approach this process by drawing on those skills of organisation you use successfully every day.

Take that shopping list, and consider the organisational skills behind it.

baking powder	frozen pizzas	fish (tomorrow)
tomato ketchup	frozen beans	carrots
(squeezy)	cat food	lettuce
loo paper	stamps	potatoes
apple juice	greens	jelly
bread	oranges	ice cream (Wed)
washing up liquid	soft fruit (cherries?	card for M
toothpaste	strawberries?)	sliced bread (freezer)
(fruit flavoured)	scrubbing brush	

A shopping list is the tip of the iceberg of domestic organisation (and disorganisation). Baking powder is there because when I wanted some yesterday there wasn't any; loo paper because there's a system for this – two rolls left and it's time to get some more. The toothpaste and jelly and ice cream oil the wheels of family relationships – but it's only because I happen to be using this week's shopping list as an introduction to the chapter that I have given a moment's thought to the planning and thinking behind it. So if the only writing you have done recently is to write shopping lists and the like, take heart! You have the skills to organise your life, and need to apply these to organising your ideas.

So how do you turn a list of items jotted down as you thought of them into a plan of action you can carry out with the minimum of running back for things you have forgotten?

Self-check

Draw up a shopping list of your own (of about 20 items), or use mine as a basis for this activity. Divide it into sensible groups according to how you would set about doing the shopping.

There are lots of ways you can divide up a list like this, aren't there? You can group things according to the supermarket section you'd find them in;

Household goods	Fruit and veg	Frozen
washing up liquid	greens	pizzas
loo paper	fruit	beans
scrubbing brush	lettuce	ice cream
	potatoes	
	carrots	

and so on.

Or you might organise your shopping differently, going to the supermarket every now and again, and doing the rest of your shopping locally; in which case your shopping list might look more like this;

Supermarket	Local
ketchup	Greengrocer : fruit
loo paper	veg
apple juice	Chemist : toothpaste
sliced bread	Fishmonger : fish (tomorrow)
cat food	Baker : bread
etc..	

Or you might organise your shopping by when you plan to do it, with the bulk of the items one day and the rest as you need it;

Monday	Tuesday	Wednesday
Bread	fish	ice cream
greens	carrots	
card for M	jelly	
stamps	fruit	
and so on		

There are lots of ways of organising shopping, and none of them is right or wrong. You choose the order that works best for you now – it may be different next week. One thing is certain, though; unless you are an extraordinarily well organised person, the original order in which you jotted down items is not the order in which you buy them.

The same applies to ideas;
- welcome and record all your ideas;
- recognise that the order in which ideas occur to you is not necessarily the best one to write them in;
- group related points together;
- use the headings to introduce the points;
- organise your ideas according to your purpose.

This is the sort of thinking, planning and organisation that underpins good, clear writing.

6.1 Paragraphs

Any writing, from a shopping list to a thesis, has divisions or sections which correspond to the organisation of ideas within them. Within sections are paragraphs; these are the basic units of ideas which make up a larger whole. Each paragraph you write should make a single point. You have already looked at paragraphs from the reader's point of view; a well organised paragraph is easy to read because the main idea comes first, and then is explained and developed. Now consider this from your position as a writer.

Writing Activity 1: Paragraphs

You may be required to carry out a piece of research or a project as part of your coursework. Below is a list of some sources of information for this sort of assignment;

employers	local interest	other students	radio
family	groups	the council	museums
newspapers	tutors	magazines	local people
library	TV programmes	Prestel/Ceefax/	advice bureaus
pressure groups	local businesses	Oracle	
	books		

● Now divide up this list into groups of related suggestions. Give each a heading. Read on when you have done this.

The headings are the important bit, aren't they? I expect some of your headings will be the same as mine and others different: there's no right or wrong as long as the divisions are sensible and include all the items. I thought I'd divide the list as follows; a slightly different grouping is suggested on P. 105.

People	Media	Organisations	Public amenities
employers	newspapers	presure groups	libraries – books
family	TV	local interest	council
tutors	magazines	groups	museums
students	Prestel etc	advice bureaus	
local people	radio	local businesses	

Look more closely at the 'media' grouping above. How might you organise the points within this section? You are now looking for ways of ordering the points you want to use to illustrate how the 'media' might be a useful source of information. You could refine your organisation like this;

Media
Printed: newspapers
         magazines
TV and radio
Information technology: Prestel / Ceefax / Oracle

Look at the subdivisions of the 'public amenity' section shown on the 'branching' plan opposite.

This plan has become an action plan; the library looks like the starting point for information of all sorts. 'People' is the other major starting point. Notice the points about libraries you might include within a paragraph on information from public sources.

● Write a paragraph on sources of information for a project based on one of these groupings.

Start with your *topic sentence*; make it clear what you are writing about; people, media, organisations, or public amenities.
After that include detailed suggestions (based on your listings) in the *body* of the paragraph.
End with a *concluding comment* – perhaps something about the value of these sources.

Writing Activity 2: The structure of a paragraph

Below is a jumbled version of a paragraph from *Effective Advertising and PR* by Alison Corke. Your task is to arrange the sentences in a logical order, bearing in mind these points about organising ideas within a paragraph. If you have access

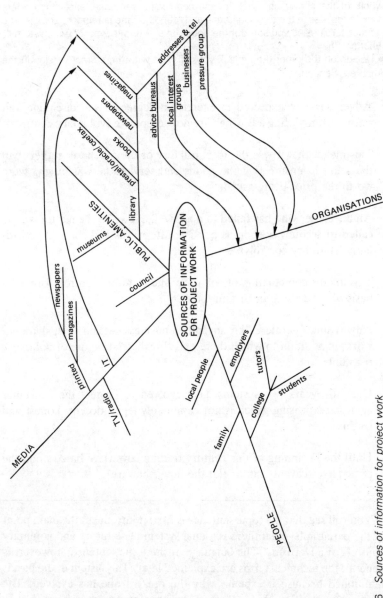

Fig. 26 Sources of information for project work

to a word processor, try using it for this activity. By using the 'Cut and paste' keys, and deleting the spaces, you will be able to reproduce these sentences so they read and look like a paragraph.

Look for the topic sentence; the one which best expresses the idea in the whole of the paragraph. Look for the concluding sentence, one which refers back to the idea in the topic sentence and rounds off the paragraph. Look for the syntactical clues as you sort out the body; 'this' refers to what? 'Two systems'; what are they?

● Decide on the order then check your answer with the correct version in the Answers Section.

Advertisers are expected to exercise a degree of self discipline and refrain from placing ads which are not acceptable (voluntary controls).

This meant that it was the responsibility of the purchaser rather than the seller to ensure that the goods and services he was buying were worth the price being asked.

An advertiser who has failed to observe the laws on the matter will be called to account as soon as possible afterwards and charged accordingly (statutory controls).

This unique combination of voluntary and statutory controls forms the basis of advertising in Britain today.

Advertising operates, like any other business, within a legal framework, in addition to which there exists a whole structure of voluntary restraints.

Over the years two systems have evolved to protect the consumer against advertising which is not completely legal, decent, honest and truthful.

Until the beginning of this century trading laws were based upon the principle of caveat emptor (let the buyer beware).

You will see that the topic sentence is first; it introduces the main point of the paragraph – that there is a dual system of statutory and voluntary controls of advertising. The language of the topic sentence, however, is general; the technical terms are explained later. The system in the past is mentioned because it explains why the present one has evolved. The writer then clarifies what 'voluntary' and 'statutory' controls mean, and concludes with a comment which refers directly and explicitly to the point in the topic sentence.

Writing Activity 3: Identifying paragraphs

The key to writing good, clear paragraphs is to be able to write clear topic sentences. Below is another extract from Alison Corke's book, reproduced without any divisions. Your task is to divide it into paragraphs. Identify the topic sentences, and see how the ideas are developed in each paragraph.

It is the IBA's responsibility to draw up a code governing the standards of practice in advertising and to see that the provisions of the Code are followed. The IBA appoints committees to give advice on the steps to be taken to exclude misleading advertisements from broadcasts, to review the Code and to advise on any other principles. In addition, the IBA is required to appoint local advisory committees representative of people living in their localities. The IBA Code of Advertising Standards and Practices is very wide ranging. It covers both general matters (eg ads should not exploit the superstitious) and very specific matters (eg ads for certain products and services such as cigarettes and undertakers are not acceptable). There are also rules governing advertising and children, financial advertising and the advertising of medicines and treatments. All TV commercials must be checked before they are transmitted by the Independent Television Companies Association (ITCA), a committee established by the ITV contractors. The ITCA is very strict in checking that commercials do not infringe either the Television Act or the Code of Advertising Practice. In addition the ITCA can and frequently does ask for scientific proof (that a shampoo really does clear dandruff, or that a detergent actually removes blood stains at lower temperatures and so on). Commercials are usually shown to the ITCA for clearance at script stage, then again as finished before they are screened. Without ITCA clearance a commercial cannot be shown.

This extract covers three main topics;
 (i) the IBA's responsibilities in relation to the Code of practice;
 (ii) the nature of this code.
(iii) the checking of TV commercials by the ITCA.

The sentences expressing these three points are the three topic sentences. Did you notice the concluding sentences too?
 (i) The last sentence of the first paragraph was not particularly conclusive; it completed the list of responsibilities (local advisory committees).
 (ii) The second paragraph ends with specific examples of the 'wide ranging' Code.

108

(iii) The third paragraph ends by reinforcing explicitly the point made in the topic sentence. The paragraph moves from 'TV commercials must be checked' to 'Without ITCA clearance a commercial cannot be shown' – a stronger restatement.

- So, before you write, plan your paragraphs;
1. Make your **main point** first; this is your topic sentence.
2. Follow it up with **linked explanation**, illustration or examples in the middle.
3. End with a comment which **links back to the topic sentence** by adding to it or showing how the examples reinforce your point or modify it.

This sounds inflexible and schematic, but the chances are you often write in this way instinctively. The advantage of planning to write in a structured way is that it gives you a clear place to start – with the main idea – when you are faced with a writing task.

Review
Writing Activity 4

Find Fig 22 (Charts 1 and 2) in Chapter 4. Write a paragraph on what you observe in each chart. Start with the main point (your topic sentence); then add detail to support and illustrate it, and conclude with a comment that refers back to the main point.

Work through the Fact Finding questions if you want to, but try and avoid looking at my comments or the commentary by New Society until you have written your paragraphs. These commentaries will indicate the sort of points you should have picked out, but they will not be identical to yours; my comments are in response to specific questions and New Society includes additional information.

6.2 Instructions

The purpose of instructions is to enable somebody new to the task to carry it out correctly and easily. Instructions need to begin at the beginning, describe each step in order and steer the person round foreseeable difficulties without overburdening them with detail. Not an easy task, particularly when the process is second nature to you.

Writing Activity 5a: Instructions

Below are instructions for wiring a plug in a confusing order.
1. Arrange the instructions in what you think is the best order.
2. Edit and rewrite them where necessary.

If you have access to a word processor, try using it for this. An advantage of a WP for ordering ideas and points is that it is easy to try out different arrangements of the text and to rewrite. You can print a good looking copy of your versions.

How to wire a plug
- Undo the large screw in the middle of the plug.
- Cut the plastic casing so that about an inch of coloured wires shows.
- Loosen the screws of the three terminals.
- You need a screwdriver and a blade such as a Stanley knife.
- Inside the plug you will see three terminals and a fuse.
- When it's open, twist the copper wires so the strands are neat.
- Most appliances have cables with three wires; brown (live), blue (neutral), earth (yellow and green).
- Make sure the wires reach far enough into the plug to reach their correct terminals. You may need more than 1″ coloured wire.
- Some appliances do not have the earth wire.
- A little less than $\frac{1}{2}''$ copper wire should be exposed.
- Take care when you cut the coloured plastic casings not to cut the copper wires.
- Insert the cable under the clamp.
- Position the clamp over the plastic casing.
- To get the cable under the clamp you need to loosen it. Loosen the two small screws on the pin side of the plug.
- Insert the copper wires to the corect terminals; brown to live (right) by the fuse, blue to neutral (left), yellow and green to earth, centre top.
- When you have finished, position the lid on the plug and tighten the central screw.
- Make sure the fuse is the correct one for the appliance.
- When each copper wire is well inserted, tighten the terminal screw to secure it.
- Your appliance is ready for use.
- Tighten the two smaller clamp screws.

How good are your instructions? Try them out yourself as you wire a plug, and then on somebody who is not confident about doing it.

Discuss with them what alterations you could make to improve your instructions.

Self-check

- Look back at your instructions on how to wire a plug. Divide them into sections which mark the stages of the process. On a word processor, insert an extra 'Return' at your divisions.

Even a simple process like this has stages; the beginning (finding tools, preparatory work); middle (the wiring itself) and end (checking, doing up the plug). These three stages correspond to three paragraphs.

Writing Activity 5b

More practice
Try writing instructions for the following, one point per line.
1. How to set up and run a word processor or computer to the point where you start to write/play/input data.
2. How to claim Income Support or Unemployment benefit.
3. How to operate a new photocopier or piece of machinery at work or at home.

You may find it quite easy to write simple instructions but need to make decisions about how much detail to include; what happens when the photocopier goes wrong? Claiming benefit may be simple in theory but many people find they encounter difficulties they had not anticipated, satisfying the 'Availability for Work' test, follow-up interviews and the like. You could use a new paragraph for this sort of detail; your readers can skip it if they don't need it.

When you are satisfied with your instructions, decide how to divide them into paragraphs. Make sure you have a topic sentence so your reader can anticipate what is coming next.

6.3 Articles

Writing Activity 6: an article

This activity is based on the following extract from 'The Business of Communicating' by Nicki Stanton. She offers 'tips' and a checklist of dos and don'ts when you are being interviewed for a job.
- Write an article giving advice on interviews based on these points.

Tips to remember
When you are in a strange, formal situation it is easy to forget the obvious things which are second nature on more relaxed occasions, so here are a few tips to remember.

- Arrive in good time – not only because it is polite but because having to rush will leave you feeling hot and flustered, and therefore nervous.
- Be neat and fairly conservative in your appearance.
- Take cues from the interviewer on degree of formality – your sensitivity to non-verbal communication should help you with this. Perhaps be a little more formal than usual – not a stuffed shirt. Be cautious about jokes, sarcastic asides, etc.
- Don't smoke unless invited to do so; and then only if you must, unless the interviewer smokes; but never if there is no ashtray in sight.
- Be prepared to take notes, if it is necessary to record information. But it might be best to ask the interviewer if he would mind if you did. Even then, don't scribble furiously all the way through.
- Be polite, but friendly and don't forget to smile (but only when it's appropriate).
- Leave promptly when the interview is over: don't hover. Smile, shake hands and thank the interviewer.

....

Summary Checklist
Before the interview
1 Be informed about the organization: its history, geographical location, general methods of doing business, reputation, etc.
2 Anticipate questions that might be asked: factual questions as well as 'trap' questions.
3 Make a note of questions you want asked.

During the interview
4 State why you are applying for the job and show you know something about it.
5 Present your qualifications in terms of having something of value to offer the company. Deal as much as possible in specific details and examples – job experiences, interests, travel, activities, offices held, organizations and school.
6 Don't depend merely on a 'smooth front' (appearance and smile) to sell yourself. Provide full information to the prospective employer.
7 Don't hesitate to admit potential weaknesses. Under no circumstances attempt to bluff or fake on these, but wherever possible make a transition from a weakness to a strength; or, at least, when

the facts justify it, show some extenuating circumstances for the weakness. (This doesn't mean supplying alibis or excuses!)

8 Generally attempt to expand your responses beyond a simple 'yes' or 'no'.

9 Treat the interviewer as a human being, not an ogre!

10 Remember the normal rules of etiquette.

11 Get as much information as possible about the job requirements and organization, and on 'sensitive' matters such as salary (usually in terms of range, or the going average).

12 Try never to have an interview concluded without some sort of understanding about where you stand, what happens next, who is to contact whom, etc.

13 Try to enjoy it.

14 Be sincere – be yourself.

(From *'The Business of Communicating'* by Nicki Stanton. P.96-8, Pan Breakthrough 1986)

Before you start there are a number of points to think out.

1. *Who* is the article aimed at? Young people entering the workforce? Older people returning to work? Keep your audience clearly in mind since this will affect what you say and how you say it.

2. *What sort* of publication are you writing for? In-house journal? Student paper? Local paper? Publications often have a distinctive style. Bear this in mind too.

3. *Plan* your article. You already have the basic material. Your task is to select from it and organise it.
   – look for points that go together
   – look for headings
   – look for paragraphs.
   • When you have done this, check with my plan opposite.

Your plan doesn't have to look like this. A plan is a shape in your head; you know what to start with, how to finish, and have a clear idea of the points you want to make in the middle. Some kind of written plan is usually a help, however. You can jot words across the page, or arrange headings down the page. Leave space for adding points and moving them around. I find branching notes a useful discipline; they make me think and keep the plan short.

4. Look at the two plans. How many paragraphs will your article have? Mine will have six: four in the body, some sort of introduction, and some concluding remarks as well. I found two of the paragraphs in the body easy to plan– 'background preparation' and 'during the inter-

113

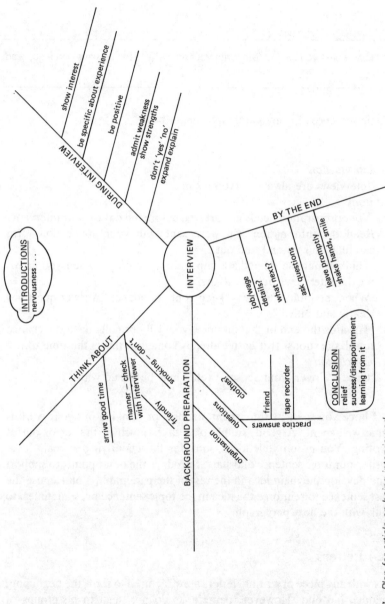

Fig. 27 Plan for article on being interviewed

THINK ABOUT
- arrive good time
- manner — check with interviewer
- smoking — don't
- friendly

BACKGROUND PREPARATION
- organisation
- questions
- clothes?
- practice answers
  - friend
  - tape recorder

INTERVIEW

INTRODUCTIONS
nervousness . . .

DURING INTERVIEW
- show interest
- be specific about experience
- be positive
- admit weakness
- show strengths
- don't 'yes' 'no'
- expand explain

BY THE END
- job/wage details?
- what next?
- ask questions
- leave promptly
- shake hands, smile

CONCLUSION
relief
success/disappointment
learning from it

114

view'. The other two in the middle needed more thought to work out what the points had in common.
5. Try following the plan for paragraphs on P. 108.

• Now, at last you can start to write your article! When you have had a go, read on.

Topic sentences for my paragraphs might be;

1. *Introduction*
   'Interviews are always nerve racking...'
2. *Body*
   'Your preparation needs to start well before the day of your interview. Read the information you were sent with your application form carefully and try and find out...'
3. 'Think about the immediate impression you create when you arrive for the interview. Be sure to arrive...'
4. 'When the interview starts, keep your confidence. Answer questions clearly and fully...'
5. 'Towards the end of the interview you will normally have the chance to ask questions. If it hasn't already come up, this is the time to...'
6. *Conclusion*
   'Once it's over, your sense of relief may be mixed with...'

I hope you see why time spent planning or thinking out your work is time well spent. A good, simple plan takes much of the terror out of writing. You group your ideas, look for the underlying or main idea, write your topic sentence and start. Introduce the other points to support and develop the main idea in the rest of the paragraph. You can use the last sentence to reinforce the idea in the topic sentence or, sometimes, to link with the next paragraph.

6.4 **Letters**

As with any piece of writing, letters are structured to show the beginning, middle and end. However, paragraphs do not need to be groups of developed ideas and often contain a single point in a single sentence.

Even the shortest letter will normally have three paragraphs.

Dear Ms Jones

Thank you for your letter of 10th April.

I can confirm that 10.30am, Thursday 2nd May is a convenient time for us to meet.

I look forward to meeting you then.

Yours sincerely,

N. Patel

The author is making three simple points. The first and last are governed largely by convention. The introductory paragraph identifies the subject immediately and connects the letter with the exchanges that have already taken place. Letters normally finish with an expression of goodwill in the concluding paragraph.

Writing Activity 7: letters

Letter 1

Your boss has been asked to speak at a company communications seminar but will be unable to do so as he will be involved in his annual visit to regional offices to discuss plans for the coming year. He has to be away from the office today and asks you to draft a letter for him to see on his return. As he leaves the office he mumbles something about 'perhaps I could get old Wainwright to do it for them'. (From *The Business of Communicating* by N. Stanton, Pan Breakthrough)

Plan the letter; think it through.
(i) What is your *purpose* in writing?
(ii) What is the *content*?
(iii) What *tone* will you adopt?
(iv) How many *paragraphs* will the letter have?

Your *purpose* is to make apologies since your boss is not free to speak, and to urge an alternative speaker. Your *content* will outline the situation and make this suggestion. Your *tone* needs to be friendly and encouraging.

There are always at least three paragraphs in a letter; if you divide your explanation of the problem (boss unavailable) and your solution (another speaker), you will have *four* paragraphs.

• Write the letter. When you have a draft, turn to the Answers Section and compare it with the letter suggested in 'The Business of Communicating.'

Look closely at the structure of this letter and the paragraphs in it.

Paragraph 1: Identifies the subject and opens on a pleasant encouraging note.

Paragraph 2: The topic sentence introduces the main idea of this paragraph tactfully – that Mr Sharp is busy. This point is explained and illustrated in the middle. In the conclusion the writer returns directly to the idea in the topic sentence – that Mr Sharp is not available.

Paragraph 3: The point in the topic sentence is to suggest an alternative speaker whose qualities are described in the middle. The last sentence returns directly to the proposal.

Paragraph 4: Although short, this expression of goodwill is important.

Letter 2

You have so far failed to pay £15 for a Green Card (insurance confirmation necessary for travelling abroad) which was issued several months ago. You have felt disinclined to offer payment until the insurance brokers asked for the money and intend now to offer only £10, since you were put to considerable inconvenience by the insurance company (for whom the brokers act). They were extremely inefficient, failing to produce the card on time despite adequate notice, and only supplying one eventually at the eleventh hour after you had made several telephone calls and personal visits. What sort of covering letter would you send with the cheque? (From *The Business of Communicating* by N. Stanton, Pan Breakthrough 1986)

This is a difficult letter to write, and whether the firm pursues you for the extra £5 or not depends largely on your skill as a letter writer. So think it through.
  (i) What is your *purpose* in writing?
 (ii) What is the *content*?
(iii) What *tone* will you adopt?
(iv) How will you *structure* the letter?

Your *purpose* is to get the firm to agree to your proposal to pay £10 instead of the £15 demanded. The *content* of your letter must outline your reasons for this proposal. The *tone* needs to be polite and firm. The *structure*? Again, first and last paragraph, and two in the middle, one to outline your grievance and one for your proposal.

● Write the letter. When you have a draft, compare it with the letter suggested by Nicki Stanton in the Answers Section.

The structure of this letter is as follows:

Paragraph 1: The first sentence identifies the subject politely and refers to past exchanges; she agrees that the bill has not been paid.

Paragraph 2: The topic sentence introduces the main idea here; the problems encountered in obtaining the card. She details these in the rest of the paragraph and concludes with a summary of these 'problems' (money, time, anxiety) indicated in the topic sentence.

Paragraph 3: is brief; it begins and ends with the writer's proposal.

Paragraph 4: closes the discussion firmly and politely – a tone which implies that she expects the firm to concede her case. Would *you* agree to her payment of £10?

For more guidance on the layout of letters, see 'How to set out letters' in the Reference Section.

6.5 Reports

'Yes, I checked the photocopier about ten minutes ago. It was working all right but the print is rather faint. I think we should add some toner soon.'

This is a good report. It is useful and short and gives clear, well structured information. A formal report supports this logical structure with conventions:

Introduction

1 Terms of reference: what you have been asked to find out:
                    (the state of the photocopier)

2 Procedure: how you found out the information:
                    (a personal check)

Body

3 Findings: what you found out:
                    (OK but print faint)

Conclusion

4 Conclusions: your conclusions, or diagnosis:
                    (needs toner)

5 Recommendations: what you think should be done:
                    (add toner soon)

These five points are the structure of any report however short or long.

Writing Activity 8

A report on the Canteen

There have been a number of complaints about the length of time it takes to get served in the staff / college / works canteen. Several people have complained that far too much of the lunch hour is taken up with queuing, and that food is cold by the time they sit down to eat it. As union/staff representative you have been asked to find out if these complaints are justified and what action should be taken if they are.

● Present your findings as a short formal report with recommendations.

How do you set about doing something like this? The structure of the report offers useful guidance.

Working on your report

1. Establish your *terms of reference*. Who has asked you for the report? What exactly have you been asked to do?

   (i) find out if the complaints are well founded. This involves fact finding; how long do people have to queue for? Is food cold by the time they reach the tables?

   (ii) suggest what action (if any) should be taken. This requires you to make judgements and specific suggestions for improvement; is an unreasonable amount of the lunch hour spent in this way? What could be done to improve the situation?

2. You then think about how to gain your information. This will be recorded in the *procedure* section of the written report. It is important to record your research methods so readers can make up their own minds about whether your methods are likely to produce a thorough and impartial investigation.

   Jot down how you would set about checking these complaints. You could

   (i) conduct a *survey* of canteen users

   (ii) distribute a *questionnaire* to all staff

   (iii) make your own *observations* during the lunch hour,

       e.g. note how long it takes for one person to reach a table and

check the length of the queue during the hour.
(iv) *interview* selected people
(v) *visit* another canteen to look at other systems.

Once you have decided on your sources and methods for gathering information, you need to give some thought to practicalities. What questions do you want to ask in your interviews and questionnaire? How will you record your observations? You will find guidance on questionaires and interviews in the reference section. Think ahead about how to present your findings; a simple graph or diagram may present some information more effectively than words. Look back to Chapter 4 for ideas.

3. The *findings* section is the body of the report. By the time you are ready to write, you will have quite a lot of material to organise. Identify your main headings and group points under them in subheadings. Often the most important points are placed first. Alternatively, the findings section begins with a statement of the current background situation and goes on to describe particular aspects or difficulties in greater detail.

4. In the *conclusions* you present your analysis of the situation, indicating the problems as you see them. It is an important section, because many of your readers will have neither the time nor the inclination to read the findings in detail – although they will probably look at your procedure to satisfy themselves that your research methods are likely to lead to reasonable conclusions.

5. You end with *recommendations* (if you have been asked for them). Here you make specific suggestions for action by the person(s) who commissioned the report to remedy the problems you highlighted in your conclusions.

● Draw up terms of reference, carry out the research and draft a report on the canteen facilities where you work or study. A version of this report is given in 'How To Draft a Report' in the Reference Section.

If this activity is inappropriate for you, try one of the following:

1. A report on the provision of play equipment or sports facilities in the local park, by a parents or park users group, for submission to the Director of Leisure services in the local council.

2. A report on the service offered by the local job centre for submission to the regional manager of the DHSS by a group of local job seekers.

3. A report with recommendations on the accessibiliity of public build-

ings and amenities (libraries, swimming pools, housing offices, Adult Education Institutes, schools etc) to people with a disability, for submission to the Chief Executive in the local authority.

4. A report on the effects of the unusually severe snow in January on the organisation in which you work. Make recommendations on how disruption could be minimised in the future.

5. A report presenting your findings and conclusions on Case Study 1, Chapter 4. See P. 80.

7 Essay Writing

Analysing the question and planning an answer

In degree and professional courses students are required to do much of their thinking through writing. This takes various forms: seminar papers, notes, reports on experimental or project work, summaries and case studies. Chapter 6 is about how to organise your ideas in any writing you do.

However, the main vehicle through which students are encouraged to think and communicate their ideas is the essay; the next two chapters take a close look at essay writing. Many courses, whether degree level or not, rely heavily on the essay as the principal means of encouraging students to show their understanding of a subject. And, of course, despite moves to diversify methods of assessment, the essay remains a firm favourite with examination boards.

In other words, you probably need to develop skills in essay writing. Even if you do not need to write essays as such, the ability to identify exactly what the question is asking of you, and to plan a relevant answer is equally important in other forms of written assignments.

Self-check

What does an essay test? Arrange the following in order of importance;
– your personal opinions on a subject
– your understanding of a subject
– your knowledge of a subject?

I would place 'understanding' a clear first, followed by 'knowledge' then 'personal opinions'. Essays are not primarily a means by which you display comprehensive knowledge. Other forms of assessment such as multiple choice questions test this much better and in subjects where a large body of knowledge is required, these are often used.

For example, this question from Economics A Level, Oxford, June 1986:

Which one of the following is likely to be the worst store of value during a period of rapid inflation?

> A antiques
> B fixed interest government debt
> C houses
> D land
> E the shares of industrial companies

Here, a student's knowledge of the subject leads to the choice of one correct answer. There is no room to explain why a particular answer is chosen, or the relative importance of several factors. Economics, as an academic discipline, has reached certain conclusions and students are expected to know these.

Compare that question with this essay title;

> Why is the control of inflation a common objective of government policy? What, if anything, might be said in favour of inflation?

People without a knowledge of economics may well have views on the subject. They, however, would be expressing their more or less well-informed personal opinions. Without a knowledge of economics they could not show an understanding of the issues raised and answer the question from an economic standpoint.

In an essay, then, you are being asked to show your understanding of a subject. Clearly, understanding follows from knowledge, but essays are not where you write all you know about x. This approach attracts universal criticism from examiners;

> 'A disturbing proportion of candidates insisted on producing general 'write all you know about..' answers, usually after latching on to a key word or phrase.. and were penalised for the resulting irrelevance.'
> (Examiners Reports on ACCA examinations, June 86)

> 'The main finding in answering this year's paper is clearly a perennial one: the inability to answer the questions set. It is possible that candidates are unaware of how seriously examiners take the wording of particular questions. Many weaker candidates seem to imagine that a question simply designates an area of study about which they are required to write all they know.'
> (from Examiners Reports, 1986, Political Studies A level, Oxford Board)

A good essay, then, is one in which you show your knowledge of a subject by demonstrating that you understand it. You do this by answering the question set.

This chapter suggests a specific and structured approach to analysing essay questions and planning answers. This sort of approach may not suit everyone; if you write competent essays already, there is no reason to change. If, however, you are aware that writing well structured, relevant essays is a problem for you then you might like to try out this practical, step-by-step approach, and later adapt it to your own way of working.

Advice is geared towards the typical exam essay, where you have three hours in which to write four essays. The principles, however, are the same for any essay, whether shorter (such as five essays in three hours) or longer, as may be the case with coursework essays and some exams.

7.1 What is the question asking?

Self-check

Below are three questions from A level Sociology papers. What are they about?
a) Examine the problems that sociologists face in defining and measuring poverty. (AEB Nov 82 639/1 Qu 3)
b) 'Unemployment has replaced old age as the major cause of poverty in contemporary Britain.' Discuss. (Oxford May 84 9848 Qu 11)
c) 'What thoughtful rich people call the problem of poverty, thoughtful poor people call, with equal justice, the problem of riches.' (R.H. Tawney) In the light of this statement, comment critically on sociological explanations of poverty. (AEB Nov 85 639/1 Qu 10)

They are all, of course, *about* poverty. The relevant extracts in the 'Reading' and 'Notemaking' chapters will give you an idea of the textbook knowledge you would need as a basis for any answer on poverty. This knowledge, however, is only a starting point for an essay. Examiners complain that candidates frequently reproduce whole sections of textbooks in answer to questions for which those sections are inappropriate or irrelevant. The message from examiners is clear; read the question to identify precisely what a particular question is asking, and plan an answer which includes only material that is directly relevant. The difficulty, of course, is *how* to do it.

Imagine, for a moment, that you are an examiner. Twice a year (or more) you have the task of thinking up questions which enable you to tell which of the hundreds of candidates taking that exam have a really good understanding of the subject and which have just learnt up last year's answers. How do you do it? You do it by setting questions on different *aspects* of the same topic on the syllabus, as in the questions on poverty above. This encourages students to

(i) write in depth on a particular aspect rather than generally on the broad topic

(ii) think flexibly about the subject by looking at it from a new angle.

This means that you, the examiner (or tutor) can see who has an understanding of the subject and who hasn't. The good candidates will see exactly what you are asking, and will write about that aspect and no other. The weak ones may have learnt up an answer to the question you set last year, or have little understanding (or knowledge) of what you have asked for this year. These are the ones who write 'all I know about..' answers.

So the first step to being a good examinee is to learn how to identify exactly what the question is asking. 'How to make up exam questions' in the Reference Section sets an exercise in making up questions. You may like to try it when you have worked through this section.

7.2 How to analyse the question

In this section we look at the three questions on poverty, and systematically analyse each one.

Essay a) Examine the problems that sociologists face in defining and measuring poverty.

1. *Identify the subject*

   This is the topic that appears on the syllabus. Obviously all questions have a subject, which is usually easy to identify. If it isn't, try this.

   – read the question, look up and ask yourself, 'What, in one or two words, is this question about?'

   – If this question was in an exam and someone asked you which questions you had done, you'd say, 'I did the one on..'

   In this case there's no difficulty. The subject is *poverty*.

2. *Identify the instruction*, the word that tells you how the examiner expects you to write. Are you asked to outline? Account for? Compare and contrast? Discuss? Each of these will require a different style of essay. The instruction here is *examine*.

3. *Identify which aspect(s)* of the subject this particular essay is asking for. These are the *key words* of the question, the ones you need to plan your answer around, and write about from the first paragraph. The key words here are '*problems* that sociologists face in *defining* and *measuring* poverty'.

This analysis gives you an outline plan;

Examine the problems that sociologists face in <u>defining</u> and <u>measuring</u> poverty.

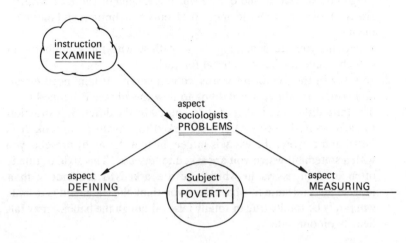

Fig. 28 *Essay a)*

Planning Activity 1

● Analyse this question in the same way;
Essay b) 'Unemployment has replaced old age as the major cause of poverty in contemporary Britain.' Discuss
1. What's the *subject?* (What's it about?)
2. What's the *instruction?* (How are you to write?)
3. What key *aspects* of the subject is this particular question asking for?
4. Are there any other *significant words* I need to take into account in my answer?

The other significant words are, of course, 'contemporary Britain'. You often need to ask questions about words like these. What does 'contemporary Britain' mean? 1960s? 70s? early 80s? late 80s? What studies will you include? Will you use current material from the press? What you decide to include depends on how you define 'contemporary'.

● Draw up an outline plan based on your analysis of the question, and then check it with mine in the Answers Section (Fig. 29).
● This essay has several differences to essay a) What are they? Make a note of the differences and what this means for the essay writer.

126

1. The first and fundamental difference is that the essay is on a totally
   different *aspect* of the same subject, poverty. Essay b) asks you to
   weigh up two factors and decide which is the major cause of poverty.
   Essay a) asks you to write about problems of definition and measurement.

   Perhaps you are beginning to sympathise with the examiner who
   gets the same textbook material for each.
2. In essay b) the significant words 'contemporary Britain' need *definition*. Answers will vary according to how this phrase is defined.
3. The third difference is that of *style*, caused by the different instruction
   in each essay. In essay a) you are asked to 'examine', to look at in
   detail and convey; the essay is largely factual. Essay b) presents you
   with a statement which you are asked to 'discuss'. This style of title is
   often used in essays in which you are asked to conclude with a
   judgement, and state to what extent you think the statement is true. It
   will rarely be totally true or totally false, although the balance may fall
   heavily on one side.

Planning activity 2

● Analyse this essay question.
Essay c) 'What thoughtful rich people call the problem of poverty, thoughtful
poor people call, with equal justice, the problem of riches.' (R.H. Tawney) In the
light of this statement, comment critically on sociological explanations of
poverty. Identify:
   1. the subject
   2. the instruction
   3. the key aspects in this particular question
   4. any other significant words to take into account?
   5. Are there any terms which need definition or querying?

The style of this question is different again; the part that follows the
quotation contains most of the important elements. But what happens if
you ignore the quotation? Your outline plan would look like Fig 30 (i)
opposite.

If you attempted to write an essay on this plan, you'd have to cover all
the textbook sociological explanations of poverty, such as those on
P. 37–39. You'd be writing a 'write all you know about' essay. Long
quotations such as this can be off putting, but once you have a rough idea
of what the question is about, go back to the quotation asking, 'What

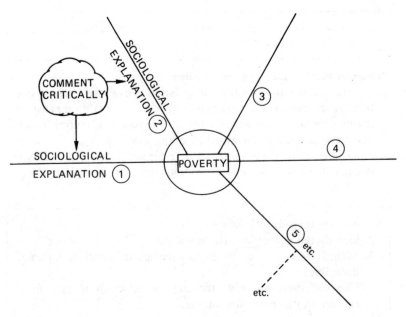

Fig. 30(i) *Essay c)*

this cast on the question?' Try and think where the quotation fits in with what you know about the subject. It will limit the scope of the question by directing you to particular aspects; here, particular theories and contrasting theories.

● Re-read the extracts on P.36–38 then work through the five stages in analysing the question and check below.

The five stages in analysing the question will lead you to
1. the *subject*, poverty;
2. the *instruction*, 'comment critically';
3. the *key aspects*; the sociological explanations which view poverty as problematic and those which view riches as problematic.
4. the *significant words*; 'with equal justice'. This is important; the essay goes further than simply asking you to give an account of various theories; you have to make some statement about whether they are equally persuasive. This comes in the conclusion.
5. Are there any words you should ask *questions* about? I think you should pause over the word 'problem'; why and how is this a problem? and think about the implications of 'with equal justice.'

• Now draw up an outline plan for an answer to this question and compare it with Fig 30 (ii) in the Answers Section.

Review of Points: Analysing the question

1. A careful *analysis* of each essay question is essential because questions on the same subject ask you to write on totally different aspects. If you write 'all I know about' a subject your essay will suffer from the defects so damningly described by examiners.
2. Questions are carefully constructed. Your task is to see how they are put together and to *identify the components*. This is a practical skill.

---

1. Identify the subject Box it.
2. Identify the instruction. Underline it.
3. Identify the key aspects in this particular question. Double underline.
4. Check if there are any other significant words to take into account in this particular answer.
5. Ask yourself *questions* about the question or phrases in it. What's the purpose of the quotation? What does this word mean? Are there two sides to this issue?

N.B. The skill of analysing a question is largely independent of the knowledge you will need to draw on in the body of the essay.

3. Notice the different styles of essay you can be asked to write. The style of the essay depends on the instruction. Some will be factual, 'outline', 'describe'; others ask you to explain, 'account for'; others to consider the arguments and evidence and to reach a conclusion, 'how far', 'discuss'.

4. Draw up an *outline plan* for your answer based on your analysis of the question. It should only take a minute or two; it is the skeleton to which you add material you want to include in your essay. The style of your plan does not matter at all. I use branching plans because I find them clearer, but if you prefer to spread your headings down the page, do so. The important thing is to leave lots of space so you can add points and move points around.

This first part of the chapter has outlined a method for analysing essay questions and planning answers. The second part looks at this process in greater detail, and offers practice and examples from a range of subject areas.

7.3 Types of question / Styles of answer

The Instruction

A recent examiner's report said that many candidates did not seem not to understand the significance of guidance offered in key words in the questions such as 'discuss', 'distinguish', 'examine' and 'outline'.

This guidance about the style in which you are expected to write, is to be found in the instruction. In some essays you are asked to make *judgements* about an issue. In the process of making a judgement or reaching a conclusion you will consider conflicting theories, factors, findings and indicate which ones you find most persuasive and why. In other essays, you will be asked to demonstrate your knowledge through your ability to define or analyse a problem or trace the consequences of a measure. While these questions are clearly more *factual*, they require as much analysis and planning as the essays which conclude with a judgement. Before you start to plan an answer it is essential to be clear about the style in which the instruction is telling you to write.

Self-check

Look back to the three questions on poverty on P. 123. In which of these are you asked to make a judgement? Which of these essays calls for a factual style of presentation?

Essays b) and c) ask you to make some kind of judgement about the problem raised in the question; 'discuss' and 'comment critically' are clear indications of this. Essay a) on the other hand, asks you to 'examine' problems – a more factual style of essay.

Self check

Read the essay titles below. In which essays are you asked to make a judgement? In which essays are you asked to show your factual grasp of a subject? Make two lists.

(i) Should the power of committees be increased? (Political Studies)

(ii) 'Districts exist on maps. People live in neighbourhoods.' Explain this statement and examine its significance, if any, for both the policy making process and the organisational structure of a local authority. (ICSA Local Govt in the Community June 85)

(iii) Do you regard *Nineteen Eighty Four* as a novel or simply as a political tract? (English A level AEB Nov 84 623/2 Qu 6b)

(iv) a) Outline the principal features of monetary policy as operated in the UK since 1979.
b) To what extent have the overall goals of macro economic policy been achieved in the UK since 1979? (Institute of Bankers Banking Diploma St 2 Monetary Economics Sept 85)

(v) Would an increase in public sector investment in present circumstances lead to an increase in employment or to inflation? (ICSA Economic policies and problems June 85)

(vi) Compare and contrast the British and American constitutions (Political Studies)

(vii) Compare and contrast the comon law defence of duress and the equitable doctrine of undue influence. What effect do they have on a contract if successfully pleaded and upon whom does the burden of proof fall? (Contract Law)

(viii) How far does the system of precedent mean that certainty is purchased at the cost of justice? (Law A level Oxford May 83)

I would say that you are asked to make a judgement of some sort in the following questions; (i) (iii) (ivb) (v) (viii). Questions (ii) (iva) (vi) and (vii) are designed to test your understanding of a subject in a factual style.

The division of essays into *'judgement essays'* and *'factual essays'* may seem an over simplifcation. In some ways it is; the further you go into a subject, the more you find that people can, and do, disagree about just about everything, even apparent facts. Equally, judgements need to be based on arguments supported by factual evidence if they are not to be merely the expression of personal prejudice and opinion. The division is useful, however, at the planning stage of an essay because it directs you to an appropriate style and structure for your essay.

7.4 Judgement Essays

What is a 'judgement essay'?

A judgement essay is one which raises issues about which different views can be held. You are expected to show that you understand the different views and interpretations, can present the evidence and conclude with a judgement yourself.

Self-check

1. Look back at the instructions of the judgement essays. List them and try and define briefly what each means and what it implies for the style and structure of the essay. Then compare your definitions with those in the glossary on P. 192
2. Drawing on your definitions and those in the glossary, list the characteristics of judgement essays.

The important points to emerge about judgement essays are as follows: You need to:
– define problematic or debatable terms;
– identify the two sides of the argument;
– present arguments and evidence to support both sides;
– make a judgement in the conclusion showing where you stand;
– bear in mind that no side or factor will have all the arguments in its favour. You may agree strongly with one view or interpretation, or the experts may have virtually reached a consensus on an issue, but the fact that the question is asked at all means that it is debatable.

Your finished judgement essay will have:
(i) a clear structure;
   an *introduction* which indicates the issues involved,
   a *body* in which you set out the arguments and evidence in support of these views,
   a *conclusion* in which you indicate your views on the subject.
(ii) two or more sides to the discussion.
(iii) a degree of complexity. Neither view will be totally right or totally wrong, although the balance may fall heavily on one side.

How to plan a judgement essay

Planning activity 3

Essay (i) Should the power of committees be increased?

- 1. Analyse the question by following the method outlined on P. 128. When you have finished, read on.

---

i) The *subject* (topic on the syllabus) is committees.
ii) The *instruction* is <u>should</u>. This is an issue about which people may disagree; it is therefore a judgement essay.
iii) The *key aspect* to discuss in the body of the essay is <u>whether the power of</u> (parliamentary) <u>committees should be increased or not</u>.
iv) There are no other *significant words*
v) Ask yourself *questions*. *What* are the arguments for increasing power? *Who* thinks this? *What* are the arguments for not increasing power? *Who* thinks this? and *why*?

- 2. Draw up an outline plan. Don't worry if you don't know anything about committees; here we are interested in the structure not the content. Before you start, work through the following guidelines.

Take a whole side of paper for this, because once you have your skeleton, you will need the space to add detail, and to move points around. Try drawing up your outline plan in this order:

1. Use the words and phrases in the question as your main *headings* so as to be sure your answer will be relevant.

2. Decide on your *conclusion*. This is common sense; you know where you are going before you start a journey. You may change your mind over detail as you go, but you must have an idea of your objective before you start any process. This applies as much to essay writing as anything else.

   In a judgement essay it is often helpful to mark your position on a sliding scale. Avoid the extremes; you are almost bound to be oversimplifying and presenting a one sided argument if you totally ignore the arguments of one side.

3. Fill out the detail of the *body* of the essay. Here you draw on your knowledge of the subject. You may have more to say in support of one view. This doesn't matter as long as you consider some of the counter arguments and evidence. Some points can be argued both ways; this is fine. It shows you understand the complexity of the issue.

4. Decide on your *introduction*. When you plan an essay in this order it is often surprisingly easy to start. You may find that a particular term needs to be defined before you can discuss it. This is often a good way to start an essay. The implications of the question may point you to a central problem which underlies the specific issues. However you start, by the end of your introductory paragraph you should be launched; the body of the essay must deal directly with the issues in the question.

5. Decide on your *paragraphs* when you have noted down the points you want to include. A typical exam essay will have:
   introduction: 1 paragraph
   body: 3, 4 or 5 paragraphs
   conclusion: 1 paragraph
A coursework essay may need to be fuller; the body can expand to consider points in greater detail, and therefore have more paragraphs. In Higher Education you will be expected to go deeper into the subject and give greater attention to the implications of detail; all this involves longer essays and, probably, longer paragraphs. As you work out your paragraphs, aim to group related points, or support a central argument with several illustrations. (Advice on writing essays is given in the next chapter.) Finally, decide on the order in which you will take your paragraphs.

• Now start writing! A plan should be an aid, not a burden, so don't spend too long on it. Don't rewrite it either. If you leave enough space for jottings and late thoughts, you won't need to.
When you have finished, compare your version with Fig. 31 in the Answers Section.

SUMMARY:

How to plan a judgement essay
1. Analyse the question (See P. 128.)
2. Plan your answer
  (i) Use the words and phrases of the question as your *headings*
  (ii) Decide on your *conclusion*
  (iii) Fill out the *body*
  (iv) Decide on your *introduction*
  (v) Decide on your *paragraphs* and their order
  (vi) Start!

Judgement Essays – Review
Here are three planning activities using the essay titles on PP. 129–30. You may want to try one or two now, or come back to them later for revision. Be disciplined about doing your version before you check.

Planning Activity 4

Essay (iii): Do you regard Nineteen Eighty Four as a novel or simply as a political tract?
1. Analyse the question
2. Plan an outline answer

Subject : Nineteen Eighty Four
Instruction : 'Do you regard..' Clearly a judgement essay.
Key aspects : is it a 'novel' or a 'political tract'.
Significant words : 'simply'.
Ask *questions* : What is a 'novel' as distinct from a 'political tract'?
These terms need defininition. 'Simply' suggests that a political tract is a lower form of life, not meeting the criteria of a novel. Is the book either of these? or a mixture – a novel with a political interest?

• Draw up your plan then compare it with Fig 32 in the Answers Section.

Planning Activity 5

Essay (v): Would an increase in public sector investment in present circumstances lead to an increase in employment or to inflation?
1. Analyse the question.
2. Plan an outline answer.

Subject : public sector investment.
Instruction : Would...? (judgement essay).
Key aspects : employment or inflation as a result of increase in investment?
Significant words : in present circumstances.
Questions : what are the main features of 'present circumstances' which will determine the effects of increased public sector investment? What is meant by this? Does this need defining?

• Draw up your plan then refer to Fig 33 in the Answers Section.

Planning Activity 6

Essay (viii): How far does the system of precedent mean that certainty is purchased at the cost of justice?
1. Analyse the question.
2. Plan an outline answer.

Subject : the system of precedent.
Instruction : How far .. (a judgement essay)
Key aspects : certainty or justice?
Significant words : at the cost of
Questions : What is precedent? How does it work? Does it result in injustice? How often? How true is the statement in the question? Fairly true? or not very?
You may like to compare this question on precedent with the one on P. 54. Ch 3. Which key aspects are asked for in that one?

• Draw up your plan then refer to Fig 34 in the Answers Section.

7.5 **Factual Essays**

In a 'factual' essay, the temptation to write 'all I know about' answers is often even stronger than in 'judgement' essays. However, as Examiners reports make clear, it is penalised just as heavily.

> 'A common failing was still the reluctance to read and answer the question set; instead candidates were tempted to write whatever they knew about the apparent subject of the question. Thus question (3) about precedent did not actually require a complete exposition of the doctrine of precedent, but asked specific questions about certain aspects of it...' (ICSA General Principles of English Law, Examiners Reports June 85)

Self-check

1. Look back at the instructions of the 'factual' essays on P. 129. List them and try to define briefly what each means and what it implies for the style and structure of the essay. Then compare your definitions with those in the glossary.
2. As you did with the instructions for 'judgement' essays, list the characteristics of factual essays.

The common theme that runs through the definitions of the instructions for factual essays is the need for *selectivity*. In a factual essay you should:
- define the terms in the question
- pick out relevant detail
- point out differences between apparently similar things
- consider an issue in detail
- support points with evidence
- be clear in tracing consequences or highlighting issues.

Planning Activity 7

Essay (vi): Compare and contrast the British and American constitutions.

With this specific question in mind, work through the following instructions on how to approach a broad factual essay. When you have finished, draw up your own plan before referring to Fig 35 in the Answers Section.

How to plan a factual essay
1. Analyse the question
Follow the method outlined on P. 128 to analyse the question:

(i) The *subject* (topic on the syllabus) is 'British and American constitutions'

(ii) The *instruction* is 'compare and contrast'.

(iii) No particular aspects are specified,

(iv) Nor are there any problematic terms.

This is a basic and very broad essay, more likely to be set as coursework to draw together and consolidate your knowledge, than as an exam essay, which tests your knowledge by focussing on a particular aspect. So it presents quite different problems at the planning stage. The problem is how to structure a mass of information, without falling into the trap of an 'all I know about' essay.

2. Draw up an outline plan

Again, leave plenty of space for your points. You may well find that the order suggested for drawing up an outline plan for a judgement essay works perfectly well for a factual essay. The only major difference concerns the conclusion. Whereas in a judgement essay, you know you need to make a judgement in the conclusion, you do not have this convenient way of ending a factual essay. Nevertheless, your essay must have a clear structure.

Try planning a factual essay in this order.

1. Use the words and phrases in the question for your main *headings*. In this essay, the instruction itself is all you have to go on; use it.

2. Plan the structure of the *body*. Make sure you
   (i) *link* points; in this example, contrast the written US constitution with the unwritten UK one. While the points are contrasting, the theme is linked.
   (ii) *develop* points. Don't just list them and leave them to speak for themselves. Points don't. Explain the consequences, effects or implications of a point you have made. Use illustrations which support the point you are making. Again, you are working towards a body of 3, 4, or 5 paragraphs.
   (iii) decide on the *order* of your points and paragraphs.

3. Plan your *introduction*. Are there any terms which need defining? This is one way of conveying that you have a precise idea of what you have been asked to write about and in a factual essay precision is particularly important. It can also be useful to make a general statement about the subject before you move on to the detail. Here,

for example, you could outline the different histories of the two countries which underly the specific differences in the constitutions.

4. Think through your essay to the *conclusion*. You will probably find you have to think harder about how to conclude a factual essay. Try concluding in one of these ways;
   - refer back to the question; underline the relevance of your essay to the title by relating the points in the body to the wording of the title directly;
   - look back to the introduction; pick up your theme and bring it up to date, perhaps by pointing to current and future trends.
   - look back at the definitions you started with; do they need modification?
   - draw your reader's attention to the most important point, factor, consideration in the body, and add a comment about it.

There are a few **don'ts** in writing factual essays:

Don't list unconnected points which end up looking like a dozen short 'paragraphs' rambling down the page. This tells your reader at a glance that you have not linked points, nor developed or illustrated them. You start and end with a list.

Don't list all your points in the introduction and recap again in the conclusion. It is unnecessary and dull.

Planning Activity 8: a highly structured question

Essay (vii): Compare and contrast the common law defence of duress and the equitable doctrine of undue influence. What effect do they have on a contract if successfully pleaded and upon whom does the burden of proof lie?

1. Analyse this question.
2. Plan an outline answer.

Unless you are a lawyer, this question is probably double dutch to you! Don't worry; your task is to identify the parts of the question and to arrange these parts to show the structure of an outline answer. Treat it like a jigsaw puzzle. Have a go before you check with my analysis.

There are two parts to this question; each is highly specific.
First part
Subject : duress and undue influence
Instruction : compare and contrast these.

Key aspects : none. The question is a direct one about these topics on the syllabus.

Significant words : 'common law' and 'equitable doctrine'. These phrases guide you to the different sources of the laws concerning duress and undue influence.

Questions : the question is direct and simple. Focus your questions on your analysis.

Second part

Subject : 'they' i.e. duress and undue influence.

Instruction : What effect? A straightforward account of the consequences of each.

Key aspects : effect on a contract and statement concerning the burden of proof in each case.

This essay is at the opposite extreme on the scale of complexity to the previous one. The instruction is the same, 'compare and contrast', but they pose totally different problems to the writer. In the first the question was straightforward; the difficulty lay in structuring an answer. Here, the question is dense and complex, but once you have unravelled it, it virtually plans itself.

• You then draw on your knowledge to work your way through the plan – in six paragraphs. When you have finished, refer to Fig 36 in the Answers Section.

Planning Activity 9

Essay (iv): a) Outline the principal features of monetary policy as operated in the UK since 1979. (15 marks)

b) To what extent have the overall goals of macro economic policy been achieved in the UK since 1979? (10 marks)

•1. Analyse this question. When you have had a go, read on.

Again, you have two linked questions here. You will often find that a question with a factual first part, asks for an evaluation or judgement in the second part.

a) *Subject*: monetary policy

   Instruction: outline (factual)

   Key aspects: principal features (be selective)

   Significant words: in the UK since 1979 (specific).

b) *Subject*: goals of macro economic policy

   Instruction: to what extent (judgement)

Key aspects: achieved (or not)?
Significant words: in the UK since 1979 (specific); the date of the general election and the introduction of new policies. Perhaps your general starting point.

The examiners commented on this question:

'This question was interpreted by candidates as an invitation to write in part a) all they knew about the conduct of monetary policy in the UK since 1979. .'(Reports of the Examiners, the Institute of Bankers Sept 85)

●2. Plan an outline answer. Don't worry if you do not know anything about the subject; concentrate on the structure. When you have finished, compare your plan with mine in the Answers Section (figs 37 and 38).

Planning Activity 10

Essay (ii): 'Districts exist on maps. People live in neighbourhoods.' Explain this statement and examine its significance, if any, for both the policy making process and the organisational structure of a local authority.
●1. Analyse this question, then read on.

Subject: local authority
Instructions: explain, examine significance
Key aspects: policy making and organisational structure
Significant words: 'districts' 'maps' 'people' and 'neighbourhoods'. These words guide you to the purpose of the quotation..
Questions: Are there are problematic words needing definition? The distinction between 'district' (an administrative division) and 'neighbourhood' (a locality with which people identify) needs to be made. What is the relationship between the two parts? These questions and your definitions will make a useful starting point.

● Draw up your plan then refer to Fig. 39 in the Answers Section.

Review
This chapter has taken you step by step from first sight of an essay title to the point where you are ready to write. Here is a summary of the processes involved:

1. **Read, understand and analyse the question**
Approach this systematically. Identify:

The *subject*. Box it.
the *instruction*. Underline it.
key aspects in this particular question. Double underline.
Are there any other *significant words*?
Ask *questions* about the question or words in it.

2. **Plan an answer**
Use words and phrases from the question as *headings*.
Then – in the order that best suits you;

decide on your *conclusion*;
fill out the *body*;
decide on the *introduction*;
decide on the content and order of the *paragraphs*;
start!

A typical exam essay will have:
Introduction: one paragraph
Body: 3, 4 or 5 paragraphs
Conclusion: one paragraph

(The section 'How to make up essay questions' on P. 198 gives further practice in analysis, by assembling questions from component parts).

The purpose of this systematic approach is to encourage a critical way of thinking. It's not true to say that any one method is the key to success, but it is true that an analytical and methodical approach – even if you are the only one who can see the method in it – is essential to good essay writing. What form this takes, the markings you make (or don't make) on exam question papers, the style of your notes, the detail of your plan is irrelevant. But, if you haven't yet developed a method that works for you, give this a try and adapt it as you go along.

8 Writing the essay

This chapter is about the practical business of translating an essay plan into an essay. Chapter 6 gives advice on how to write paragraphs and arrange the points within them and chapter 7 discusses how to analyse essay titles. This chapter picks up from here and considers how to structure essays and make the paragraphs in them work for you in answering the question set.

8.1 **Paragraphs: structure**

Self-check

Look back to chapters 1, 6 and 7. Skim read to pick out the main points about paragraphs and paragraphing in these chapters.

These chapters stress that *paragraphs should have a structure*

- A paragraph has a main idea.
- This main idea is usually expressed clearly in one sentence, the 'topic sentence'.
- This topic sentence is usually the first in the paragraph.
- Paragraphs themselves have a structure; a beginning, middle and end. The sentences in the middle explain, develop or illustrate the main idea in the topic sentence. The last sentence often returns to the idea in the topic sentence to show how it has developed.

This structure has a purpose;

- to make it easier to *read*; skim reading is easier in a well written piece because the main idea in each paragraph is first. Closer reading is more effortless because one idea is developed before you move on to a new one.
- to make it easier to *plan*, to link related points and plan the overall structure and length of your work;

– to make it easier to *write*. When you write, whether it's a letter, an article or an essay, start each paragraph with a clear statement of the point you are making, then add detail. You start a new paragraph when you want to make a new point.

This chapter aims to be as practical as possible. The extracts are not 'model' answers although some, obviously, are better than others. All are taken from essays of mature students taking 'A' levels in one year. Some are written as coursework essays, some under exam conditions. They are reproduced as they were written, often with errors of punctuation and expression uncorrected; these will be for you to identify and correct in proof reading exercises in the reference section.

Writing paragraphs in essays
The points noted about the structure of paragraphs can be translated into a *paragraph plan*:

1. *Start with the topic sentence*
   – to express the main idea
2. *Explain or define*
   – any abstract or problematic terms
   – to clarify or develop the topic sentence
3. *Discuss one example in some detail*
   – to show your evidence
   – to support the main idea
   (Mention one or two more examples briefly
   – to widen the discussion, if appropriate)
4. *Conclusion*
   – to show the relevance of the examples
   – to link back to the idea in the topic sentence
   – in first and last paragraphs, to show link with title.

Essay Activity 1

Below are two paragraphs from students' essays. For each decide
1. What is the main idea? Where is this expressed most clearly?
2. What is the function of the sentences in the body of the paragraph?
3. Does the paragraph end well?
4. Do you think the paragraph is well written?
Then compare your answers with mine in the Answers Section.

Paragraph 1
A hierarchical court structure is very important because the standing of a precedent is governed by the status of the court which decided the case. Decisions of senior courts, if found to be relevant, are treated as 'binding' on the lower courts, so that the judge must follow the reasoning and apply it to the case before him. Generally the superior courts are also bound by their own previous decisions. The major exception is the House of Lords. Prior to the 1966 Practice Statement the House of Lords was bound by its own previous decisions as was clearly stated in *London Street Tramways Co v LCC (1898)*. In 1966, however, it issued a statement saying that in future it would exercise the right to ignore earlier decisions.
(Mary: 'Precedent is an excuse for a judge to follow unthinkingly and mechanically what previous judges in a different social climate have decided.' Is this necessarily true? Law A level Oxford May 85)

Paragraph 2
Durkheim saw the rate of suicide as a social fact. He found that suicide rates varied between countries and within them but remained at a steady level. Thus he discounted individual reasons for committing suicide and developed his theory of social integration to account for it. Durkheim used official statistics for the bulk of his research, he believed these statistics were social facts. They provided him with objective quantifiable data. He did not use participant observation to investigate the meanings people gave to suicide, he sought to explain it. His sociological theory, the questions he would ask (what causes suicide?) is tied up with the methods he uses.
(Colin Gayle 'Sociological theory and research methods are well nigh inseparable.' Discuss.)

Essay Activity 2

In the paragraph below, the sentences are not in order. This is a jumbled version of a short answer to a question on the story '*The Boarding House*' in *Dubliners* by James Joyce. Your task is to order the sentences so they make a well written paragraph. If you have access to a word processor use it for this. Type out the sentences, move them around and print your versions.
Remember the paragraph plan:
Topic sentence – which expresses the central idea;
Body – which explains and illustrates this;
Conclusion – which shows how the detail in the body relates to the main idea in the topic sentence.

• When you have a version you are satisfied with, compare it with the original and note the comments in the Answers Section.

In what ways is this story humourous?

Doran's naive description of how Polly seduced him is so full of innocence that the reader cannot fail to see the humour.

Joyce's use of this phrase causes the reader to be further amused at Doran's expense.

He is naive and gullible and yet sees himself as superior to Polly and her family.

Without a doubt the joke is on Doran.

As they are conning him this difference between Doran's opinion of himself and the truth is highly amusing.

He has been totally fooled by Polly and her family.

Doran himself unwittingly supplies the humour.

'He had a notion that he was being had' is an absolute understatement.

8.2 Paragraphs: relevance

What's your point?
You need to be clear about the point you want to make in a paragraph before you start to write. It sounds like a statement of the obvious, but if you are not absolutely clear about the point you want to make and its relevance to the title, you won't be able to express it clearly, nor relate it to the title. These students were all clear about what they wanted to say; this led to good, clear writing.

Essay Activity 3

Below are two paragraphs from the body of an essay on the play 'Othello' by Shakespeare. The title is: 'Outline the parts played by Emilia and Roderigo and show the various ways in which they contribute to the dramatic interest of *Othello*.'

The task here is to improve them.

1. What is the main point in each paragraph?
2. Is this idea clearly stated anywhere?
3. With the minimum of rewriting, recast each paragraph so that there is a clear expression of the main idea in the paragraph and it directly answers the question.

Act 4 Sc 3 is a dramatic interlude where Emilia and Desdemona confide in each other. Emilia comes across as warm, caring and worldly; she has no illusions about men. 'But I do think it is their husbands fault if wives do fall.' Desdemona, by contrast, is naive and because of her sheltered upbringing knows little of the ways of the world. This scene is important for the audience because it is a build up of tension and feeds into the tragedies of Act 5.

Emilia is the first person to arrive on the scene after Othello has murdered Desdemona. Genuinely grieved and shocked by her mistress' death, she courageously challenged Othello in spite of his superior strength: 'Thou hast not half the power to hurt me as I have to be hurt'. Emilia then realises her husband's treachery, 'Villany, villany, villany – O villany! I thought so then.' Iago is directly exposed by Emilia before he kills her. Othello then realises how he has been duped by Iago as the tragedy unfolds itself.

(Mary)

Paragraph 1

Qu. 1. The point is that Emilia and Desdemona are contrasting characters and that this contrast is dramatically important in this poignant scene.

Qu. 2. The idea is not stated where the reader registers it effortlessly – in the first sentence. It is there in the third sentence, 'Desdemona by contrast . . .', but in an essay, especially an exam essay, it needs to be placed where the material in the body of the paragraph can be seen to follow from it logically, supporting and developing it.

Qu. 3. Little rewriting is necessary; just add a topic sentence. The conclusion is good; it links the paragraph to the title by showing Emilia's contribution to the 'dramatic interest' of the play.

Paragraph 2

Qu. 1 & 2. What is the point here? There are several points; Emilia is the first to arrive after Desdemona's death; she is courageous; she realises her husband's villany; Iago is exposed by Emilia, then kills her; Othello realises he has been duped. But what is the main point?

There is no main point as such. The paragraph is a summary of the events of this part of the scene, but summarising, however skilful, is not what this question wants. It is too detailed for an 'outline' and does not directly show Emilia's contribution to the 'dramatic interest' of the play. The point behind this retelling of the plot is, I think, that *Emilia is the means by which the pace of the drama is quickened and the plot unfolds.* Her contribution to the dramatic interest is direct and considerable; this needs to be said. You should never leave your reader to work out your point; your tutor will scrawl 'What's your point?' and an examiner will penalise you for retelling.

Qu. 3. More rewriting is needed here; start with the point, then select your detail to support and illustrate it. You could use the highlighted sentence from the commentary above as the basis for your topic sentence.

The topic sentence and the title

It is not enough, of course, to write well constructed paragraphs. Each paragraph of an essay must be directly relevant to the title, and must be seen to be so from the first sentence.

Essay Activity 4

Below are extracts from two politics essays on: 'Should the power of committees be increased?' This title is analysed on P. 132 Ch 7.
As you read ask yourself questions about
(i) *relevance*: is this paragraph answering the question?
(ii) *structure*: what is the point being made in each paragraph? is this idea clearly expressed in a topic sentence? does the rest of the paragraph support and develop this idea?

Extract 1: taken from the beginning of an answer to the question.

There are in fact two main types of committee in the UK; standing committees and select committees. Standing committees have a legislative function only. The work of the standing committee is utilized during the normal passage of a bill through Parliament, after a bill has received its second and main reading, it is presented to one of the standing committees for detailed consideration and amendment before being represented in its amended form to the legislature for further debate.

Select Committees are established mainly to deal with issues concerning certain subjects. For instance there is a select committee on agriculture and one on science and technology. Select Committees may also be established to deal with a controversial issue of the time, for instance the Westland committee was recently set up to investigate that affair.

Committee members are certain select MPs who are given a short term appointment to sit on the committee. It is argued that the time they are with the committee is too short for them to become fluent with its operation and procedure to be of any real use to the committee. (John)

Relevance This beginning does not look as if the essay will answer the question. It should all be about the *power* of committees; should it be increased? or not? It is a judgement essay, so the introduction should set the context for arguments and evidence for and against increasing power, leading to a conclusion in which the writer states his or her own view. The first two paragraphs do not address this question at all. The last one touches on it. However, the idea is not explained or expanded and two sentences do not add up to a paragraph.

Structure: the topic sentence of the first paragraph ('two main types of committee . . . standing . . . and select . . .') introduces the points made in the first two paragraphs (the nature and functions of committees), but makes no mention of power. Already the answer is adrift from the question. The third also starts with a statement which does not address the question of power.

• Now turn to P. 189 in the Reference Section and read the comments on extract 1. On the basis of these, try rewriting the extract to produce a good introductory paragraph and the topic sentence (only) of the second paragraph, to begin the body.

Extract 2: taken from the body of another answer to this question.

If the power of committees were increased it would take away power from the House of Commons, it is argued. This argument can be 'derailed' by the fact that committees would be beneficial in presenting more of a chance for the MPs on the committees to debate, scrutinize and so reach a more accountable, representative result on the issue in question. Committees would provide more depth to the resulting Bill or issue in question.

Increasing the power of committees also might mean making MPs full time which has its advantages and disadvantages. If they were full time they would all be able to attend their relevant committees and play a fuller role in the business at hand. As committees are held in the morning they would be free to attend. As most MPs are at the moment part time this would need to change for committees to play a fuller role in Parliamentary affairs. Salary should be increased so that MPs would be prepared to take on their new roles and then not have other jobs which had previously taken up their spare time. Some people argue that MPs would become narrow without outside interests i.e. teaching jobs, jobs in business or in the city. This can be 'waylaid' by the fact that committees would mean they could divert their interest into the committee and become more specialized and professional in outlook.

The power of committees should be increased by increasing their number so that Parliament can be made more accountable, and also interest groups adhered to as well as the executive, departments and civil servants be more accountable and answerable to the House of Commons and the electorate. Increasing their number would mean more work could be considered and more answers to questions could be found in a more informal but professional way.

(Jackie)

Relevance The writer is clear about what the question is asking and every paragraph starts with a topic sentence that links the point to the question.
Structure The point of each paragraph is expressed in a topic sentence at the beginning and the rest supports and develops the idea fairly well, although awkward expression causes difficulties in places. The points are
Para 1: to answer the argument that to increase the power of committees would decrease the power of the House of Commons;
Para 2: a consequence of increasing the power of committees would be full time salaried MPs.
Para 3: increasing the power of committees by increasing their number, workload and accountability.
Style The essay needs proofreading and some rewriting to improve readability and flow. Clearer and fuller topic sentences and sharper concluding sentences would make the argument clearer.

- Now look at the detailed comments on the extract on P. 190. On the basis of these, rewrite paragraph 2 so the points are used more effectively in answering the question.

Essay Activity 5

Mark an essay
Below is a complete essay on the same title, set as coursework, so longer than an exam essay. Read it, as if you were an examiner. Make a note of the

comments you would make if you were marking it on a piece of paper placed next to the text.

Should the power of committees be increased?

1   Parliament is made up of two houses, firstly the House of Commons and secondly, the House of Lords. Over the years the power of the House of Lords has been reduced dramatically, and many people feel that the House of Lords has now become nothing more than a debating chamber with no real power. As the power of the Lords has been reduced, the Commons has become more powerful. As the work increased in the House of Commons the need for more committees became apparent. At present in the Commons there are about eight standing committees and about a dozen select committees.

2   The functions of a standing committee is to scrutinize a Bill and present the government of the day with their findings. The government is under no obligation whatsoever to use the findings given by the standing committee. A standing committee is appointed by the Speaker in consultation with the party leaders. A lot of lobbying takes place towards the standing committee from pressure groups and occasionally foreign powers take an interest. This has recently brought a lot of criticism; a member of the committee at present looking into the channel tunnel has been accused of being in the pay of the ferry companies.

3   Select committees' main functions are to scrutinize the Executive. Many people feel that they are needed to check civil service power. This is all very well but civil servants have the right not to answer questions in front of the committee, and this power was exercised in the recent case of Westland helicopters.

4   When people are chosen to go onto the committees, they are all MPs (many people feel that most are yes men) and this can be argued is not in the best interests of the country. Members of the committee do not stay long enough to really achieve anything worthwhile and may not have the knowledge of the subject needed for a proper investigation.

5   The biggest argument that people who oppose the Committee system we have at present use is that the findings can be ignored by the government. On the other hand, recently, during the Westland affair, a committee caused the resignation of Michael Heseltine. This can be seen as the influence of committees getting stronger. In 1981 the streets of many cities of mainland Britain erupted into the worst scenes of street rioting seen for years. In Brixton one of the areas worst hit by the rioting a Committee was set up headed by Lord Scarman to look into the reasons for the outbreak of violence and to try to stop this sort

of disturbance from happening again. When the findings were published no action relating to them was taken by the government.

6   Unlike the United States of America, committees do not initiate legislation. Also unlike the US where committee findings are taken seriously and can even result in the downfall of a president, e.g. Nixon in the Watergate scandal, in the UK since 1979 275 reports have been published and only four of them have been discussed by the House of Commons.

7   A few reforms for the committee system have been put forward recently these are that standing committees should be turned into specialist bodies who would debate policy and their findings would be respected and used by the government. People from outside Parliament should be able to sit on committees who have an expertise in the subject under discussion. Select Committees should have their power increased and extended to be able to call up people to give evidence.

8   Most MPs in the House of Commons are in favour of a committee system because the object of a committee is to collect information and to let the House of Commons and public know what is going on. Although most MPs are in favour of the committee system, they are not in favour of any reform because it would take the power away from the House of Commons and history has told us that politicians have never been in favour of letting go of power. It can also be said if the power of committees was increased, too much power would be in the hands of a nonelected body. And is this democratic?

                                                                        (Julian)

The writer of this essay has a lot of good, current material, clearly has a mind of his own and has understood the issues about power. However, the reader ends up feeling confused; the essay lacks structure and has sketchy punctuation.

1. The *introduction* starts off quite well, but tails off with a factual comment (about the number of committees) when it should be returning to the question of power. Add a concluding sentence: for example

    ' . . . the need for more committees became apparent. Today, many people feel that the power of Parliament has shifted from both Houses to the committees and that it is in the interests of democracy to halt or even reverse this process.

    There are, however, powerful arguments in favour of increasing the power of committees . . . (topic sentence, para 2) . . .'

2. The first sentences of the paragraphs are not topic sentences. They often do not express the essential point of the paragraph nor show how this point goes towards answering the question – of whether the

power of committees should be increased or not. For example, paragraph 5 starts with a sentence which indicates that it will be about how government can ignore the findings of committees. It then mentions the case when a committee caused the resignation of a government minister (Heseltine) – an example of power. Compare also the first sentence of para 2 of the original with the topic sentence suggested above.

3. The *body* is not well planned. An essay should be planned by points and, in a judgement essay, arguments supported by evidence, not by listing the facts of a subject. For example: paragraphs 2 and 3 describe the functions and powers of standing and select committees. The same material could be used to support (in one paragraph) an argument about present lack of power to affect government decisions (2) or to check civil service power (3).

The body of the essay is repetitive, a consequence of not planning by points but by general topic headings. For example, points about the powerlessness of committees to force government action are made in paragraphs 2 and 5.

4. The essay does not have a clear *conclusion* in which the writer gives his view. It is a judgement essay, so it needs to end with a judgement. My impression, from the weight of evidence he presents, is that, on balance, he is in favour of increasing the power of committees, but he does not say so explicitly. Instead, he draws back from the question by describing MPs' views which appear to contradict his own. This is confusing to the reader and leaves the essay hanging – without a judgement.

This list of weaknesses reads like a damning catalogue of faults. The reason it is worth working on an essay like this is that it is good enough to be much better.

Essay Activity 6

Using the material in this essay, plan an exam answer to this essay question. This means:

> Introduction – one paragraph;
> Body – 3, 4 or 5 paragraphs;
> Conclusion – one paragraph.

Use the outline plan on P. 224 of the Answers Section (Fig 31a) as your starting point. On the basis of the extracts you have read

1. Decide, provisionally, on your conclusion. By how much should the power of committees be increased? By a lot? or not much? Mark your position on a sliding scale between 'Not at all' and 'Yes, absolutely'.
2. Work out the body. Re-read Julian's essay looking for points. First, look for the main arguments and decide which side of the debate they support. Second, look for the detail and evidence that supports the points in the headings.
3. Decide on your introduction.

Then compare your plan with the detailed plan on P. 225 (fig. 31b)

8.3 Writing introductions

How much can you tell about an essay from the introduction? The answer is, of course, 'a lot'. The purpose of this section is to demonstrate this, and give you a practical understanding of what makes a good introduction.

The introduction is where you

(i) show that you have grasped exactly what the question is asking:

(ii) indicate the issues you plan to develop in the body of your essay.

Essay Activity 7

Below is the first draft of the introductory paragraph to the following essay:
In what respects do you think standards in television may be in decline?

What is shown on our television screen is determined by a host of factors. Commercial television's immediate concern is to guarantee an audience for their advertisers. This prompts the BBC into reacting in order for them not to lose their audience. Added to this is the pressure from the public for a varied menu of programmes which are restricted greatly by the censor's increasing wish not to allow the public to decide what they want to watch.

(Leo)

Is it a good opening paragraph to this essay title? To what extent does it correspond to the paragraph plan on P. 143?

It is quite a good introduction. The topic sentence introduces the main idea, that there are a 'host of factors' to consider. The next three sentences 'unpack' this idea, indicating what some of these factors are; pressures on commercial TV; pressures on the BBC; pressure from the public. The idea in the topic sentence is well explained and developed by well chosen supporting evidence. The paragraph then tails off with a comment about censors. The points in the paragraph are not linked directly to the title of the essay, which is about standards declining. There is no conclusion.

• Before you read Leo's redrafted version on P. 235 of the Answers Section, try rewriting the end of the paragraph to include a concluding sentence which links the whole paragraph directly to the title.

Essay Activity 8

Below are some introductions to a sociology essay. The title is: 'Sociological theory and research methods are well nigh inseparable.' Discuss.
    Before you read them, think about the question and analyse it:

  (i) what is the *subject*?
 (ii) what is the *instruction*? Is it a judgement essay or a factual one?
(iii) what *aspects* are you being asked to consider?

Now read the introductions. Record your opinion on each one; does it look as if the essay will answer the question? Has the writer understood the issues? Is it easy to read and understand? Too long? Too short? Too detailed? Too vague? And, of course, decide whether you think it would get a high grade or a low grade in an exam.

When you have finished compare your views with mine in the Answers Section.

---

1. Auguste Comte (1797–1858), the founding father of sociology, regarded sociology as a science. He argued that natural science methodology would produce a positive science of sociology. Positivists believe that the natural laws of science are applicable to the study of man. Matter is affected by external stimuli, e.g. regulated heat temperature will bring water to boil. Man is also affected by external stimuli. Rather than being independent of his environment, his actions are controlled by his surroundings.

2. Sociology is basically the study of the views, behaviour and attitudes of society. There are so many different aspects or parts of society, so many different angles from which to look at these, it is seldom that there is a uniform view on a particular subject in society only schools of thought which emerge from these differing views.

3. Sociological theory cannot be separated from the methods used to conduct the research. The positivist sociologist argues that the me-

thods and logic of natural science can be used and applied to the study of man. Phenomenologists however argue that because man has a consciousness he cannot be treated as an object because the variety of factors which are affecting his behaviour are so great. There is a constant argument between positivist and phenomenological sociologists. Both use different research methods which are closely linked to the theory which the sociologist adopts. Therefore in answer to this question it is necessary to discuss both perspectives and explain the links between theory and method.

4. The type of research methods that sociologists choose are mainly based upon which theoretical approach they take. These are divided into two major camps; the positivist approach and the interactionist approach. Those sociologists who take a positivist approach to the study of society believe that sociology is a science which should follow the rules and methods of the natural sciences. While the interactionists argue that the subject matter of the social sciences cannot be studied in the same way as the subject matter of the natural sciences.

5. Sociology uses various methods to carry out research. When a sociologist wishes to carry out research on a certain topic he can choose from various methods which can give qualitative as well as quantitative information.

6. A sociological theory involves an explanation or description of how society works. Thus Marx's view on stratification involved an account of classes. His theory of social stratification was built on a description of classes as explanation of this. Another example of a sociological theory is in the area of suicide. Durkheim's theory of suicide was based on a social law. The level of suicide is dependent on the level of 'social integration' in a society. Different methods of investigation are used to investigate society. These methods result in different types of data being produced.

7. The relationship between theory and research methods are closely interwoven and inter-related with one another. Sociologists hold different theories; sometimes they may agree with a certain notion or concept, whilst others very often hold conflicting and contradictory ideas in order to give the best analysis of various groups in society, and society's effect upon them.

Self-check

1. How much can you tell about an essay from the opening paragraph?
2. What do you look for in an opening paragraph? Make a list of dos and don'ts for writing introductions. Then compare your list with mine below.

Do:
- start with a topic sentence that indicates that the paragraph and essay which follows will be directly relevant to the title.
- try and ensure that this sentence catches the attention of your reader.
- indicate the concerns if not the specific topics with which you will deal in the essay.
- relate this explicitly to the question as you conclude.

Don't:
- set out all your wares in the first paragraph. This is for the body.
- be too general and vague either. This gives the impression you don't know your subject.
- deal with only one or two of several views or perspectives. Set out a framework, and deal with the 'camps' in the body.

Essay Activity 9

Below is a second set of introductions from exam essays on *Nineteen Eighty Four* by George Orwell. The title is:
'Consider the importance of the past in *Nineteen Eighty Four*.'

● First, analyse the question as suggested on P. 128: subject, instruction, key aspects. Then give some thought to what you might expect to see in an introduction. Here are some specific points for you to consider:

a) What is the difference in the way the phrase 'the mutability of the past' is used in (1) and (2)? Which do you think works better? Why?
b) Both (2) and (4) use the same quotation. Do they make equally effective use of it? Why?
c) Are there any oddities of grammar, expression or fluency that bother you as a reader?
When you have considered these, go on to form your view on how good the following essay is likely to be. My views are given in the Answers Section.

1. The past in Nineteen Eighty Four proves to be an extremely important factor. The whole book is based around the past on two different levels. The first is that one may connect 1984 with the second world war. And secondly, the book is concerned a great deal with the mutability of the past.

2. The importance of the past to Nineteen Eighty Four is summed up in the Party slogan; 'Who controls the past controls the future, who controls the present controls the past.' The mutability of the past against the objective reasoning of Winston's memory are the two major factors of the society Orwell portrays.

3. The past is important in Nineteen Eighty Four as it was a time when there was more freedom and a different way of life. For Winston Smith it is important as he remembers pieces of dreams of his family and he knows that there is something special missing now which he had in the past. Big Brother is now in power and the Party is controlled with extreme, stringent rules.

4. 'Who controls the past controls the future; who controls the present controls the past.' An apt description from an inner party member in Nineteen Eighty Four. Total annihilation of the past meant that there were no comparisons, no memories and certainly, no records.

This was the last question on a three hour paper and the students responded with short paragraphs – a sensible reaction to pressure of time although the essay is unlikely to attract top grades. In the introduction to a factual essay of this sort you need to show that you have a grasp of the issue, (the past), and to indicate the areas you will develop in the body of the essay.

Review

This review is a practical activity in applying points made in these chapters about writing essays. Below is a short exam answer to the same essay question on Orwell.
1. Paragraph it. Look for
    – topic sentences;
    – concluding sentences to each paragraph.
2. Be an examiner.
    – Does the introduction look as if it will answer the question? Any changes needed?
    – Are the paragraphs in the body relevant to the question? Does each have a topic sentence? Does this topic sentence relate the content of the paragraph directly to the question? How many paragraphs are there in the body?
    – How does the essay conclude? Do you think it is a good conclusion? Why?
3. Draw up the plan of this essay. Show the introduction, conclusion and main points in the body.

Compare your reactions with the comments on this essay on P. 191.

158

Essay title: 'Consider the importance of the past in 1984'

Throughout *Nineteen Eighty Four* Winston Smith is pre-occupied with thoughts of the past. He dreams of incidents that happened many years before; he remembers his mother; he remembers holding a piece of 'evidence' against the party. It is his ability to remember events in the past that distinguishes him from other party members. It could be argued that his memory of the past was the cause of his defection. It was essential for the party to eliminate all traces and records of the past as far as possible. Records and accounts of life before Party rule would provide society with a comparison. It could provide them with an objective view of the Party. Winston Smith undertakes the difficult quest of trying to find out what life was actually like before the party. He does this because he can just remember a time when things were different. Control of the past is also important as it provides a Party record. Winston Smith's job at the Ministry of Truth is to change newspapers and other records, so that the outcome of events matches earlier predictions or corresponds with earlier events. The past is most important to the party because through controlling the past the Party can control people's minds. The longer the Party rules, the more it will control the past and consequently people's minds. This is illustrated by Winston's discovery that the Party had told Julia that they had invented the aeroplane. Personal control of the past forms the basis of the principle of 'doublethink'. Winston Smith cannot 'doublethink' and hence he retains a mental record of that which has happened before him. This is the root cause of his defection. It is illustrated when O'Brian produces the photograph of Jones, Aaronson and Rutherford itself 'proof' of the Party's falsification of the past, and shows it to Winston during his torture. He then burns it. Winston remembers seeing the photograph; O'Brian does not. The Party aims to control the past so that people only live for the present and remember nothing that has gone before. As a result people will adopt an attitude of universal passivity regardless of circumstances; no laughter; joy or sadness. George Orwell has shown us the great importance of the past in a society and has given us a harsh warning as to the possible consequences if it were to be controlled.

(John Gorczkiewicz)

9 Remembering

"If I had perfect recall, I'd get full marks in the exam." True or false?

It has to be false, doesn't it? Few exams are intended to test your A–Z knowledge of a subject. The purpose of any assessment procedure is to assess understanding, and you show this by your ability to select only those facts and arguments the question asks for. For this you need a firm grasp of the essential body of knowledge of your subject – which, obviously, you need to remember. This chapter considers a number of approaches to the question of how to improve your ability to remember things.

People differ in the methods they use for remembering things, and, as you know yourself, you use different methods for remembering different things. For example, how do you remember when someone is coming to tea or supper? How do you remember your cash card PIN number? I write down appointments and then all I have to do is to remember to look in the diary by the phone. The advice for cash card numbers is quite the opposite – not to write them down – so you have to invent ingenious ways of remembering them. The purpose of this chapter is to prompt you to think about how your memory works best, and to offer various suggestions for you to try out and adapt, and, if you wish, take further.

The chapter has two parts. The first is a Case Study, and follows the practical line of enquiry of the Case Studies in chapter 4. The context is a debate between 'experts' on study skills about how to memorise and you have to make up your mind about how valid and useful this advice is.

The second part of the chapter considers how you learn and memorise and offers practical activities to try out. It is then up to you to decide how useful they are and when you might use them.

9.1 Case Study: Make up your mind

In this case study, an 'evaluation' of the material takes the place of the 'Find Out' questions in Ch 4. There are three extracts to refer to;
A. the graph on P. 48 Ch 2 from *Use Your Head* by Tony Busan and the comments that follow;

B. the extract below from *Mastering Study Skills* by Richard Freeman
C. the extract. opposite from *Teaching Students to Learn* by Graham Gibbs.

Evaluation question
Do any of the three authors offer advice or comments you find either interesting or helpful?

Extract B

On the whole, we find it difficult to recall events in our lives. Unless 11 May 1965 had a special significance for you, it is unlikely that you can recall a single event of that day. In other words, we quickly lose the capacity to recall events. Even at the end of one hour's lecture, most students find it difficult to recall the first half of the lecture. After two hours or so, half the lecture will have been forgotten. The forgetting curve is shown in Figure 2.2.

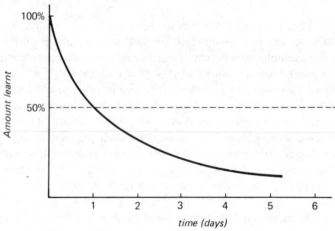

Fig. 2.2 The forgetting curve

I.e. we very quickly lose half the material learnt, but after that, the decline is slow. How can this initial loss be prevented?

There are few aspects of learning of which teachers and lecturers are so ignorant as they are of memory. It is widely believed that each of us possesses a faculty called 'memory' and that some of us have better memories than others. It is also widely held that practice in memorising poems or chunks of the bible helps to develop our memories. Both these beliefs are fantasies. A person who is good at memorising material is a person with good study habits – no more and no less.

From *Mastering Study Skills* by Richard Freeman (Macmillan 1982).

Extract C
The forgetting curve

The main characteristic of memory, highlighted in advice (cf. Buzan 1973) is usually that things are forgotten very quickly indeed unless something is done about it. There is frequent reference to the dramatic and awe-inspiring forgetting curve (cf. Freeman, 1972). . .

Graphs of the curve appear in all sorts of study skill books, usually displaying a bold disregard for labelling or graduating the axes or saying from whence the curve came. In fact it comes from Ebbinghaus (1885). He himself learnt long lists of nonsense syllables (e.g. FUJ, BEH, . . .) until he could remember them all. Then he waited for various lengths of time and saw how many times he had to go back through the list before he could remember them all again. His measure of retention was, therefore, how much effort had been saved in relearning the list. He found that after about twenty minutes he had to look through the list half as many times as he had done originally. This is interpreted by Buzan (1973) as meaning that fifty per cent of all learning is forgotten after twenty minutes. As any elementary educational psychology textbook will tell you there are some problems with such an interpretation:

1. The material Ebbinghaus used is absurdly unlike academic material. If you use meaningful material (e.g. lists of words or sentences) even within the other constraints of the experimental paradigm, the curve is *much* flatter, (e.g. Tyler, 1933). Obviously one remembers many things indefinitely.
2. The method of learning is absurdly unlike student learning. Going through and through a list may be all that one can do to memorize unconnected meaningless material. Students naturally adopt far more efficient strategies for learning meaningful material, unless advised otherwise. Clearly most things are 'memorized' in one trial, without any conscious effort. For example, do you remember your journey to this room this morning? Simply interacting in a meaningful way with the world results in a memory trace being formed. Our main problems are in *retrieving* such traces.

3. The method of testing memory is absurdly unlike student assessment. We do not put students through an examination again and again until they are word perfect and then see how long that took compared to such perfect mastery during the previous term. When people are asked to remember sentences, they remember the *meaning* without the surface *form*. For example you can probably remember the gist of how I opened this chapter without remembering the exact words I used. We make sense of our experience and automatically store in memory the sense we have made. If I tested you on your verbatim recall of the first sentences of this chapter you would score very poorly indeed, even if you had remembered the important things about it.

4. A good deal of the forgetting in the Ebbinghaus paradigm had been found, by the 1950s, to be due to 'interference' from the learning of other lists *prior* to the one tested, or *between* learning and recall of the one tested, rather than simply to passive decay of the memory trace. The more similar the interfering lists are, the more forgetting takes place. The learning of the crucial list is not *unique* enough to distinguish it in memory from memory traces of other lists of nonsense syllables. This is very unlike the learning situation facing students. If you were to test students on the exact form of words used in one of two different lectures on the same general topic, then presumably the similarity of the phrases habitually used would cause them problems in distinguishing one lecture from the other. But if you were to test them on their understanding of some concept or principle from one lecture then the similarity of conceptual framework from the other lecture would obviously *help* and not interfere.

Rehearsal

Clearly the forgetting curve is of extremely dubious relevance to student learning. This has not prevented Buzan (1973) and Main (1977), for example, from going on to give advice to students on the basis of what happens to this curve when you rehearse.

A graph is prepared, based rather loosely on Jost's law (1897). It is derived from exactly the same experimental paradigm as Ebbinghaus employed. Successively relearning the list of nonsense syllables results in successively shallower forgetting curves. It is concluded, in study skills advice, that to slow the relentless march of forgetting, you need to *rehearse* your material, at successively longer intervals. This must involve, says Buzan, rehearsing your notes immediately, after one day, one week, one month, etc. Apart from all the objections to the evidence for this phenomenon, outlined above, there are bizarre possibilities in store for any student who should follow such advice. A conventional student attending, say, four lectures a day and also taking

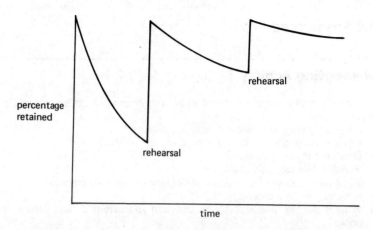

notes from, say, two text sources a day, would, after only five weeks, be rehearsing 120 sets of notes a week! I have never met a student who would be willing to undertake such a task.

From *Teaching Students to Learn* by G. Gibbs, Open University Press, 1981.

Evaluation Activity:

● Work through these questions and compare your answers with mine in the Answers Section.

i) What are the two topic sentences in the Freeman extract? Does the rest of the extract support these two points?
ii) What are a) the similarities and b) the differences between the graphs presented by Freeman and Buzan?
iii) From your overview of the Gibbs extract
   a) what is the main point in each of the two sections? (see topic sentences)
   b) How many 'problems' with Buzan's interpretation does he identify?
iv) From your detailed read, what are these problems?
v) How do Gibbs and Buzan differ over 'rehearsing' or reviewing material learnt?
vi) According to Gibbs, how do students memorise things?

● Now write your own evaluation: Do any of the three authors offer advice or comments you find either interesting or helpful? This activity resembles a short piece of academic criticism. The questions have taken you through the first step, to establish, as far as it is possible in short extracts, the views of different authors. The second step, to evaluate this in the light of your own views and experience, is an individual matter. I am not going to comment; you may find it interesting, however, to discuss the points raised with other students, tutors or friends.

9.2 **Memorising**

Memorising Activity 1

You have a lot of information stored away in your memory. Let's see if you can retrieve a little:
1. What did you have to eat last Saturday evening?
2. What is the phone number of someone close to you?
3. Finish the rhyme that starts
   'Twinkle, twinkle, little star'.
4. What two concepts are used by sociologists in defining poverty?
5. How do you tie a shoelace?
6. What is the first practical step in analysing an essay title suggested in this book?

How did you set about remembering these things?
1. You may remember exactly what you ate last Saturday evening, particularly if it was in some way different to the general run of Saturday evenings. Equally, you may have started with a complete blank, and had to coax memories out. You think of Friday and Sunday – anything different about them? You need a starting point, and then help yourself along; where were you that evening? who with? did you cook supper? what were you wearing? If you carry on like this for a while, you will reach the particular item you were looking for – what you ate. You will also have drawn out of your memory a full picture of the evening. The memories are there; it's a question of retrieving them through *linking* and *association*.
2. People have various tricks for remembering things like phone numbers: adding up bits of the number, splitting numbers into two digit numbers, or simply learning them. Obviously it helps if you have known the number for a long time or use it frequently.
3. You will probably never forget the nursery rhymes you learnt as a small child, although if your upbringing was not typically British, you may not know this one. This has *rhyme* and *rhythm* to help you. You would have started to learn the sounds of these words before you understood them.
4. Have you read chapters 1 and 2? If you haven't, the question of remembering does not arise. Even if you have, however, you might still not have remembered the concepts of 'absolute' and 'relative' poverty. Why is this?
   – Sociology is not your subject, so you had no reason to learn them;
   – you classified the extracts as 'reading exercises' and considered the content unimportant;
   – it was new to you and did not make much sense to you.

These reasons are primarily to do with *motivation* to learn and *understanding*. You are less likely to remember things you are not interested in or don't understand.

5. You never forget how to tie shoelaces, but in case you think it is easy, watch a child trying to learn how to do it. It's a *skill*; you observe, you copy, you try, you do.

6. Like (4), if you haven't read the chapter, you can't expect to remember, but if you have, I hope you remembered that Step 1 is to identify the subject. If you did not remember this, look again at your motivation. How important is essay writing in your course? How conscientious are you about doing the Self Checks and Activities? If your answer to questions of this sort is 'not very', your memory probably obliged by editing out this information!

Review

What practical points about how to remember can you take away from this activity?

1. You remember a lot without making a conscious effort and you don't have to worry about overburdening your memory. Our memories, fortunately, are not like arcade shove ha'penny (or 10p) machines; things don't drop over the edge when you add new items!

2. The problem is often simply a question of *retrieval*.

3. Your *motivation* as you learn is probably the most important single factor. It is much harder to make up later for a low level of interest at the time of learning. If you are interested, you make sense of things as you learn, and connect up new information with things you know already.

4. You need to *understand* what you are trying to learn. The process of making sense of material when you come across it is a much better guarantee that you will remember it than to rely on feats of memory. The chapters on reading and notemaking offer practical guidance on making sense as you go.

5. There are certain items you simply need to *memorise* – phone numbers, dates, studies, formulae, quotations. Be clear about what the essentials are since there are usually fewer of them than you fear, and develop knacks for learning them.

6. You learn skills by *doing*. This comes after observation, understanding, trial and error. Many study skills come into this category.

Memorising Activity 2

Memorise the following information – you will be tested on it afterwards.

1. Write down the 7× table and the 13× table, and learn them.
2. Learn these rhymes;
    i) 30 days hath September, April, June and November,
       All the rest have 31, save February alone
       which has 28 days clear,
       And 29 days each Leap Year.
    ii) i before e except after c.
    iii) Learn the first two verses of this extract from the poem, 'The Old
       Sailor' by A. A. Milne.

    There was once an old sailor my grandfather knew
    Who had so many things which he wanted to do
    That, whenever he thought it was time to begin,
    He couldn't because of the state he was in.

    He was shipwrecked, and lived on an island for weeks,
    And he wanted a hat and he wanted some breeks;
    And he wanted some nets, or a line and some hooks
    For the turtles and things which you read of in books.
                    ....
    So he thought of his hut . . . and he thought of his boat,
    And his hat and his breeks, and his chickens and goat,
    And the hooks (for his food) and the spring (for his thirst) . . .
    But he never could think which he ought to do first.

    And so in the end he did nothing at all,
    But basked on the shingle wrapped up in a shawl.
    And I think it was dreadful the way he behaved –
    He did nothing but basking until he was saved!

3. You probably know several mnemonics. Learn these;
    i) Many Very Excellent Men Jump Sideways Using New Plimsoles.
       This mnemonic reminds you of the names and order of the planets:
       Mercury, Venus, Earth, Mars, Jupiter, Saturn, Uranus, Neptune,
       Pluto.
    ii) Every Good Boy Deserves Favour. In music E, G, B, D, F are the
       notes written on the lines in the treble clef.
    iii) All Cows Eat Grass, A, C, E, G are the notes written between the
       lines in the bass clef.
4. Learn this list of items;
    oak   marrow
    robin   magpie

carrot	forget-me-not
daffodil	radish
dandelion	washing line
sparrow	lime
lettuce	blackbird
tulip	sycamore

Now for the TEST.
1. What is 5 × 7? 9 × 7? 5 × 13? 8 × 13?
2. How many days are there in a) June b) July?
3. Are these words correctly spelt; receive their retreive?
4. Write out the first two verses of 'The Old Sailor'.
5. In what order are the planets?
6. Write out the complete list of items from Activity 4.

And now mark yourself!

Knacks for Memorising

Far more important than how you did are the techniques you used for remembering.

1. You were probably more confident with your 7× table than your 13× which is more likely to be new to you in this form. You learn these by recitation and *rote learning* and, if you depend on them, you need to overlearn, as with the tables you learned as a child. Test yourself on your 13× table next week.

2 and 3. There are two questions you need to ask to check successful learning;
  (i) did you remember the rhymes?
  (ii) could you *apply* them easily?

4. 'The Old Sailor' has a lot going for it – apart from its description of a syndrome we all recognise. The poem relies on ancient story telling techniques which only survive spontaneously today in rhymes for children. It has a regular and catchy rhythm, regular rhyme, simple language. Even if you didn't remember all the words, you can probably tap out the rhythm, and fill in some rhymes. This is what makes (some) poetry – certainly the sorts of *jingles* you might use as an aid to memory – easy to remember.

5. *Mnemonics* of various sorts underpin many systems for memorising. Tony Buzan introduces a system in 'Use Your Head', and develops these ideas in other books. These systems use numbers, rhyme, colour, association to create vivid and often improbable or vulgar mental pictures to aid memory.

6. Probably the best approach to this is to sort out the items into *categories*. It is easier to remember things that relate to each other and make sense in their groupings. Overall, all these are things you might find in a garden so they are not a random collection of items. If you divide them like this the list is broken up and makes sense;

Trees	Vegetables	Flowers	Birds
oak	marrow	daffodil	magpie
lime	carrot	dandelion	robin
sycamore	radish	tulip	sparrow
	lettuce	forget-me-not	blackbird

Did you remember 'washing line'? As odd one out you may have found it stood out – or have forgotten it. Try tying it in – to a tree, with a blackbird on it – anything that helps you to remember. You may have found the short groups easy to remember; if you didn't, try some tricks; birds, for example, M & S, B & R, (shops); flowers, DDT (guaranteed to kill all flowers!) and forget-me-not.

In any course of study, you have a lot of material to remember. Fortunately, it is not just a question of memorising unconnected facts. If you are having difficulty, consider your motivation in learning the information, and act on your conclusions.

Make sure that you really understand what you are trying to learn. Read critically, make notes selectively, ask yourself questions as you go. First establish the concepts you need to understand your subject. Then learn the essential formulae, quotations, studies, diagrams etc. that you need to show your understanding. For this try out a variety of techniques, and don't persist with methods that don't suit you. Have confidence in your memory; the information is there – your task is to retrieve it.

References
Tony Buzan: Use Your Head (BBC Publications 1974)
Speed Memory (BBC Publications 1984)

10 Being Assessed

Assessment, in one form or other, is an integral part of any course. It is more than a necessary evil; getting feedback is part of the pleasure of a course. Your work is the basis of dialogue between you and your tutor and part of the process by which you set yourself objectives and progress in your studies. However, there can't be many people who feel this positive about assessment as exams loom, an interruption in your life which produces some apparently random results a few weeks or months later.

Most of this chapter is concerned with exams and the period leading up to them, since these are the high – or low – spots of the year if your course ends with them. First, though, think about the assessment procedure itself and your part in it. In courses which are based on some form of continual assessment, this self-assessment is essential.

10.1 The Assessment Process

Self-check

Who are the parties to the assessment procedure on your course? What is the role of each?

The parties to any assessment procedure are:
1. you
2. your tutor(s)
3. an external moderator or examiner.

The role of each varies widely, as you saw from the extracts from syllabuses in the introduction. Some courses are based largely or wholly on coursework, while others, which require as much coursework, are assessed entirely on performance in an exam.

1. **Your role** is to take responsibility for your own learning. You are the person who determines more than anyone what you get out of your course. You need to:
   – prepare for classes (do reading set etc)

– complete and hand in assignments/essays on time
– read, understand, discuss and act on tutor's comments
– learn from other students.

Every now and again, perhaps once a month, or when you get your work back, it can be helpful to ask yourself structured *self assessment questions*:
– What am I good at?
– What have I got better at?
– What are still my weaknesses?
– What do I need to work on next?
– What use do I make of my tutor?
– Do I discuss points I'm unclear about?
– Do I learn from other students in discussion or in activities, e.g. project work, revision groups?
– Am I getting the work done?
– Do I need to organise my time better?

The process of answering questions such as these in your head will normally be enough to suggest what to work on next. You may find it helpful to jot down your answers from time to time.

2. **Your tutors' role** is to help you to learn and be successful in your studies and it is up to you to make the best use of them. You need to respect people's different teaching styles but recognise that no one can teach effectively without adequate feedback from students. So:
– ask questions when you need to clarify a point;
– discuss your tutor's comments on your work;
– consult your tutor for guidance on your progress: where you are going wrong, where you've improved.

Your tutor may also be involved in a more formal assessment procedure. This may include:
– a *profile*, in which you and your tutor agree which objectives you have and haven't (yet) fulfilled.
– an *oral assessment* or interview. Your tutor should be able to give you specific guidance on what is expected. It is then up to you to act on it. Be realistic about this dual role; your tutors are involved in making an objective evaluation of you – they will be willing you to do well but can't make too many allowances! You should do well if you are realistic in your preparation.

– *agreement with a moderator* to standardize marking. Again, your tutor will be operating within clear guidelines but moderators respect tutors' views, so do make full use of your tutor in your preparation.

3. **The examiner or moderator** is rarely the white haired ogre the title conjures up. Most are practising teachers whose own students are being examined by someone else and are well aware of the difficulties experienced by both students and tutors. Typically, the procedure for marking exam scripts is like this; examiners ('Assistant examiners') are given a marking scheme, which outlines how marks should be awarded. After they have provisionally marked some scripts, examiners hold a standardisation meeting where unforeseen problems are raised, and responses to these agreed. The marking scheme is then amended to cater for answers or problems that had not been anticipated. Any queries that arise after this are referred directly to the Chief Examiner. Moderators do much the same, but as they visit schools and colleges for discussions with tutors they appear to be more 'human'.

10.2 **The Revision Period**

And so to exams. In the course of the year you will have developed certain skills as well as knowledge of your subject. In the exam and the period leading up to it, you will draw on all your study skills, with the added ingredient of pressure.

When do I revise?
1. *Start revising now.* You could be one month into your course or one month before an exam when you read this. If you have just started your course get into the habit of regular reviews of material covered (see Chapter 2). This will make it easier to extract main points and summarise when you come to the final revision period.
2. *Draw up a revision timetable* for the five or six weeks before the exam. Make a list of the topics to revise, and plan your allocation of time on an overall week by week basis. Each week decide exactly what you are going to work on and when you are going to do it.
3. *Organise your time.* You will have to find more time for study in these weeks. Look at your 'Time finding' Sheet (Chapter 5) and see where you can carve out some extra time. You should know by now when you work most effectively so try to use these times as far as possible. You will probably have to use other times as well, but don't overdo it. Do keep time for relaxation, and don't cut down on sleep. Common sense tells you that lack of sleep makes you tired, tense, irritable,

forgetful and inefficient at whatever you are doing. But common sense is often one of the first casualties in the exam period; don't let it be for you.

How do I revise?
Any way that works for you. But if you find yourself asking the question, try out some of these suggestions:
- *Ask other students/friends what they do* and try it if it seems sensible.
- *Be clear about what you need to know*. Your syllabus and coursework is your starting point. Fortunately, in most subjects you probably don't need to remember a massive amount of facts, although there are a minority of exams (such as the final qualifying exam for doctors) that do require a comprehensive mastery of detail. In most subjects and at most levels you need to understand principles, theories, ideas. When you have this understanding, facts and detail make more sense because they have a purpose and a link.
- *Learn your basics* the main points and supporting detail: graphs, statistics, cases, formulae, quotations, studies. Look back to Chapter 9 for suggestions on this.
- *Rewrite your notes in a shortened form* as a basis for this learning. Try and reduce a topic to a series of key points (and illustrations) which trigger associated knowledge and ideas. Use no more than a side of A4, well spaced. Look back to Chapter 2 for suggestions on grouping and linking ideas.
- *Use cards*. Cards are a useful discipline in picking out essential points and are handy for carrying around to revise from at odd moments. They are also useful when you are thinking about how you might use the information. You can put them on the table and move them around to show the connections between topics.
- *Practise using your knowledge*. Learning up a topic is only the first step towards being able to use it in an exam. When you have revised a topic, think immediately about how you might use it. Look at past papers and pick out three questions on the same topic. Analyse each question – subject, instruction, aspect (See Chapter 7) and plan an outline answer to it on a single side of A4 or a card.

Be clear about why you are doing this; it's not in the hope that the question will come up again – assume it won't. You're doing it so you can think about the topic from different angles and see how you can draw on the same body of knowledge in different ways depending on how the question is worded. Look back to the three questions on 'poverty' (P. 123); this should also remind you that writing 'all I know about . . .' answers (which rote learning revision often leads to) is not going to get you far in an exam.

- *Look at past exam papers* primarily for this purpose. You can try question spotting for fun – but expect to be wrong. It helps to be familiar with the appearance of the paper (print size, colour, layout), the rubric or instructions (e.g. 'three questions of which at least one must be from each section'), and the style of questions.

- *Form a revision group with other students* This can be really helpful and a welcome antidote to the isolation which can set in when classes end. Other people bring different insights, understanding, views and levels of interest to a topic, and this can help to clarify your own views and understanding. Teach each other certain topics; give verbal outlines of answers from notes. However, if it stops being helpful or degenerates into too much time wasting, be disciplined enough to stop.

- *Write timed answers* to some exam questions. You may want to allow up to five minutes longer than you will have in the exam, because you are writing without the sense of pressure and the adrenalin that speeds you up in an exam.

- *Handwriting*: show an example of your handwriting from a timed answer to three or four people you trust to give you an honest (but not lugubrious) comment on its readability. If your handwriting is hard to read, it undoubtedly places you at a disadvantage with the examiner who will probably have a couple of hundred scripts to mark in a couple of weeks.

  - Try writing bigger/smaller. Standard size writing of 8 or 9 words per line tends to be easier to read than very large or very small writing.
  - Experiment with different pens or biros. Some pens change the way you write or slow you down. This may be no bad thing.
  - Write less. Think and plan more.
  - Concentrate on improving the formation of three or four letters. Identify which cause the most difficulties and misunderstandings and work on them. I have every sympathy with people with poor handwriting, but unfortunately, sympathy is not enough. Bad handwriting creates a bad impression, and will drop you a grade; if great tracts of your papers are virtually unreadable, how can the examiner give you marks for what you've written?

10.3 Exams

Exam preparation

Look at the syllabus and past papers for your course. What styles of question will you have to answer in the exam? Obviously, I can't comment directly on what you need to prepare for; as long as you know, that's all that matters!

The types of answer required are likely to be similar to those indicated in the extracts from syllabuses in the introduction, and this book suggests approaches to the main ones:
- essays; what instructions does your exam board favour?
  Are most essays factual or judgement essays? See Chapters 6, 7, 8.
- case studies (use the contents and index to select relevant sections, but see especially Chapters 4 and 6).
- various forms of business communication, such as letters and reports. (Chapter 6 and the Reference Section)
- analysis of data (Chapter 4)

In addition to these, short written answers and multiple choice questions are often set. The conventions of these vary from subject to subject. A data response question for Business Studies requires a practised and trained approach specific to the subject, quite different to the approach required by, for example, an English Comprehension exercise.

In the exam

Read the exam paper carefully There is nothing new about this advice, but it is probably one of the most ignored under the pressure of the exam. The three activities that follow present you with some examples in the hope that they convince you that you really must

read the instructions and
read the questions carefully.

Assessment Activity 1

Re-read the extract from *Teaching students to learn* by Graham Gibbs on P. 16 then answer the following multiple choice question. Uncover only the question.

Graham Gibbs objects to the 'forgetting curve' because
   a) the Ebbinghaus material on which it is based is out of date
   b) it has been used by too many study skills experts
   c) it has little relevance to students
   d) Ebbinghaus used nonsense syllables.

This question is typical of multiple choice questions in that none of the options is totally wrong – all are mentioned by Gibbs, but (c) is the best summary of Gibbs' objections. You *must* read all the options in a multiple choice question before you decide which is right.

Assessment Activity 2

Which of the outline answers (A–F) fulfil the requirements of the question?

Using *one* of the following to illustrate your answer:
banking; the retail distribution trade; building societies; insurance;
describe how *four* of the facilities below are used by your chosen
example

a) Laser printers   d) Computer based information services
b) On-line facilities e) Magnetic strips
c) Micro-computers f) 'data-post'

(5 marks per item)
(Data Processing Level 1 CACA)   Total: 20 marks

A Describe how laser printers are used in banking, the retail distribution trade, building societies and insurance.
B Describe how on-line facilities, micro-computers, magnetic strips and 'data-post' are used by building societies.
C Write about how computer based information services and 'data-post' are used in banking, insurance and actuarial work.
D Give a brief account of business applications of laser printers, micro-computers, computer based information services and 'data-post'.
E Describe how the retail distribution trade uses 'data-post', computer based information services, micro computers and on-line facilities.
F Outline the pros and cons of dot matrix and laser printers in building societies and insurances businesses

Whatever you decided, you probably have some sympathy both for the candidates, many of whom found this question confusing, and for the examiner with a marking scheme which can only award marks to answers and parts of answers directly relevant to the question asked. I hope you correctly identified B and E as relevant answers.

Assessment Activity 3

Let's suppose that from your researches into past papers you were expecting a question on a language paper which starts like this:

The following passage contains about 750 words. Write a precis of this passage in not more than 250 words summarising the main points in clear, connected English (50 marks).

When you enter the exam room and turn over your paper, the question before you starts like this: .

a) Read the following extract and summarise the main points of the argument in not more than 150 words of continuous prose. (35 marks)
b) How effective is your precis in communicating the style and content of the original piece? (15 marks)

• What is the main difference in what you are being asked to do?
• How would you cope with a surprise like this?

Changes in the style and presentation of exam questions happen more frequently now as exam boards seek greater flexibility from candidates.
I hope you would:
1. Notice it.
2. Keep cool. The skills required by a restyling of a question are the same; only the form is different. You are well prepared.
3. Do exactly as the question asks. Write 150 words for (a) and use your judgement, within the overall allocation of time to marks in the question for (b).
4. Allocate your time and effort according to the marks the question attracts. The question is marked out of 50 in a 2 hour exam marked out of 100, so allow one hour for this question. In a question of this sort you will have to allow a lot of time for reading and understanding the passage, picking out main points, making notes. But be aware of the 35/15 distribution of marks and plan accordingly.

So do read your exam paper carefully!

Budgeting time in the exam
You must allocate your time according to the marks a question attracts. If you have four questions to answer in three hours, each marked out of 25, divide your time equally between them. If question 1 is marked out of 40 and the remaining three out of 20, simple arithmetic tells you that you should spend twice as long as question 1. This section is about the arithmetic of exams. Again, I hope to persuade you to act on it, by working it out yourself.

A time budget
How do you allocate time in a '4 questions in three hours' (or 5 or 3 questions) paper? Simple arithmetic suggests 45 minutes each, but if you allow a full 45 minutes on the first two questions, you are bound to be short. Why?

- You need time to read the paper and finalise your choice of question, 5–10 minutes.
- You need time to check over your script at the end; another 10 minutes, say.

This leaves you with 40 minutes for each answer, including 5 minutes for analysing the question and planning an outline answer. So the most you would be writing for is 35 minutes per answer. You can vary this slightly, allowing up to 45 minutes overall for one and 35 for another question, but don't go above or below these limits. Why?

Assessment Activity 4
Examination Arithmetic

Below are the marks awarded to three (fictitious) students on one paper, followed by a table showing the correlation between marks and grades at A level. The paper is marked out of 100 and each question carries 25 marks.

Question	Student 1	Student 2	Student 3
1	18	14	16
2	17	15	13
3	10	12	13
4	9	14	0

Scheme for marking and grading papers at A level
Grade A   70 and over
    B   60–69
    C   53–59
    D   46–52
    E   40–45
    N   35–39 (narrow failure)
    U   Ungraded

1. What mark and grade does each student get? Are these as you expected?
2. What can you deduce from these marks about the approach of each student to the exam?
3. Can you make any suggestions as to how any of these students might have improved their grade by reallocating time?

Student 1 54% Grade C. This student is clearly very able and completed two excellent A grade answers but the low grades for the last two indicate very sketchy answers from a candidate of this ability. At least s/he avoided a disaster by dividing what little time was left between the last two questions. If this candidate had allowed equal time for each question, a couple of marks might have been lost from the first two answers but many more would have been gained from the last two. Instead of a comfortable B this student passed with a poor C.

Student 2 55% = Grade C. This student approached the exam systematically and allocated time carefully producing a range of competent, not brilliant, answers. This candidate obtained the best result of the three.

Student 3 42% Grade E. This candidate came near to outright failure. Question 1 was obviously the best topic and it looks as if the candidate spent far too long on it. It did not pay off; the answer got three marks above what seems to be the norm for this student. This in no way makes up for the void in question 4. Even a weak answer would have picked up some marks; 4 marks would have produced a D grade and 11 marks a C. This is well within the student's capability.

Conclusion Examination arithmetic is compelling, isn't it? The moral of the story is not that the average student does better in exams, but that the other two went down one or two grades simply because they were not strict about how they used their time. Divide your time equally and attempt all questions; a sketchy last question or notes is much better than nothing. **Never leave a void!**

A final Self Check

1. The question on P. 175 (Assessment Activity 2) is taken from a 3 hour paper in which the candidate has to answer five questions, carrying equal marks. How long should you allow for
   i) each question
   ii) each of these subsections?

2. Get hold of copies of recent past papers in your subject. Work out how long you should allow for each question and parts of questions. Work out
   (i) reading/choosing time
   (ii) overall time for each question
   (iii) allocation of time within each question allowing for planning, writing, subsections (if any)
   (iv) time at the end of the exam for checking. Then try it out by doing a paper. Make adjustments to suit you.

Post script
After the exam, forget it. If it's the first of several, take time off, relax. If it's the last, enjoy the freedom. Make a point of meeting and exchanging addresses with people you want to keep in touch with, because people tend to go their own ways as soon as exams are over.

Part 3

Reference and Answer Sections

11 Reference Section

11.1 **How to get the most from your dictionary**

The first part of this section follows from 'Why use a dictionary?' on P. 54
Chapter 3. The first six headings below correspond to the headings there.
You can use a dictionary to:

1. *Check the meanings of words*
   'Spurious', 'judicial', 'precedent' are words you might have checked.
   You may know the meaning of the last one but want to know what it
   means in this legal context.

2. *Check the meaning of idiomatic expressions*
   Look up 'lip-service'.

3. *Check how to pronounce a word*
   How do you pronounce 'spurious'? Compare the way this word is
   marked with 'spurn', 'sputnick' and 'sputter' further down the page.

4. *Find out what a familiar word means when it's used in an unfamiliar*
   way
   Look up 'distinguished'. What does it mean here?

5. *Find out what part of speech a word is*
   This is not just for grammar buffs but can help you to establish
   meaning and pronunciation:
   > 'distinguished' as in a 'a distinguished visitor' is an adjective
   > describing the noun 'visitor'. The word in the Law question is a
   > verb, meaning 'to point out the difference of . . differentiate,
   > draw distinctions.' (Concise Oxford Dictionary).

   It can also help with spelling. Is 'practise/practice' correctly spelt in
   these examples?
   > 'With practise you will improve.'
   > 'I'm practising my handwriting.'

(The first example should be 'With practice, you will improve',
'Practice' here is a noun.)

6. *Learn to identify the roots of words.*

   This helps to increase your vocabulary, and enables you to have an intelligent guess at the meaning of a word.

   Look up 'judicial' and 'justice'. Identify the Latin root of these words and make a note of a dozen words which share the root, and their meanings.

   Most prefixes come from the Latin. Once you know what the prefix means, you can recognise it in other words.

   What does 'pre-' mean?

   What do these words mean; predictable, prejudice, premature?

   Other examples of prefixes are; pro-, con-, anti-, ante-, trans-, sub-. Check their meanings and note 3 or 4 words that use each prefix.

7. A dictionary can tell you something of the *history* of a word, and the languages and cultures it came from.

   Look up 'groundsel'. What do you learn about the medical uses of this plant in the past?

8. And, of course, you use a dictionary to check *spelling*, as long as you know the first few letters – 'negotiate' or 'negociate'?

How good is your vocabulary?
How many of the following words could you a) define precisely and b) use correctly?

alleviate	enumerate	paradox	marginal
covertly	equilibrium	propensity	organic
endemic	ideological	velocity	prevalence
cartel	inferred	horsetrading	quasi-
differential	mitigate	incur	viability

This matters, because all these words are taken from recent exam papers in social science and business subjects. Obviously, if your understanding of a word is hazy, your grasp of what the question is asking will be hazier still. So make a point of looking up any word you don't fully understand, and note examples of how the word is used.

A final check
1. *How up to date is your dictionary?* Does it list: laser, cassette, duvet, biro, microfiche?

2. *Can you use the information in the dictionary?*
   The dictionary definition of a word is only the starting point to understanding it and being able to use it or explain its meaning to someone else.
   Look back to (6) above. Could you explain the meaning of these words and use them correctly?

(i) *predictable*; 'forecast, prophesy' (COD) ie: you can tell what will happen.

(ii) *prejudice*; 'preconceived opinion, bias'. ie: making up your mind about someone or something before you have first hand experience of them or it. The inclusion of 'bias' in the dictionary indicates that if you do this you are likely not to see the objective truth!

(iii) *premature*; 'Occurring, done, before the usual or proper time'. The word could be used in these contexts;
   – 'It would be premature to issue a statement now; we don't know what their proposals are yet.'
   – 'The baby was premature, born four weeks early.'

11.2 **How to check alphabetical order**

Finding things listed alphabetically can be easier said than done. Since it is an essential skill whether you are looking for sections in a filing cabinet, or entries in a phone book, dictionary, library card index or microfiche, this section is here to give you practice if you need it.
If you don't find the entry you want immediately
  (i) Check the spelling. Clark? Clarke? Clerk?
 (ii) Look at the order of the letters well into the word.
       eg. Cowdrey, Cowdroy, Cowdry?
(iii) Check the first names or initials.
       eg. Clark, S.; Clark S.N.; Clark, Thomas; Clark, Tony.

Reference Activity 1

Below is a sketch of the author catalogues in a public library of names beginning with 'C' and a list of books and publications filed under 'C'.

1. In which drawer would each card be filed? The drawers are numbered for ease of reference.
2. Arrange in order the cards that would be found in drawer 14.

1 BUTT —CAML	5 CHAMBERS — CHAU	9 COB -- COLLING	13 COT — COX, P
2 CAMM — CARN	6 CHAV — CHRISTMAS, M	10 COLLINS, A — COM	14 COX, R — CROSN
3 CARO — CAS	7 CHRISTMAS, N — CLARK, W	11 CON — COOK, W	15 CROSS — CUR
4 CAT —CHAMBERL	8 CLARKE, E —COA	12 COOKE —COS	16 CUS —DAT

Malcolm CRAIG, *Investing to survive the '80s; inside information for businesses and investors*
CHILD POVERTY ACTION GROUP, *National Welfare Benefits Handbook*
Vivian J. COOK, *Young children and language*
Ernest CLARKE, *Chemistry objective and completion tests for 'O' level*
CONSUMERS ASSOCIATION, *The Which? Book of Money*
Robert CLARK, *Police and the Community; an analytic perspective*
Marianne CRAIG, *Office workers' survival handbook; a guide to fighting health hazards in the office.*
Malcolm CRAIG, *Successful investment*
A. J. T. COLIN, *Programming for microprocessors*
Brian CLARK, *Whose life is it anyway?*
Malcolm CRAIG, *Invisible Britain; Handling money? Discover how to get the best deal.*
Alastair COOK, *The Americans; fifty letters from America on our life and times*

When you have finished, check your order in the Answers Section.

11.3 How to Punctuate

This section is intended as a simple outline of the basic rules of punctuation. If you find you need a more comprehensive guide or further practice, there are plenty of books which offer this.
'Punctuation' (Books 1–4) by T. G. Ledgard (Cassell 1977) are excellent for students of all ages although designed for schools.

Full stop

A full stop is used at the end of a sentence. This is the most important piece of punctuation because it divides writing into sentences, the basic units of sense. If you have difficulty identifying sentences and using full stops, look for guidance from a friend, tutor or a book.

Reference Activity 2

1. Punctuate this passage:

This candidate came near to outright failure question 1 was obviously the best topic and it looks as if the candidate spent far too long on it it did not pay off the answer got three marks above what seems to be the norm for this student this in no way makes up for the void in question 4 even a weak answer would have picked up some marks four marks would have produced a D grade and eleven marks a C this is well within the student's capability.

Turn to P. 178 (Chapter 10) and compare you punctuation with the paragraph 'Student 3'. You will note that I used two semi-colons. It is perfectly correct to use full stops here instead. It is not correct to use commas. (See below).
2. Turn to 'Paragraph 2' P. 144 Ch 8. By changing two commas to full stops, correct the punctuation in this paragraph.

Capital letters

Use capital letters
1. To start sentences.
2. For names of individual people, places, days, months, organisations, products, etc.; Jane, Dr. Richard Williams, France, Monday, July, the National Extension College, Whiskas.
3. For the titles of books and films: Macmillan Professional Masters 'Eastenders', 'Panorama'.

Check your handwriting to make sure your capital letters look different to your lower case letters. They should be taller and are often differently formed.

Commas

They must not ever be used as an alternative to full stops. They have several uses:
1. To mark off items in a list
   eg. Common sense tells you that lack of sleep makes you tired, tense, irritable, forgetful and inefficient at whatever you are doing, P. 171)

2. At the end of each line of an address (handwritten or typed using 'closed' punctuation).

3. To mark off a phrase which is not absolutely essential to the sentence. A single comma is used when the non-essential word or phrase comes first:

   eg 'Fortunately, in most subjects you probably don't need to remember a massive amount of facts.'

   A pair of commas is used when the non-essential word or phrase comes in the middle of the sentence:

   eg 'Do you remember, for example, your journey to this room this morning?'

4. To mark off direct speech from what comes before or after it.

   e.g. 'The fact is,' said Norman Fowler, 'that we are providing more and better patient care than at any time in the history of the health service.' (P. 81 Ch 4).

5. To mark off phrases beginning with words like when, after, unless, although when they come at the beginning or middle of a sentence.

   eg 'After they have provisionally marked some scripts, examiners hold a standardisation meeting where unforeseen problems are raised.'

   'She decided that, as she had worked since breakfast, it was time for a break.'

Self Check

Punctuate this passage:

> This must involve says Buzan rehearsing your notes immediately after one day one week one month etc apart from all the objections to the evidence for this phenomenon outlined above there are bizarre possibilities in store for any student who should follow such advice.

Check it with the last paragraph of the extract from Graham Gibbs P. 162) See if you can explain why each comma is used.

Apostrophes
have two uses only.
1. *To mark missing letters*

I don't know	= I do not know
She'll wait	= She will wait
It's Sunday	= It is Sunday
They could've come	= They could have come

2. *To show belonging*
i) where something belongs to one person or thing use 's
   - Tom's football
   - Write up your notes from today's class.
ii) where something belongs to more than one, add an apostrophe to the
   plural or 's to the plural form of the word:
   - the children's school
   - the boys' shoes.
Notice the difference between this and 'the boy's shoes' – only one boy.
People often scatter apostrophes around whenever they see an 's'. Don't.
The rules for the use of the apostrophe are straightforward.

Quotation marks and speech marks
Use inverted commas, either singly (') or in pairs (") to surround words
which are
1. spoken
   "The National Health Service is safe in our hands," said Margaret
   Thatcher.
2. taken from another writer.
   - Winston Smith cannot 'doublethink' so he retains a mental record of
   that which happened before him.
   - The 'young elderly' group has not increased much.
   'Doublethink' is George Orwell's phrase, quoted in an essay on
   Orwell. The 'young elderly' is a phrase used by health service
   specialists, so I use quotation marks in my commentary on Fig 24 P. 88.
3. The titles of books and films are usually enclosed by quotation marks
   except in printed matter where they are often set in italics..

Layout for quotations
1. If the quotation is short, continue writing on the same line, enclosing
   the quoted words in quotation marks, as above. Quotations in essays
   should normally be short and so set out like this.
2. If you are quoting more than one line of poetry keep to the line
   structure of the poem, starting a new line, slightly indented, for each
   new line of poetry.
3. If the quotation is long, such as a lengthy extract from a speech, start a
   new line and indent the whole extract slightly.
4. If quotation marks (or speech marks) are used in a narrative (story or
   story-like account), start a new line for a change of speaker, or an
   interruption.
5. All punctuation relating to the quoted words should be inside the
   quotation or speech marks.

The example below is a fanciful reconstruction of the context in which Norman Fowler gave the speech quoted on P. 81.

The Right Honourable Norman Fowler rose to his feet amid rapturous applause from the floor. 'You know, Madam Chairman,' *he began, glancing over his spectacles and surveying the sea of upturned, expectant faces*, 'at times I have difficulty in recognising some of the descriptions of the National Health Service used by our opponents. They say it is in decline, run down, being cut. Yet what are the facts?'

At this point, he paused. His attention seemed drawn to the front row. Strange noises were coming from the direction of a large and hitherto enthusiastic supporter.

'*Aaaagh!' she gasped, 'Oooh! It's, it's . . ' and she fell to the floor clutching her chest.*

'The fact is,' *he continued, with a little less assurance* . . . . .

Semi-colons
These are used
1. instead of full stops where you want to show a close link between two (usually short) sentences:
   eg 'Have confidence in your memory; the information is there.'
   (See the punctuation passage under 'full stops' above.)
2. and can be used instead of commas to separate items in a list, when each item has several words.
   eg 'The SSCC made several recommendations: that the lunch hour should be extended till 2.00pm; the barrier relocated; the staff vacancy filled immediately; and that a second till be introduced.'
   (based on the recommendations of the report on P. 207).

Colons are used to show that something is to follow, usually a list. (See the example above).

Further practice
The best way to learn to punctuate well is to pay close attention to the punctuation of your reading matter. Make a habit of looking closely at the punctuation of perhaps one paragraph in the course of each reading session.

You make like to try using a tape recorder. Record yourself reading an extract from a book or article at a normal speed, then play it back, stopping to allow yourself time to write it down. Compare your punctuation with the original. You can try this with your essays too. Record what you'd like to say, and worry about the punctuation afterwards when you have written a draft.

11.4 **How to Check Your Work**

Before you hand in a piece of work, whether coursework or an exam
script, check it for
- errors in accuracy: spelling, punctuation, wrongly used words;
- readability and flow;
- clarity of structure. You may be able to insert, for example, a topic
  sentence which makes your point better, or links it more explicitly to
  the title.

In the three pieces below, the comments on the *left*, under 'Proof
reading' show corrrectable points of this sort. The 'Reader's Comments'
on the *right* suggest structural changes that would improve these extracts
from students' work. Many are beyond the scope of a proof read; they
point to the sort of critical thinking about the structure of an essay you
need to do as you plan and write (cf: the original and revised essay plan
on pages 224 and 225 of the Answers section).

Extract 1 (follows on from p. 148)
Essay title: Should the power of committees be increased?

PROOF READING

READERS COMMENTS

Unnecessary

Omit

Full Stop

No new
paragraph
Too vague

Comma

There are ~~in fact~~ two main types of
committees in the UK; /standing committees
and select committees./ Standing committees
have a legislative function only. The work
of the standing committee is utilized during
the normal passage of a bill through
Parliament. After a bill has received its
second and main reading, it is presented to
one of the standing commitees for detailed
consideration and amendment before being
represented in its amended form to the
legislature for further debate.
Select Committees are established
mainly to deal with/issues
particular
(concerning certain subjects) For instance, there
is a select committee on agriculture and one on
science and technology. Select Committees
may also be established to deal with a
controversial issue of the time, for
instance the Westland committee was recently
set up to investigate that affair.

Add topic sentence
to link with question
eg. 'In recent years
the business of
Parliament has
increasingly been
carried out by
committees...

Omit. Too much detail
for introduction. Shift
to body.

Omit. Too much detail
for introduction.

Return to question. Add
concluding sentence to
relate paragraph to
power and topic
sentence. eg. 'Since
committees now conc
themselves with issues
ranging from (x) to (y)
the question arises....

repetitive + vague Committee members are ~~certain~~ select
MPs who are given a short term appointment
to sit on the committee. It is argued that
the time they are with the committee is too
short for them to become fluent with its
operation and procedure to be of any real
use to the committee.

This is the main point here. Express in topic sentence and relate to question of power

(John)

Extract 2 (follows on from p. 149)

PROOF READING

READER'S COMMENTS

Awkward expression. Rephrase.

Wrong word. Restructure.

If the power of committees were increased ✓
it would take away power from the House of
Commons, it is argued. This argument can
be 'derailed' by the fact that committees would
~~be beneficial in presenting~~ (more of a chance)
for the MPs on the committees to debate,
scrutinize and so reach a more accountable,
representative result on the issue in
question. Committees would provide more
depth to the resulting Bill or issue in
question.

overlooks

Topic sentence indicates main point + relation to power.

Increasing the power of committees also
might mean making MPs full time (which has
its advantages and disadvantages) If they
were full time they would all be able to
attend their relevant committees and play a
fuller role in the business at hand. As
committees are held in the morning they
would be free to attend. (As most MPs are at
the moment part time this would need to
change for committees to play a fuller role
in Parliamentary affairs) Salary should be
increased so that MPs would be prepared to
take on their new roles and ~~then~~ not have
other jobs which have previously taken up
their (spare) time. Some people argue that MPs
would become narrow without outside
interests (ie) teaching jobs, jobs in business
or in the city. This can be 'waylaid' by the
fact that committees ~~would mean~~ they could
divert their interest into the committee and

meetings

such as.

However as full time MPs & members of

Clearer topic sentence with wider scope to cover whole paragraph. Relate directly to question of power.

Omit. You go on to discuss these so. you don't need this statement.

Omit. Repeats point in previous statement.

Style

(i.e. = that is) Awkward expression + unclear

become more specialized and professional in outlook.

    The power of committees should be increased by increasing their number so that Parliament can be made more accountable, and *responsive to* also interest groups adhered to ~~as well as~~ *and* the executive, departments and civil servants be more accountable and answerable to the House of Commons and the electorate. Increasing their number would mean more work could be considered and more answers to questions could be found in a more informal but professional way.

                        (Jackie)

[margin notes: Add Concluding sentence about effect of this on power.

Meaning ?

Add concluding sentence about the effect of this on power.]

Extract 3 (follows on from p. 158)

Essay title : 'Consider the importance of the past in 1984'

    Throughout *Nineteen Eighty Four* Winston Smith is pre-occupied with thoughts of the past. He dreams of incidents that happened many years before; he remembers his mother; he remembers holding a piece of 'evidence' against the party. It is his ability to remember events in the past that distinguishes him from other party members. [It could be argued that his memory of the past was the cause of his defection.]

    It was essential for the party to eliminate all traces and records of the past as far as possible. Records and accounts of life before Party rule would provide society with a comparison. It could provide them with an objective view of the Party. Winston Smith undertakes the difficult quest of trying to find out what life was actually like before the party. He does this because he can just remember a time when things were different.

    Control of the past is also important as it provides a Party record. Winston Smith's

[margin notes: Weak conclusion. Link character + concerns of W.S. with Orwells' concern about the past and totalitarianism.

Add concluding sentence linking with topic sentence.]

job at the Ministry of Truth is to change
newspapers and other records, so that the
outcome of events matches earlier
predictions or corresponds with earlier
events.

Too short – undeveloped. Give eg + show why this is important

✓

Good topic sentence.

The past is most important to the Party
because through controlling the past the
Party can control people's minds. The longer
the Party rules, the more it will control
the past and consequently people's minds.
This is illustrated by Winston's discovery
that the Party had told Julia that they had
invented the aeroplane.

Develop. Mention 'Newspeak' central to this.

Add concluding sentence

Personal control of the past forms the
basis of the principle of 'doublethink'.
Winston Smith cannot 'doublethink' and hence
he retains a mental record of that which has
happened before him. This is the root cause
of his defection. It is illustrated when
O'Brian produces the photograph of Jones,
Aaronson and Rutherford itself 'proof' of
the Party's falsification of the past, and
shows it to Winston during his torture. He
then burns it. Winston remembers seeing the
photograph; O'Brian does not.

Good topic sentence

✓

✓

Good use of example ✓

Comma

Add sentence to link this explicit with topic senten

The Party aims to control the past so that
people only live for the present and
remember nothing that has gone before. As a
result people will adopt an attitude of
universal passivity regardless of
circumstances; no laughter, joy or sadness.
George Orwell has shown us the great
importance of the past in a society and has
given us a harsh warning as to the possible
consequences if it were to be controlled.

✓

A good concluding paragr. adding a personal insight to directly relevant concluding remarks.

(John Gorzkiewicz)

A competent exam essay.

11.5 How to Interpret Instructions in Essays

This section takes the form of a glossary of the most frequently used
instructions in essay questions. Each entry starts with the definition given

in the Concise Oxford Dictionary. It is well worth checking to see if your subject has any 'favourite' wordings; individual boards and examiners often have their own styles. All the essay titles used in the book are listed here under the appropriate instruction.

Account for: 'explain the cause of'. This instruction indicates a factual essay. You show your grasp of the subject by your ability to identify and explain why something happens.

e.g. Account for
  a) France selling wine to the United Kingdom and the United Kingdom selling whisky to France;
  b) France selling cars to the United Kingdom and the United Kingdom selling cars to France.
  (Economics A level Oxford Board June 83)

Analyse: 'Examine minutely the constitution of . . ascertain the elements of'. Here you break down a subject into parts. You need detail and clarity in your presentation of information in this factual essay.

e.g. 1 Analyse, with examples, the ways in which major groups bring pressure to bear on government in Washington.
  (Political Studies A level Oxford Board June 84)

e.g. 2 Critically analyse the factors which should be taken into account when considering copying and/or printing in respect of: a) initially installing equipment; (10 marks)
  b) making copies of a particular document. (7 marks)

(ICSA Part 2 Office Administration and Information Systems June 85)

The addition of 'critically' here stresses that you are not to regurgitate factual information, but to use this information as a basis for an intelligent check list of factors.

Assess: 'estimate the value of'. Here you need to identify a number of items/factors/methods and make some judgement about them, their effectiveness or consequences.

e.g. "The press leads rather than reflects public opinion."
  Assess the accuracy of this statement in respect of the:
  a) 'popular' press;
  b) 'quality' press.
  (Government and Politics A level AEB 609/2/01 Qu 5)

Comment: 'write explanatory notes on'. This instruction is asking for your informed reactions to an issue or view. There is limited scope for your views within the subject discipline.

e.g. 'What thoughtful rich people call the problem of poverty, thoughtful poor people call, with equal justice, the problem of riches.' (R. H. Tawney)

In the light of this statement, comment critically on sociological explanations of poverty.

(Sociology A level AEB Nov 85 639/1 Qu 10)

(see P. 126 Ch 7 for analysis and plan of this question)

Compare and **contrast**:

Compare: 'to liken, to pronounce similar to';

Contrast: 'to set (two things, one with another) in opposition, so as to show their differences.'

With 'compare and contrast', you are required to consider (usually) two things (policies, approaches, ideas, methods) and to point out, firstly, similarities between them and secondly, differences.

With 'compare' on its own, indicate differences in the context of your discussion of similarities.

'Contrast' asks you only to discuss differences.

Both instructions indicate a factual style of essay.

e.g. 1 Compare and contrast the British and American constitutions. (Political Studies)

e.g. 2 Compare and contrast the common law defence of duress and the equitable doctrine of undue influence. What effect do they have on a contract if successfully pleaded and upon whom does the burden of proof fall?

(Law A level) (See P. 136 and 138 for analysis and outline plans of these questions)

Consider 'weigh the merits of'. This rather general instruction leaves you with some careful planning to do as you decide which aspects to introduce to your essay. The examiner is looking for thoughtful angles to the subject.

e.g. Consider the importance of the past in *Nineteen Eighty Four* (by George Orwell).

(See P. 156 Ch 8 for introductions to this essay and P. 158 for a complete essay)

Define 'to declare exact meaning of'. A definition is short and is often necessary in essays which do not specifically ask for one. When you are asked to define a term, this is usually because it is in some way problematic and the examiner wants to know if you have understood it and how you intend to use it. It is normally followed by a second part to the question.

e.g. The use of computer aided design (CAD) and computer aided manufacture (CAM) has increased dramatically during the last five years. Define briefly what you understand by these terms and then explain the social and economic consequences of their introduction.

(Design and Technology A level London Board June 1986)

Describe: 'recite the characteristics of'. Beware of interpreting this as an invitation to 'write all I know about . . ' in a factual essay. Pay close attention to the rest of the question.

e.g. 1 Describe the means available to a type of local authority of your choice to ensure an equitable distribution of its services to those in most need.

(ICSA Services Administration by Local Authorities 1985)

e.g 2 Describe the skills required of a manager responsible for the effective running of a functional department within an organistion. State the type of functional department you are considering.

(ICSA management: Principles and Policy June 85)

Discuss: 'to examine by argument, to debate'. Here you are asked to identify an issue, often two sides of a debate within a subject, to present arguments and evidence to support each view and to show where you stand in relation to the debate in the conclusion. The scope for expressing personal opinions is often quite limited.

e.g. 1 Sociological theory and research methods are well nigh inseparable.' Discuss.

(Sociology A level) See P. 154–5 Ch 8 for work on this question.

e.g. 2 'Unemployment has replaced old age as the major cause of poverty in Britain'. Discuss.

(Sociology A level Oxford Board May 84) See Chapter 7.

e.g. 3 See under 'distinguish' for a different style of discussion. Here you are asked to present pros and cons as a basis for a judgement by a third party (an employer).

Distinguish: 'To see, point out the difference', often between two things that tend to be confused. It is often used in the first part of a question, followed by an evaluative or searching second part.

e.g. Distinguish between self administered pension schemes and managed funds and discuss the factors to be considered by an employer when deciding between them.

(ICSA Pensions and Insurance Administration, Pilot paper 1986)

Do you regard/think/agree . . These direct questions, apparently asking for your personal view, require the same structured presentation of both sides of the issue or argument as any other judgement question. Make your position clear in the conclusion.

    e.g. 1 Do you regard *Nineteen Eighty Four* as a novel or simply as a political tract?

        (English A level AEB Nov 84 623/2 Qu 6) See P. 134 Ch 7 for a plan of this essay.

    e.g. 2 See Law question P. 54 Ch 3

Evaluate 'ascertain the amount of'. Here you present a number of factors or issues, weigh up supporting evidence and make a judgement about the merits of the case. As in any question requiring a judgement, no single factor will have all the arguments on its side.

    e.g. 1 Evaluate the case for more open government in Britain.

        (Government and Politics A level AEB June 86 609/2/01 Qu 1)

    e.g.2 Evaluate the competing claims of the following to be indicators of a country's standard of living:

        a) GNP at factor cost perhead;

        b) consumers' expenditure per head;

        c) the stock of durable goods held by consumers.

    (Economics A level Oxford June 85)

Examine: 'investigate, scrutinize. . inquire into'. This requires you to consider an issue in detail, and to show clarity in tracing causes or consequences or highlighting issues.

    e.g. 1 Examine the problems that sociologists face in defining and measuring poverty.

        (Sociology A level AEB Nov 82 639/1 Qu 3) See P. 124–5 for a discussion of this question.

    e.g. 2 'Districts exist on maps. People live in neighbourhoods.' Explain this statement and examine its significance, if any, for both the policy making process and the organisational structure of a local authority.

        (ICSA Local Government in the Community June 85)

        (See P. 140 Ch 7 for an analysis and P. 233 for an outline plan of this question)

Explain: 'to make known in detail: make intelligible'. This introduces a factual essay in which you pick out detail which clarifies or accounts for something. It is often followed by a more evaluative second part, as, in eg 2 above.

e.g. 1 Explain how the law gives protection against racial and sexual discrimination.
(ICSA Industrial Law and Practice June 85)
An essay which answers the question 'Why?' will be an explanation.
e.g. 2 Why is the control of inflation a common objective of government policy?

How far . .? Like 'to what extent' (below), this instruction indicates that there are no simple answers to this question. You have to identify and discuss the issues and show your own position in the conclusion.
e.g. How far does the system of precedent mean that certainty is purchased at the cost of justice?
(Law A level Oxford May 83) See P. 135 and 228 for analysis and plan.

Outline 'description of essential parts only'. Select only the main features, leaving out the minor details. Aim to give a 'bird's eye view' of the topic. Expect a second part to the question, requiring more detail or an evaluation.
e.g. 1 a) Outline the principal features of monetary policy as operated in the UK since 1979.
b) To what extent have the overall goals of macro economic policy been achieved in the UK since 1979?
(Institute of Bankers Banking Diploma St 2 Monetary Economics Sept 85) See P. 139 and 231 for analysis and outline plan.
e.g. 2 Outline the parts played by Emilia and Rodrigo in Othello and show the various ways in which they contribute to the dramatic interest of the play. (English A level) See P. 145 for work on this essay.

Show how: here you have to demonstrate that you can use your detailed knowledge of the subject to prove a point or establish a theme.
e.g. 1 See above.
e.g. 2 Show how in Nineteen Eighty Four the author (George Orwell) reveals a deep concern for the value and power of language.
(English A level AEB Nov 85 623/2 Qu 6b)

Should . . . ? As with 'do you think. .', 'would. .' it is tempting to make a snap answer in favour of one side and to pursue this through the essay. In general, be wary of this; the fact that the question is asked at all indicates that the issue is complex. Treat it like any other judgement essay, and make your views clear in the conclusion.
e.g. Should the power of committees be increased?
(Political studies A level) See Pages 132, 147–153, 224–5.

State: 'Express fully or clearly in speech or writing'. The main features should be given, briefly and clearly. See eg 2 under 'describe' above.

To what extent: This is an important and frequently used insruction in judgement essays. As with 'how far', you show your familiarity with the subject by your ability to present arguments and evidence on both sides, and conclude with your views on a sliding scale somewhere between 'Not at all' and 'totally'. If you agree wholeheartedly with one of the extremes, you are likely to be oversimplifying.

e.g. 1 See 1b under 'outline' above.

e.g. 2 To what extent are judges and magistrates independent?
(Law A level Oxford May 84)

Would. . See 'should. . ' above. There are probably more of these 'direct questions' than ones with a classic instruction. Stop and think; what is this question really asking? Is it a factual or a judgement question? and structure your answer accordingly.

11.6 How to Make up Exam Questions

This activity is intended more as a game than as a crash course in becoming a Chief Examiner. Nevertheless, I hope it will underline some of the points about the structure of exam questions made in chapter 7. In this chapter, the activities involved analysing exam questions to highlight their component parts. Below you have the components of essay questions ready to be assembled for next summer's exams in Sociology, Economics, Law and Politics. They are divided into sections which roughly correspond to the headings used to analyse the questions: subject, instruction, key aspects and significant words.

Reference Activity 3

The parts of ten past exam questions are jumbled up. Your task is to shuffle them around to produce as many viable exam questions as possible. If you can, make a photocopy of the page, and cut up the questions. This will make it easier to move them around and try different combinations. It is also interesting to work with someone else; see how many ways of asking questions on the same subject you can find between you.

For each question, start with a *subject* and an *instruction*. This will often produce a viable question, but be too broad and dull for an exam. Experiment with different combinations to produce different basic questions. Then add *a key aspect*. Experiment with several key aspects; see how a different aspect completely changes the question. Finally add a phrase containing *significant words* If you think your question needs to be clarified or made more specific. Not all questions will have this addition. Good luck!

SUBJECT	INSTRUCTION	KEY ASPECT(S)	SIGNIFICANT WORD
the term 'de-industrialisation'	Consider	the strengths and weaknesses of	
in the distribution of population since 1945	What are	independent	as it exists in the US
import controls	Discuss	as a source of law	on the political scene in Britain
alternatives to local authority rates	Evaluate	the differences in the way consensus and conflict theorists view	
the 'professions'	Discuss	is necessarily a conservative force in society	as applied in the British legal system
equity	Examine the view that	the meaning and significance of	as methods of financing
open government	Discuss	the economic arguments for and against	
judges and magistrates	Examine	the economic consequences of	in the context of the UK economy
the system of judicial precedent	What are	the effects of changes	
religion	To what extent are	the advantages and disadvantages of	both in the past and at the present day

Fig. 41   *The Components of a question*

11.7 How to set out letters

Fig. 42 **A formal letter**

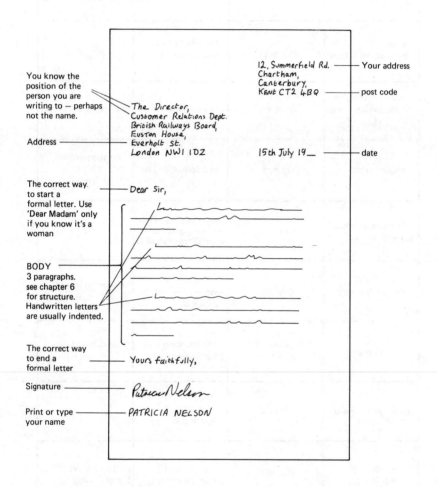

In brief: a formal letter
begins **'Dear Sir'**
and ends **'Yours faithfully'**
(Formal: you have not met, you do not know the name of the person you
are writing to; the business is formal)

Fig. 43 **A less formal letter**

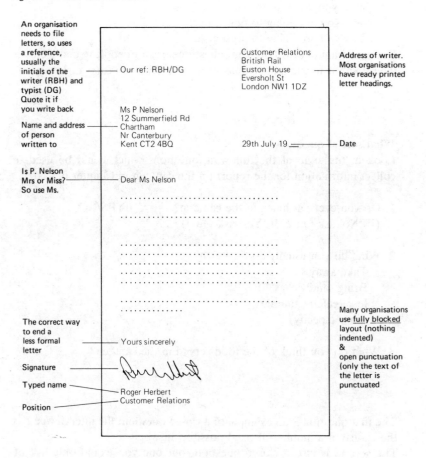

An organisation needs to file letters, so uses a reference, usually the initials of the writer (RBH) and typist (DG) Quote it if you write back — Our ref: RBH/DG

Name and address of person written to — Ms P Nelson / 12 Summerfield Rd / Chartham / Nr Canterbury / Kent CT2 4BQ

Customer Relations
British Rail
Euston House
Eversholt St
London NW1 1DZ

Address of writer. Most organisations have ready printed letter headings.

29th July 19 ___ — Date

Is P. Nelson Mrs or Miss? So use Ms. — Dear Ms Nelson

. . . .
. . . .
. . . .
. . . .
. . . .
. . . .
. . . .
. . . .

The correct way to end a less formal letter — Yours sincerely

Many organisations use <u>fully blocked</u> layout (nothing indented) & open punctuation (only the text of the letter is punctuated

Signature —

Typed name — Roger Herbert

Position — Customer Relations

In brief: a less formal letter
begins '**Dear Ms** (or **Mrs, Miss, Mr** Nelson)
and ends '**Yours sincerely**'
(Less formal: you know who you are writing to; you may (or may not) have
met; you want to adopt a more friendly, personal tone. Where people
correspond on a personal and fairly equal basis, the opening
'Dear Patricia Nelson' is sometimes used. Don't use this yourself unless
you are sure it is appropriate)

11.8 **How to draw up a questionnaire**

First be clear about
> *what* you want to find out;
> *how* you are going to find it out;
> *how* you are going to present it.

You may want to distribute your questionnaire for people to complete on their own, or to use it as the basis for interviews you carry out yourself.

What sort of questions?
Look at the style of the following questions which could be used to collect information for the report on the canteen in Chapter 6.

1. Do you ever eat lunch in the canteen?   YES/NO
   (If 'No' ask Qu 2. If 'Yes' ask Qu 3)

2. What do you usually do for lunch?
   > Take away
   > Bring sandwiches
   > local cafe/restaurant
   > other (specify)

3. What do you think of the food served in the canteen?

The first question is an example of a **closed question;** the interviewee has the choice of a number of fixed possible answers.

The second is also a closed question, but one you would only ask of people replying 'No' to Qu 1.

The answers to closed questions are easy to sort and can be presented clearly as percentages, as a bar or pie chart.

The third question is an **open question** – useful if you are interested in people's attitudes. You often gain unexpected information by allowing people to give open ended answers in this way, but it can be more difficult to decide what to make of the information and how to present it. Most questions on a questionnaire should be 'closed'; in an interview you may want to include more 'open' questions.

The *wording* of questions is important. When you have decided on the questions you want to ask, try them out on two or three friends. Check:

- did they understand the questions?
- did they produce the sorts of answers you expected?
- were there too many questions? too few?

Then decide:
- how many people you want to complete the questionnaire;
- who they should be: men/women, students/staff, management/ employees etc.;
- who you want to interview;
- what different questions you want to ask.

If you decide to use a *tape recorder* for an interview, practise with it first. Set the counter at 0 for the interview and when you play it back, stop it when you come to an interesting bit. Note the number on the counter;

e.g. 15–20 problems with delivery of salad ingredients
      32–39 staff shortages

(from interview with canteen manageress)

Presentation
When you have your completed questionnaires, decide how you want to present the results. You could use a bar or pie chart to show where people eat, for example. This might show at a glance that people are not using the canteen. Bear in mind your presentation when you are working out your questions.

11.9 **How to carry out a survey**

This section is based on Writing Activity 8 P. 118

'Survey' is a term used to describe a number of types of fact finding activity. I use it here to describe a way of recording your own *observations*. Decide:

1. *what* you want to find out;
    i) how long does it take for one person (yourself?) to reach a table from the time they first joined the queue?
    ii) how long is the queue at various points in the lunch hour?
2. *why* you want to know;
    because this will give hard factual information you need about how much of the lunch hour is necessarily spent in the canteen.
3. *How* you are going to find it out.
    Record information for (i) on a prepared sheet, such as (44a) below, and for (ii) on a sheet such as (Fig. 44b) below.

Time person joined queue

Time person reached food counter

Time joined checkout queue

Time sat down

Time person finished eating

Fig. 44a *Survey Sheet 1*

Minutes after arrival	Time	Number of people in queue
0		
5		
10		
15		
----- etc		
60		

Fig. 44b *Survey Sheet 2*

How to present your findings

Look back to chapter 4 for suggestions on the various ways you could present findings. Below are examples of how information recorded on these survey sheets could be presented.

The findings from Survey 1 could be presented as a *pie chart*, showing the entire lunch hour, and how much of the time was spent on the various processes involved in eating lunch in the canteen.

The findings from Survey 2 could be presented as a *bar chart*, using graph paper. Mark out

 (i) the vertical axis to show the number of people queuing at any one time;

(ii) the horizontal axis to show the five minute divisions on your survey sheet.

(See charts in the completed report on P. 206 below)

11.10 **How to draft a report**

Below is a version of the report suggested in Activity 8 chapter 6.

Report on the serving system in the canteen
I. Terms of reference

In response to a number of complaints from staff and students about the length of time spent queuing in the college canteen (and the resulting cold food), the Vice Principal asked the Staff Student Consultative Committee to report on the serving system in the college canteen and to make recommendations for improvements.

II. Procedure

This report was compiled on the basis of
i)   a questionnaire sent to all staff and students who used the canteen on Monday March 25th.
ii) Interviews with Mrs Doreen Watkins, the Canteen Manageress and two members of her staff;
iii) Surveys based on personal observation of the canteen during the lunch hour on 25th March.

III. Findings

1. *The present situation*
i)   Lunch is served between 12.30 and 1.30pm. About 170 meals are served, ranging from the simple snack (drink and sandwiches) to a 2 course meal.
ii) People queue to be served at the food counter, where they make their selection, then queue again to pay at the till. Fig 47 shows the length of the queue for the food counter on a typical day, 25th March, and Fig 45 shows the breakdown of the lunch hour of one student who arrived at the peak time of 12.30pm.

2. *Staff problems*
Interviews with Mrs. Watkins and her staff showed that
i)   the canteen is short staffed because of an unfilled vacancy. In addition the canteen staff have been badly affected by colds and flu this winter. The number of assistants at the counter has been reduced to two.
ii) Mrs. Watkins tried to introduce a 'fast lane' system for serving snacks and drinks, but had to drop the experiment. The barrier restricts access to the counter and people who approached the exit point for drinks had caused an obstruction. In addition, some members of staff had taken advantage of the 'fast lane' to order full meals. This led to further delays and caused ill-feeling in the queue.

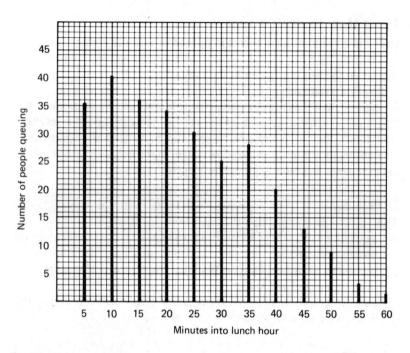

Fig. 45 *Column graph showing the length of the canteen queue during the lunch hour on March 25th*

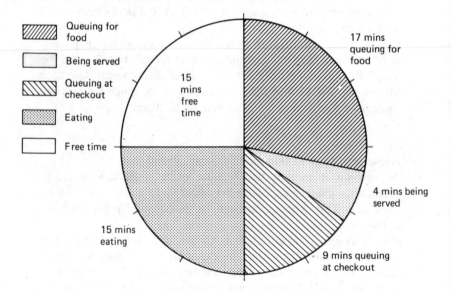

Fig. 46 *Pie Chart showing how the lunch hour is spent*

iii) Mrs. Watkins had been told last year that the college could not afford a second till.

iv) The canteen staff are under great pressure to produce 170 meals in one hour. They feel that criticism directed at them is unfair.

IV. Conclusions

The SSCC concluded that the criticisms of the serving system in the canteen with the resultant cold food are largely justified. Although the queue is much shorter by 1.00pm, this does not allow enough time for lunch. The single queues, first to the counter and then to the till, were felt to be the main cause of the delay. This has already resulted in students and staff going elsewhere for lunch and failure to take action to remedy this will further reduce the numbers of people using the canteen.

V. Recommendations

The SSCC recommends that
1. The lunch 'hour' is extended to 2.00pm to ease pressure on the canteen;
2. The barrier is relocated to allow a 'fast lane' for drinks and pre-packed snacks only, and a 'slow lane' for full meals;
3. That immediate action is taken to fill the staff vacancy
4. That a second till is acquired and staffed to allow a second queue to form at peak times, 12.30–1.15.

    D. O'Connor, Chair, Staff Student Consultative Committee
    15th April 19..

11.11 How to Fix an Average

Have you ever wondered where the two sides of a pay dispute get their figures from? One side claims that the average earnings of employees is £100 a week. The other maintains that it is over £200. The conciliation board states that it is £120. They can't all be right, can they? Is someone lying?

The answer is that they can all be right; it all depends on which method they use to calculate a perfectly truthful 'average'.

It's done like this. Let's suppose the weekly earnings of the people employed by this company are as follows;

As you can see, there are *three* figures for 'average earnings';
(i) The *arithmetical average*, worked out by adding together all the figures and dividing the total by the number of figures in the sum: £5470 ÷ 21 ≃ £260. This tends to produce a higher figure because it includes a couple of very high earners, which brings the 'average' up.

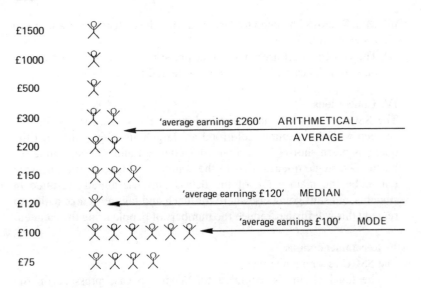

Fig. 47 *Average weekly income of employees of Fixit PLC (Pictogram or pictorial chart)*

(ii) The *median*, which is the one in the middle. This is an 'average' in that half the employees earn more than this and half earn less.

(iii) the *mode* is the figure which crops up most often. Here it shows what most people earn, what 'the average employee' gets. Median and mode methods of calculating averages tend to produce lower figures.

This is how various interest groups can use the same figures to convey a quite different picture of the same situation. So how do you know how an 'average' is calculated? Often you don't, so be sceptical of figures until you have found out how they were arrived at. You can become more critical and ask questions about sources of information. (What questions would you want to ask about the source of information in Fig 47?) And you can keep your eyes open. How was the figure for 'weekly earnings' on Chart 1 P. 75 calculated? Do you think this gives a fair picture of men's and women's earnings? How do you think the 'weekly averages' in Chart 2 were worked out?

Further reading:

How to Lie with Statistics by Darrell Huff, Penguin (1973) gives an informative, entertaining and easy to read account of how figures, charts and diagrams can be used to deceive, and how to spot the deception.

Plain Figures by Myra Chapman (HMSO 1986) gives comprehensive and clear guidance on how to present statistical information using tables, charts and graphs.

12 Answers Section

Chapter 1

Reading Activity 2

1. Two purposes are mentioned in the topic sentence of the first paragraph; to choose the right person for the job or to select someone with potential.
2. The first sentence of the second paragraph tells you what the paragraph is about – skills needed for interviewing – but it doesn't give you the precise information you need to answer the question. Do you read the rest of the paragraph, or skim on? Skim on – you can always come back.
3. The first words of the paragraph, 'subjective misjudgement' are clearly a reference back. So here's your answer to question 2. On reflection, this explains 'halo and horn', doesn't it?

Reading Activity 5 – Self check
You should have something like this;

> One of the earliest systematic studies of <u>poverty</u> was conducted by Seebohm <u>Rowntree</u> in 1899 in the city of <u>York</u>. . . .
>
> Rowntree calculated a <u>minimum weekly sum</u> of money which, in his opinion, was 'necessary to enable families to secure the necessities of a <u>healthy life</u>.' Those whose <u>income fell below</u> this sum were defined as poor. This concept of poverty is known as <u>absolute</u> or <u>subsistence</u> poverty. Rowntree admitted that it was 'on the side of <u>stringency</u> rather than extravagance' being 'the lowest standards which responsible experts can justify.' These experts included members of the British Medical Association who drew up a diet sheet which contained food with adequate nutritional value at the lowest possible cost. Presumably Rowntree expected the poor to be able to select and purchase cheap but highly nutritious food.

Reading Activity 7
Angela unfortunately, will not be able to claim benefit in September because she will not have been claiming for three months before starting

the course (see box 4). She should claim again on December 1st, by which time it will be three months since she became eligible for benefit. She must also explain that the course is part time, well under 21 hours, that she is available for work and willing to give up the course immediately if she is offered a suitable job (see box 3).

David can continue to claim benefit and study. He should point out that the course is described as 'part time', designed for people like himself and that he is available for work and willing to take a job if he is offered a suitable one. (If Linda gets a job meanwhile, most of her earnings will be set against the benefit he draws for the family.)

Chapter 2

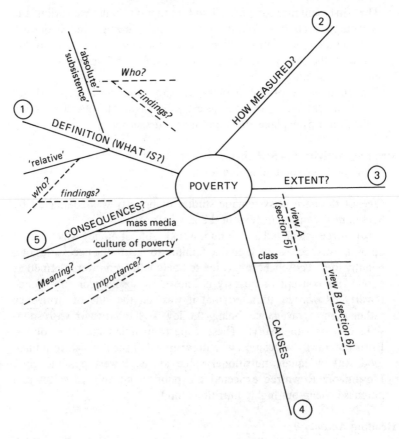

Fig. 10 *Notemaking Activity 3. Notes A*
Outline notes based on authors' (four) questions with one added heading (consequences). Complete the notes starting with points indicated in italics.

211

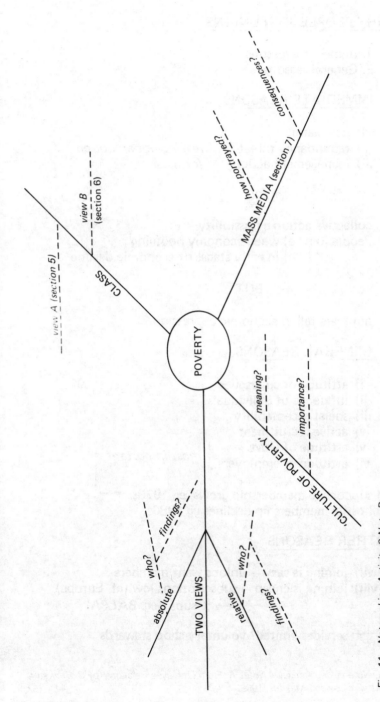

Fig. 11 *Notemaking Activity 3 Note B*
Outline notes based on my understanding of issues. Complete these notes starting with points indicated in italics.

WHY PEOPLE JOIN UNIONS

1. Immediate reasons
2. General reasons

1. IMMEDIATE REASONS

i) pay claim
ii) redundancy threat ⎱ *leaving not an option*
iii) management action ⎰ *for most*

<u>SO</u>

collective action a possibility
People join   a) when economy booming
             b) in early stages of economic decline

<u>BUT</u>

numbers fall in economic depression.

2. GENERAL REASONS

i) attitude of colleagues
ii) influence of individuals
iii) social acceptability
iv) active recruitment
v) attitude of Govt.
vi) attitude of employers. ⎱ *most important* ⌐

If supportive membership grows, eg 1970s. ◄—┘
If hostile membership declines eg 1980s.

OTHER REASONS

vii) joining is easy — unions want members
viii) joining is cheap — subscriptions low (cf. Europe)
                   — few % subs. (eg. BALPA)

—► services limited? voluntary shop stewards

Fig 12.   *Notemaking Activity 4 Notes A. From* Employee Relations, *by C. Brewster,*
Macmillan Professional Masters, 1989.

213

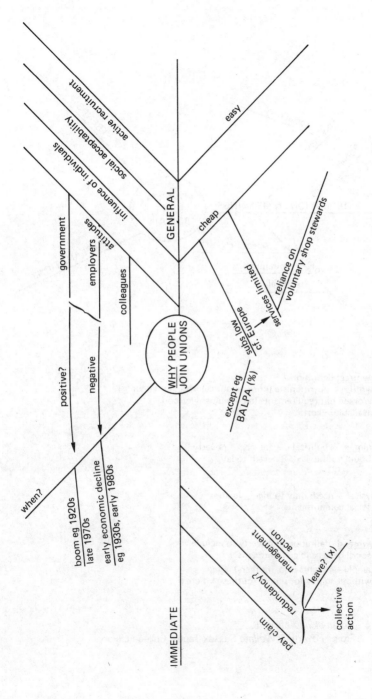

Fig 13. *Notemaking Activity 4 Notes B. From* Employee Relations *by C. Brewster, Macmillan Professional Masters, 1989.*

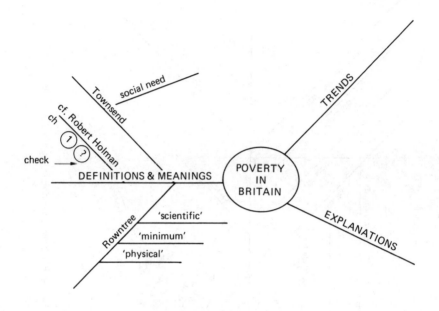

Rowntree: definition
Scientific — nutritionists (knew about calories, not vitamins)
   Worked out requirements (men/women) → food
   available → cost.

Minimum — political debate about poverty.
   Could not be 'lax'. Relevant today.

Physical — needs only (hunger), ignores
   social commitments.

Townsend: definition of poverty to include
   social needs and commitments
Example — Parents (esp. mothers) going
   without to pay for school (outings, kit etc.)

Fig. 14 *Notemaking Activity 6*
        From: *Poverty & Welfare* Sussex Tapes, College Library.

Chapter 3

Research Activity 4

1. Which ? magazine, published by the Consumer Association. The December issue of each year contains a comprehensive index. Each month carries a limited index to update.
2. ABC Rail Guide.
3. Roget's Thesaurus will give you the most comprehensive list. Take some time to find out how to use it.
4. You can get this information from the prospectuses, or from one of a number of guides.

    A comparison between the entry qualifications of these two institutions is interesting; PCL accepts a wide range of routes to their degree course – five in all. Manchester wants good Maths, and three high 'A' level grades, preferably not Law! Both stress that they welcome applications from mature students without conventional entrance qualifications.
5. The Shorter Oxford Dictionary gives this information. You could try an etymological dictionary too. Look in the front of the dictionary to find out what the abbreviations mean.

    'Star' – from the ancient languages of northern Europe as well as Latin, 'stella' and Greek (OE=Old English, OS=Old Saxon, OHG=Old High German, ON=Old Norse). It probably originates from the Aryan culture which was shared by Europe and much of Asia, echoed in the modern 'tara' (star) in Indian languages.

    'liberty' – from Latin via French;

    'freedom' – from ancient northern European languages;

    'commuter' – recently from the USA, although the word 'commute' meaning to change, is recorded in English in 1633 and derived directly from the Latin.

    'town' – from northern European languages including Celtic and Old Irish. The 'tun' 'ton' 'dun' is to be found in modern place names – London, Tunbridge. Note the changes in meaning, from fort, to enclosure, manor, land of a village, group of buildings to the modern 'town'.

    'homosexual' – 'homo' comes from the Greek meaning 'same', not the Latin for 'man'. 'Sex' is from the Latin.

    The arrival of a word in a language brings with it concepts and clues as to the way of life of its users. Stars were as important to our ancestors as commuters are today. You may like to ponder the difference betwen 'liberty' and 'freedom'.
6. Find the relevant graph in Social Trends, published annually by the CSO (Central Statistical Office).

The rise in private medical insurance from 1966 to the 1980s has been remarkable. Is it levelling off now?
7. A handbook of company information, Kelly's or Kompass gives comprehensive information on companies.

Boots employed 60,000 people in 1985 – is it more or less now?
8. This is one of the many intriguing bits of information in Whittacker's Almanack.

'l.c.' for lower case, and 'run on' for continuing paragraph.
9. A dictionary gives the meaning, a starting point for understanding the usage of words and abbreviations.

'viz' (videlicet) means 'namely'; **'ibid'** (ibidem) means 'in the same place', showing that the reference comes from a book previously mentioned. **'sic'** means 'thus', used when the reader might think there was a mistake, because a remark quoted contains an error.

Research Activity 6
1. 'stock' (after 'Breeding in farming!') lead me to 'stock control' 658.78.
2. 'Alcoholism' referred me in a cross reference to 'Addiction'. One of the headings here is 'Welfare services' 362.29.
3. The question on the closed shop leads you to 'Trade Unions', with 'unions' a subheading of 'Trade' 331.880.
4. You may have tried several headings such as 'food' here. The correct term for what one eats habitually is 'Diet' 613.2.

Chapter 4

Fact finding Activity 1
1. In 1974 i) 53% girls, 36% boys were employed without part time study.
   ii) 61% girls, 62% boys were employed in total.
   iii) The major difference here is the high percentage of girls (over half) who were in employment without part time study. Although the percentage in employment is almost identical, boys did much better in terms of on-going training and education.
2. In 1984 i) 13% girls and 10% boys were employed without part time study.
   ii) 17% girls, 18% boys were employed in total.
   iii) About a quarter of the age group is involved in YTS, more boys than girls. Even so, unemployment is three or four times as high among school leavers. More young people, especially girls, stay on in education, particularly in FE.

3.   i) Apprenticeships and day release have virtually disappeared between 1974 and 1984.

ii) Boys have been particularly affected by this, with only 8% on these schemes in 1984 compared with 26% in 1974.

Fact finding Activity 2

1) In 1976 19% girls and 21% boys left school with no GCE or CSE grades. This had dropped by 1986 to 10% girls and 13% boys.
2) In 1976 12% girls and 14% boys left school with 2 'A' levels or equivalent. By 1986 this had risen to over 14% girls and almost 15% boys.
3) Altogether 59% girls and 53% boys left school in 1986 with more than one good 'O' level – a figure worked out by adding together all those with more than one 'O' level. The figures for 1976 were 52.5% and 49%. This shows an upward trend in qualifications gained by school leavers, particularly marked in girls.

Fact finding Activity 3

Below is the commentary by the authors of Social Trends which accompanied this chart. Notice how a commentary picks out only the main features of a chart and expresses these in clear, connected writing. Figures are rounded so the writer can get the message across without confusing detail.

In 1984/85, *34 per cent of boys* and *46 per cent of girls* leaving school in England & Wales held a GCE 'O' level grade A–C or CSE grade 1 in *English*, the highest proportion for any subject.

Mathematics was the next most frequently obtained qualification for both boys and girls, with 33 per cent of boys and 28 per cent of girls holding this level of qualification on leaving school. Only 10 per cent of girls leaving school were qualified at this level in Physics compared with 22 per cent of boys; for Chemistry the corresponding figures were 11 per cent of girls and 16 per cent of boys. Between 1970/71 and 1984/85 the proportion of boys leaving school with 'O' level *Physics* increased by 7 percentage points, while for *Mathematics*, the increase was 6 percentage points. For girls the largest increases amongst the major subjects were for *Mathematics*, *Physics*, *Chemistry*, and *English*. (My italics.)

Fact-finding Activity 4

i) a) 325,000 men took non advanced Engineering and Technology courses – some 40% of the entire intake of males into colleges,

b) 87,000 took advanced courses, one third of the intake.

ii) The figures for women are 21,000 and 4,500 respectively, a tiny 6% and 5% respectively of the intake for these subjects.

iii) a) At non-advanced level the two most popular vocational subjects were Social, administrative and business studies (213,000) and Professional and vocational subjects (121,000).

b) At advanced levels Business etc studies attracted 55,000 women students and Education came second with 34,000 students. Very few women took Professional and vocational courses at a higher level.

iv) The percentage figures show the concentration of women in certain subject and vocational areas most clearly; at non-advanced level, a massive 82% students taking Medical, health and welfare courses are women, as are 74% of those on social, administration and business courses. On advanced course, 71% students taking Medical, health and and welfare, and 67% those on Education courses are women.

Fact-finding Activity 5

1. 26% women work full time and 16% work part time.
2. The occupations with the highest proportions of women are, in order:
   i. Catering, cleaning, hairdressing etc (76%)
   ii. Clerical and related (74%)
   iii. Education, health and welfare (69%)
   iv. Selling (57%)
   v. Painting, assembling, packaging etc (45%)
3. These are also the occupations with the greatest demand – or flexibility – for part time workers.

Fact finding Activity 6

i) The five least well paid occupations (top on the chart) correspond closely to the occupations employing most women, as seen in Fig 21.

ii)

Occupation	Men	Women	Difference
Bar Staff	£123	£89	£34
Nurses	£164	£143	£21
Primary teacher	£227	£198	£29
Secondary teacher	£233	£201	£32
Academics	£321	£229	£92

iii) In late 1979 to early 1980 women's earnings were closer to men's than at any other time covered by this chart. Since then, women's earnings have slipped to about two thirds of men's.

Fact finding Activity 7
  i) From 1979 full time employment for both men and women declined, more sharply for men than for women.
 ii) Until 1979 self employment had declined slowly. Since then it has increased sharply.
iii) From 1971 to 1985 there was a marked increase (50%) in the number of women with part time jobs, and a steady decline in full time jobs. The figures for the last year shown in the graph, 85/86, show an interesting reversal of this; the 10% drop in part time jobs is almost matched by a rise in full time jobs. But remember that this graph shows proportional changes only; because more women work full time than part time, there is still an overall loss of jobs for women.

Fact-finding Activity 8
Document 1 Norman Fowler's speech
Facts stated;
Point 1. More patients being treated than ever before ($4\frac{1}{2}$ million more than in 1978), consisting of
    i. One million more in-patient cases treated ('last year' ie 1985) than in 1978.
    ii. 400,000 more day cases treated.
    iii. $3\frac{1}{4}$ million more outpatient attendances
Point 2. Waiting lists are lower than when the Conservatives came into power (1979).

Mr Fowler is claiming that the NHS is in a healthy state and is offering the nation better health care under the Conservatives than ever before.

Document 2: extract from Observer
Point 1. There are 36,000 fewer beds in 1985 than in 1979, a reduction of 10% in the total number of beds.
Point 2. Patients are being discharged from hospital sooner than before.
Point 3. The number of people over 75 has increased by 20% since 1979.
Point 4. Day care has increased.
Point 5. A brief reference is made to 'increasing waiting lists'.

This article takes the view that not only have the number of beds been reduced while the needs of the population have increased but that the quality of care offered to patients has suffered under this Government.

Fact-finding Activity 9
1. The total number of 'discharges and deaths' in 1978 was 6,710,000 and in 1985 7,884,000. The increase is 1,198,000 – well over one million.

2. In 1978, 667,000 and in 1985 1,166,000 day cases were treated, an increase of 499,000.
3. In 1978 20,337,000 out-patients were treated and in 1985 23,096,000, a figure arrived at by adding accident and emergency outpatients to others. The increase is 2,759,000, over $2\frac{1}{2}$ million.

Fact-finding Activity 10
1. In 1979 there were 461,000 beds available and in 1985 421,000. Clearly this is a decrease, of 40,000. The Observer's figure of 10% is about right.
2. In 1979 in-patients stayed an average of 8.4 days, and in 1985 they stayed for 6.7 days. These figures were worked out by averaging the length of stay of the three groups of patients given in each year. This is a drop of 20% overall – a much faster turnover that allows more patients to be treated. This trend is confirmed by reference to the number of patients treated per bed. The figure for 1979 is not given but by comparing the figure for 1976 with more recent years, the trend is clear. In the five years to 1976 there was an increase of just over 1. In the five years from 1981 – 86 this has risen to 3.5 – a considerable increase.

Fact-finding Activity 11
1. The 'young elderly' group has not increased much – by about half a million.
2. The over 75 age group has increased much more over this period, from roughly 2 million to approaching 4 million. I found the easiest way to work this out was to mark off the measurements on a piece of paper and measure them against the grid.
3. The trend for the future is for a sharp increase in the numbers of people over 75, particularly those over 85, while the 'young elderly' remains almost unchanged.

Fact-finding Activity 12
1. In 1985 there were 802 thousand people on the waiting lists, fewer than the 828 thousand in 1979 but more than the 736 thousand in 1981.
2. In 1985 three out of nine specialities had longer waiting lists than in 1979, compared with seven in 1981.
3. By the 30th September 1986, the total number waiting for in-patient treatment had risen to 830,600 – a figure higher than in 1979, which would have undermined his point about a reduction in the waiting lists.

Chapter 6
Writing Activity 2
The paragraph reads like this:

Advertising operates, like any other business, within a legal framework, in addition to which there exists a whole structure of voluntary restraints. Until the beginning of this century trading laws were based upon the principle of caveat emptor (let the buyer beware). This meant it was the responsibility of the purchaser rather than the seller to ensure that the goods and services he was buying were worth the price being asked. Over the years two systems have evolved to protect consumers against advertising which is not completely legal, decent, honest and truthful. Advertisers are expected to exercise a degree of self-discipline and refrain from placing ads which are not acceptable (voluntary controls). An advertiser who has failed to observe the laws on the matter will be called to account as soon as possible afterwards and charged accordingly (statutory controls). This unique combination of voluntry and statutory controls forms the basis of advertising in Britain today.
(from *Effective Advertising and PR* by Alison Corke P.82, with some minor changes of punctuation, (Pan Breakthrough 1985)

Writing Activity 7
Letter 1
  Dear Mr Leverton

I was very interested to hear of your plans for a Company Communication Seminar – an initiative which I'm sure will be welcomed by the impressive number of firms taking part.

Spring is always a hectic time of the year for me because I make my annual visit to each of our regional offices to discuss plans for the coming financial year. As you can imagine, it is quite a task fitting all these visits in and, having made the arrangements so far ahead, I must stick to the time-table. Unfortunately, on the date you have asked me to speak, I shall be in Scotland.

However, can I suggest my colleague Mr David Wainwright, who would make an ideal alternative speaker. He has ten years' experience in Industrial Relations and Employee Communications during which time he has himself initiated several successful ventures and would, I am sure, be happy to speak on 'Tell or Listen?' if he is free. Let me know if you find this an acceptable suggestion and I will ask him to contact you.

Best wishes for a successful seminar.

Yours sincerely,

R. Sharp.

Letter 2

Insurance and Mortgage Brokers Ltd
Sharp Hill
Sheffield S37 4BS

Dear Sirs,

Thank you for the statement indicating that I still owe you £15 for the Green Card issued at Easter. I seem unable to trace an invoice for £15. However, I accept that as yet I have not settled the bill.

You will probably recall the considerable problems I encountered trying to extract this card from Sure-All Insurance in time for my departure. Despite having given the required notice for the issue of a Green Card, I had still not received it 24 hours before my expected departure. I was therefore obliged to make two special trips into town to fetch the card, both without success, although I had been told it would be ready on both occasions; two phone calls to you and one to the ferry company to inquire about my position if I sailed without it; and finally another trip into town to fetch a specially issued card – all at my expense in terms of money, time and unnecessary anxiety.

Since I regard £15 as an excessive charge for the work involved in issuing a certificate to demonstrate that I am already insured, and since I incurred considerable expense in trying to obtain the card, I am therefore enclosing a cheque for £10.

Unless you advise me otherwise I shall assume that Sure-All agree with me that under the circumstances £10 is more than adequate.

Yours faithfully,

Helena Smailes (Miss)

(Both from *The Business of Communicating* by N. Stanton. Pan Breakthrough 1986)

Chapter 7

Essay b)   **Unemployment has replaced old age as the major cause of** poverty **in contemporary Britain. Discuss.**

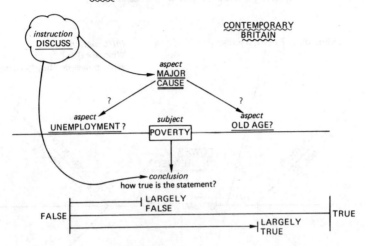

Fig. 29   *Planning Activity 1*

Essay c)   'What thoughtful rich people call the problem of poverty, thoughtful poor people could, with equal justice, call the problem of riches,' (R. H. Tawney)

In the light of this statement, comment critically on sociological explanations of poverty.

(ii)

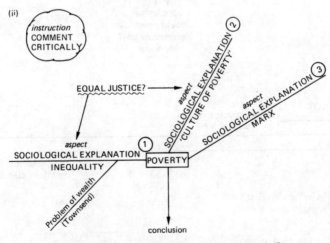

Fig. 30(ii)   *Planning Activity 2*

224

Essay i)   **Should** the power of committees be increased?

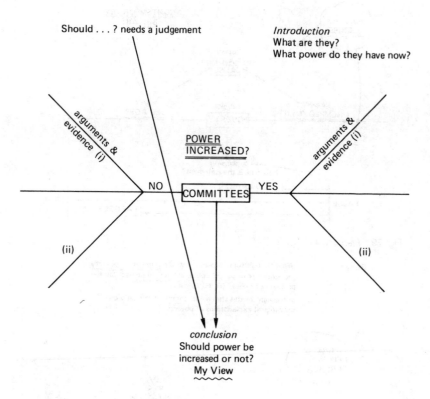

Should . . . ? needs a judgement

Introduction
What are they?
What power do they have now?

arguments &
evidence (i)

POWER
INCREASED?

arguments &
evidence (i)

NO   COMMITTEES   YES

(ii)   (ii)

conclusion
Should power be
increased or not?
My View

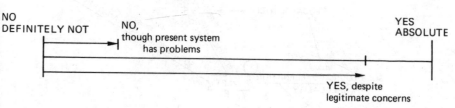

NO
DEFINITELY NOT

NO,
though present system
has problems

YES
ABSOLUTE

YES, despite
legitimate concerns

Fig. 31a   *Planning Activity 3*

Essay ii)

Should the power of [Committees] be increased?

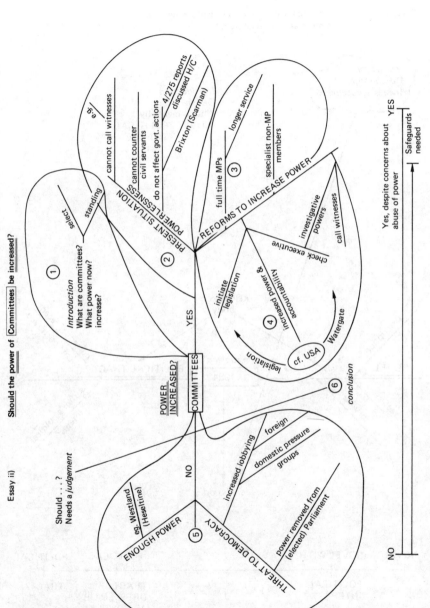

Fig. 31b *Revised Plan. This plan uses the material from essay on P. 150, replanned around points, arguments and evidence.*

Essay iii)   **Do you regard** Nineteen Eighty Four **as a** novel **or**
simply as a political tract?

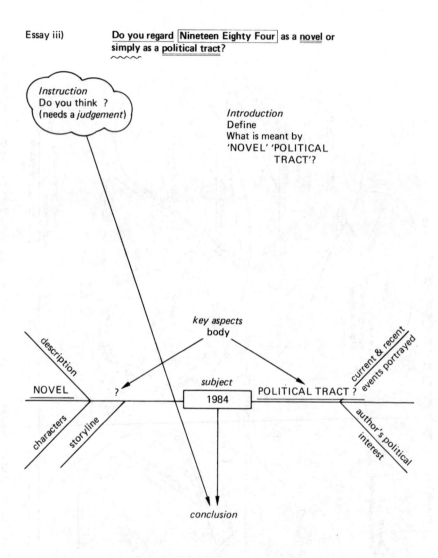

Fig. 32   *Planning Activity 4*

Essay v)   Would an <u>increase</u> in public sector investment in present circumstances lead to an increase in employment or to inflation?

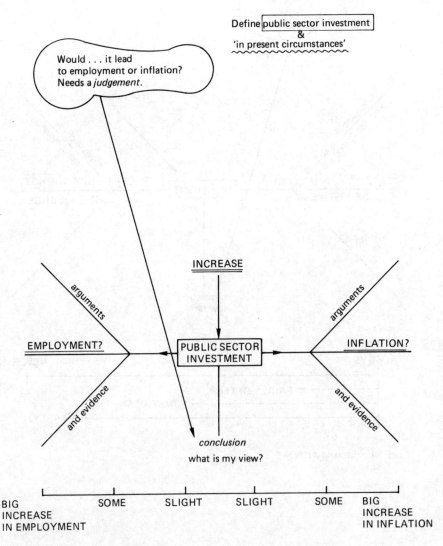

Fig. 33   *Planning Activity 5*

Essay viii) How far does the [system of precedent] mean that certainty is purchased at the cost of justice?

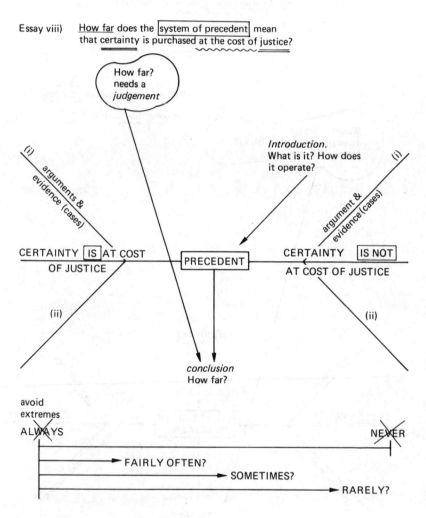

Fig. 34 *Planning Activity 6*

Essay vi)   Compare and contrast the British & American constitutions.

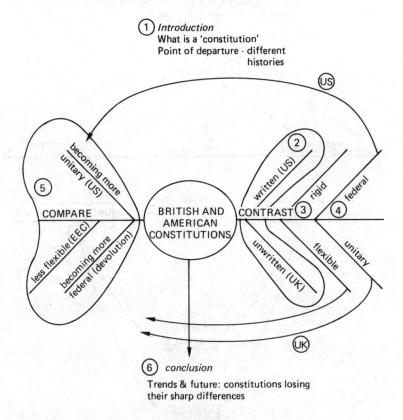

Fig. 35   *Planning Activity 7. A broad factual essay*

In a broad, factual essay it is important to structure the mass of information in the body. The numbers show a possible order for paragraphs. The contrasting features are more striking than the similar ones, so more space is devoted to them!

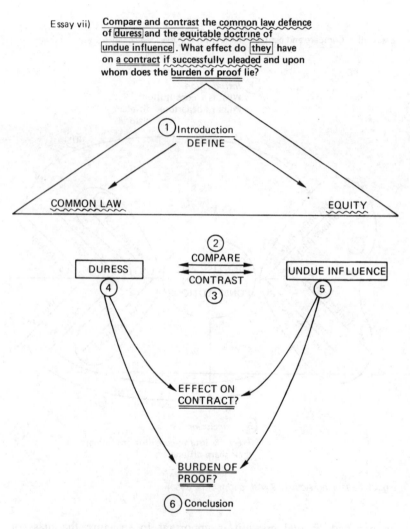

Fig 36 *Planning Activity 8. A complex question*

In a highly structured question it is essential to analyse the question carefully. Check that you cover all the points in the question in the headings of your outline plan.

Essay iv) a) <u>Outline</u> the principal features of ⎢monetary policy⎢ as
operated in the <u>UK since 1979.</u>
b) <u>To what extent</u> have the overall ⎢goals of macro economic policy⎢
been <u>achieved</u> in the UK since 1979?

If you have no knowledge of the subject your outline
plan might look like this;

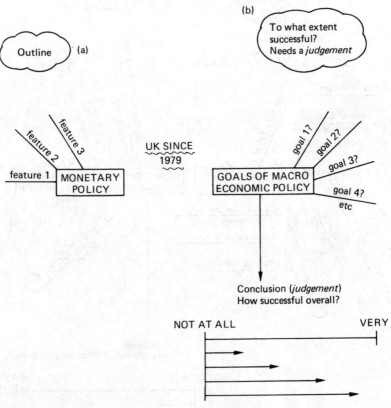

Fig. 37   *Planning Activity 9. A two part question, part factual, part judgement*

The skill in analysing a question is largely independent of your
knowledge of the subject.

If you know something about the subject your outline
might look like this.

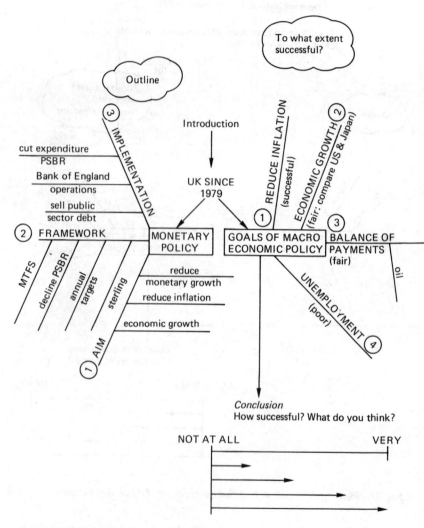

Fig. 38 *Essay (iv) Cont.*

This shows how you can add detail to an outline plan. How many
paragraphs should this essay have?

Essay ii)   '<u>Districts</u> exist on maps. People live in <u>neighbourhoods</u>.'
                  <u>Explain</u> this statement and <u>examine its significance</u>,
                  if any, for both the <u>policy making process</u> and
                  the <u>organisational structure</u> of a ⬜local authority⬜ .

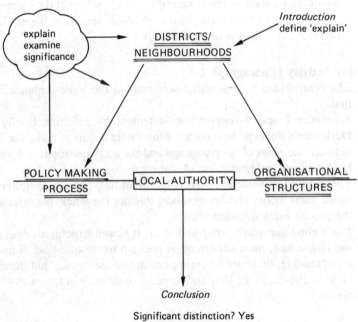

Fig. 39   *Planning Activity 10*

Chapter 8

Essay Activity 1: paragraph 1

1. This paragraph is about how legal precedent works through the hierarchical court system. This is stated clearly in the topic sentence which introduces the paragraph.
2. The rest of the paragraph develops this point; sentences 2 and 3 explain how this works in practice; sentence 4 points out the exception (House of Lords) and sentence 5 adds detail to this last statement and supports it by reference to a specific case.
3/4. The end of the paragraph would be better if it were more explicit about the position of the House of Lords at the top of the hierarchy and so related to the main point in the topic sentence. It's not bad, however; the point is there implicitly.

Essay Activity 1: paragraph 2

1. The central idea here is stated succinctly in the topic sentence, the first.
2. Sentences 2 and 3 support the statement by referring briefly to Durkheim's findings. In sentence 4 the writer begins to make the link between the point of the paragraph and the essay question. In 5 and 6 he describes Durkheim's use of statistics.
3. The concluding sentence makes the direct link beween Durkheim's sociological theory and his methods; this ties the whole paragraph to the precise essay question set.
4. It is a good paragraph, crisp and clear. It is well structured, does not use jargon and, most important, is relevant to the question. It needs proof reading; there are errors in punctuation (see under 'full stops' in How to Punctuate P. 184) and some inconsistency in tenses towards the end.

Essay Activity 2

Doran himself unwittingly supplies the humour. He is naive and gullible and yet sees himself as superior to Polly and her family. As they are conning him, this difference between Doran's opinion of himself and the truth is highly amusing. Doran's naive description of how Polly seduced him is so full of innocence that the reader cannot fail to see the humour. Without a doubt the joke is on Doran. He has been totally fooled by Polly and her family. 'He had a notion that he was being had' is an absolute understatement. Joyce's use of this phrase causes the reader to be further amused at Doran's expense.
(Rose, with minor alterations.)

This paragraph also starts with a short, clear statement of its subject in the first sentence; it contains clues ('unwittingly') which the writer picks up and illustrates later in the paragraph. Sentences 2 and 3 add the detail the reader needs to appreciate the point in 4. 5 and 6 make direct comments which relate the incident to the central point about humour and 7 draws the reader, by good use of quotation to illustrate a point, into the humour of the text. The last sentence shows how the material in the body of the paragraph develops and illustrates the idea in the topic sentence; we now know what the writer originally meant by 'unwittingly' having seen how the humour arises at Doran's expense. It is a good single paragraph answer to the question; well structured, with good use of example to back up and illustrate the central point. You might like to suggest alternatives for 'conning' and 'absolute' which are a little slangy for an essay.

Essay Activity 7
Second draft

What is shown on our television screens is determined by a host of factors. Commercial television's immediate concern is to guarantee an audience for their advertisers. This promotes the BBC into reacting in order for them not to lose their audience. Added to this is the pressure from the public for a varied menu of programmes. The censors, on the other hand, increasingly seem to be trying to restrict the viewers' right to choose for themselves. The final product is one, therefore, which has very little to do with artistic merit, but is shaped by outside forces. Some people would say that this leads inevitably to standards declining.

This is now an excellent introduction. The conclusion has made the direct link of the ideas in the introduction to the essay questions. The reader now has complete confidence that the essay will be both relevant and interesting. This extra zip comes from his inclusion of a new — and stimulating — thought in the conclusion; of the opposition between 'artistic merit' and 'outside forces' in Leo's discussion of whether standards are declining.

Essay Activity 8
Comments on introductions:

1. You don't expect to find such a direct start to an essay. This could work if the detail moves back straight away to the underpinning point – different approaches taken by sociologists to the study of people in society. Here it doesn't; positivists . . . heat, temperature . . boil . . The paragraph has got stuck on 'positivism' which is not

appropriate for an introductory paragraph. This should come in the body; the introduction should 'unpack' the issues in the question. The hope for this essay, since it is fluent and shows a grasp of concepts, is that the body will look at other theories and methods, and the whole will reach a judgement in the conclusion which refers directly back to the question.

2. The first sentence (apart from the 'basically' which is unnecessary and simplistic) is a reasonable opening sentence. The reader expects it to be explained and related to the question in the rest of the paragraph. Rather than becoming more specific, however, this paragraph (which is not sufficiently long for the development of any point) becomes more general giving the impression that the writer has little idea of the sociological issues the question is asking for. An introductory paragraph should give some indication of what these 'schools of thought' are, or at least of the outlooks and thinking they represent. Unless the next paragraph starts immediately with sound relevant material, I doubt if this essay will pass.

3. This essay starts with a categorical verdict on the question. To start with the conclusion does not give the writer much scope to 'discuss' the issue as the question asks. The essay looks as if it will be a rehearsal of theories and methods – as the writer states in the last sentence. The writer probably has good knowledge of sociology but is presenting it in a rather dull way. It is a frequent complaint of social science examiners that candidates tend to present theories and studies uncritically. This essay will probably be a safe but unremarkable pass.

4. This essay starts similarly, but the slight differences make it a better introduction. 'Mainly' in the first sentence suggests a less categorical approach to sociology and research methods and gives the writer scope to suggest that not all sociologists fit into the positivist/ interactionist camps. The jargon is simply explained, and, while the positions and methods of the two major schools are set out, detail is kept back for the body of the essay. This has the makings of a good pass.

5. This introduction is poor. The first sentence is a statement of the obvious, and there is no indication that the candidate understands the terms 'qualitative' and 'quantitative'. Technical terms and jargon are a liability, particularly in an introduction, unless you can demonstrate that you understand the concepts they represent.

6. This topic sentence makes an intelligent comment which suggests a thoughtful and analytical turn of mind. The brief accounts of Marx and Durkheim which follow, however, do not work, and leave the reader with a lot of thinking to do if we are to see the connection with the opening sentence. It is the task of the writer, not the reader/

examiner to make these connections. This candidate should have left these points to the body and concentrated here on the thinking behind the theories instead of leaving it to the last sentences. He may be trying to outline the material in the body – the 'this is what I'm going to say' approach to essay writing. This is not a good idea as it damages the structure of the essay and is dull and repetitive. Nevertheless, the candidate seems to have a grasp of issues. The essay could develop into a reasonable pass.

7. The topic sentence suggests that this candidate has understood something of the complexity of the relationship between theory and methods. Complexity is fine if the writer offers the reader clear pathways through it; this looks doubtful in the rest of the paragraph. The image of sociologists agreeing and disagreeing with notions or concepts does not contribute much to an understanding of the relationship between sociological theories and methods. Nevertheless, I am prepared to read on – this paragraph ends with a suggestion that the candidate has some insight into sociology as an evolving and dynamic subject. If so, the essay could be a reasonable pass.

Essay Activity 9
Comments on Introductions:

1. The main problem with this paragraph is lack of fluency. It does not read well, and the ideas seem oversimplified and undeveloped. The phrase, 'mutability of the past', is deposited without any comment which gives the impression that the writer is not sure what it means. This may be unfair, but it does not look like an essay that will attract a high grade.

2. This paragraph packs much more into the same space. The student clearly understands the phrase because it is used in pointing the contrast to Winston's own memory. It is also connected to the major theme of the reconstruction of the past by the party. This promises to be an intelligent essay.

3. Detail about Winston's dreams detracts from the central political point about control of the present and future through control of the past. It is competent however – a pass.

4. This is the pithiest paragraph of all, and it illustrates how much you can pack into a few lines when you are short of time, if you think before you write! As well as showing a grasp of the central political point concerning the past, the writer shows knowledge of the book (who made the comment), and in three short phrases indicates the topic (and topic sentences) on the three paragraphs in the body of the essay.

Chapter 9

Evaluation Activity

i) The Freeman extract has two main themes, introduced in the topic sentences: that we find it difficult to remember events and that teachers know little about the memory.

ii) The essential message of both graphs is that we quickly forget a lot of what we have learnt, but the graphs differ in detail. Buzan shows material memorised dropping to 10% two days later, compared with Freeman's five days. Unlike Freeman, Buzan does not suggest that anyone starts with 100% information retained, but that the amount of information retained increases by about 10% immediately after a learning period as it 'sinks in'. Whereas Freeman's diagram is intended only to show what happens to the unfocussed memory, Buzan's purpose is to show how the amount of information retained can be maintained by repeated review.

iii) You should overview a passage of this length to locate information. The main point of the first section deals with the background and origins of 'the forgetting curve' and four objections to it. The second queries its relevance to student learning.

iv) The problems Gibbs identifies with the 1885 Ebbinghaus material are:

1. that the material used was meaningless and unlike academic material;
2. students do not learn in this way, and are naturally more efficient;
3. students are not tested on rote learning, but on meaning and sense;
4. the scientific basis of the experiment on which the curve is based is questionable and so is its relevance to student learning. The use of similar material in tests causes 'interference' in recall, but it positively helps learning when it comes to understanding concepts.

v) Buzan recommends systematic and regular review of material to maintain knowledge. Gibbs queries the scientific basis for this advice and raises the practical problems facing students trying to follow it (120 sets of notes after 6 weeks).

vi) Gibbs suggests that
   - many things are memorised effortlessly when they make sense;
   - meaningful experiences leave traces in the memory. The problem is to 'retrieve' these;
   - people remember meaning, not form;
   - links between concepts help understanding.

Part III
Reference Activity

1. These cards should be filed in drawers 14, 6, 11, 8, 11, 7, 14, 14, 9, 7, 14, 12.
2. In drawer 14 the three books by Malcolm Craig come first; *'Investing to survive the '80s', 'Invisible Britain . . . , 'Successful Investment'.* The book by Marianne Craig is fourth.

Index

activities, xi
advertising, 106–7
A Level, x
  see under individual subjects
alphabetical order, 18, 59, 183–4
apostrophe, 186–7
article, 110–114
aspect (of question), 124, 128
assessment, 169–178
  methods, xvi–xvii
  oral, 170
  process, 169
association, remembering by, 164
average, 75
  arithmetical, 207
  how to calculate, 207–8
author, 60

banking (essays), 130, 139, 197, 231–2
blurb, 60
body,
  essay, 131, 133, 137, 152
  paragraph, 104, 114, 142–8
  report 117
book
  how to find, 58
  surveying, 60
boys
  occupations, 65
  O level passes, 68–9
  qualifications, 67
BTEC (Business and Technician Education Council), x
Buzan, Tony, 48, 159, 163

CACA (ACCA) (Chartered Association of Certified Accountants), 122
canteen, report on, 118–9, 202–7
capital letters, 185

card,
  index, 57
  revision, 172
  source, 61
case studies, 64–80, 80–90, 159–163
catalogue,
  author, 57
  classified, 57, 59
  computerized, 57
  subject, 57, 59
charts,
  bar, 69–70, 204
  horizontal, 72–4, 76
  pie, 65, 204, 206
categories, 168
Ceefax, 51, 104
classification number, 56, 61
classmark, 56
colon, 188
commas, 185
  inverted, 187
conclusion
  to essay, 131, 132, 137–8, 152
  to paragraph, 104, 107, 114, 142–4
  to report, 118
conclusions, draw, 67
  in reports, 119, 207
contents, 61
Child Poverty Action Group (CPAG), 21–3

Daily Mail, 24
Daily Mirror, 24
data, interpretation of, 64–90
day cases, 81, 85
day release, 66
definition of terms, 126
Department of Education and Science (DES), 68–69, 71
Dewey Decimal, 5, 55–7
diary, 93

dictionary, 53–4, 181–3
Disraeli, 90

earnings, men and women, 74–8
Economics essays, 7, 122, 130, 135, 193, 196
edition of book, 60
editorial, 3
elderly, 87–8
employment, men and women, 78–9
English essays, 130, 134, 145–7, 156–8, 191–2, 194, 196–7
Equal Opportunities Commission (EOC), 65, 71–3, 79
essay, 121–158
    analysing questions, 121–129, 141
    factual, 136–140
    instruction, 129–130, 192–8
    introduction to, 131, 133–4, 137, 151, 153–7
    judgement, 130–5
    mark, 149–152
    planning, 121–141
    (see also separate headings)
essay questions
    analysis, 124–141
    components, 128, 21
evaluation activity, 159–163
exam questions, 123, 173, 199
    make up, 198–9
    see under individual subjects
exams
    instructions, 174, 192–8
    papers, 171–8
    preparation, 173
    results, 67–70
    timing, 176
examiner, 171
Examiners Reports, 122, 129, 136

fact, in argument, 24, 80
factual essays, 136–141
    dos and don'ts, 137–8
    planning, 136–8
fiction, 54
findings, 119, 205
    presentation of, 204
flowchart, 58
forgetting curve, 48, 161–3, 174
Fowler, Norman, Rt Hon, 6, 80–1, 86, 89–90

Freeman, Richard
full stop, 185
Further and Higher Education (FHE), 71

GCSE (General Certificate of Secondary Education), x
Gibbs, Graham, 161–3, 174
girls,
    occupations, 65
    O level passes, 69
    qualifications, 67
graph, 48, 73, 75, 76, 79, 87
    column, 206

headings, 39, 59, 137
Hacker, Jim, 90
handwriting, 173
Haralambous, M, 14–16, 37–9
hospital
    beds, 82–3
    services, 84–5

ICSA exam questions, 129, 140, 193, 233
ideas, organising, 103–117
idiom, 181
index,
    book, 61
    card, 57
    subject, 57
in-patient, 81, 84–5
instruction, in questions, 124, 127–130, 192–8
instructions, writing, 108–110
interview, 119, 205
interviews, 8, 110–113
introduction,
    dos and don'ts   156
    to essays, 131, 133, 137, 151, 153–7
    paragraphs, 114
    reports, 117
ISBN, 57

jingles, 167
Joyce, James, 144
judgement essays, 131–5
    planning, 132

key aspect (of questions), 124–8, 132, 134–5, 139–141

key words, 18, 31
knowledge, 121–2, 159

Law essays, 54, 130, 135, 138, 144, 194, 197
letters,
  formal/less formal, 200–1
  layout, 200–1
  writing, 114–7
library, 50–63, 105
  lending, 54
lists, 93

main idea, 11, 31
markers, 12, 21, 43
Meacher, Michael, 80
median, 75, 208
memorizing, 164–8
memory, 48, 159–163
men,
  earnings, 75–6
  subject choice, 71
  unemployment, 78–80
microfiche, 57
mnemonics, 61, 166
mode, 208
moderator, 171
motivation, 165, 168

National Health Service, 64, 80–90
NEBBS, xiv
New Earnings Survey, 75–6
newspaper, 3, 23–4, 82–3
New Society, 75–6
notes, 27–49
  branching, 28, 33–40
  Guidelines, 30
  from lectures, 42–7
  linear, 27, 31, 40, 28, 31–2, 41
  points, 41
  review, 47–8
non-fiction, 56

observations in reports, 118
Observer, 82–3, 87–8
occupations, men and women, 76
  low paid, 77
Oracle, 51, 103
organisation, personal, 93
Orwell, George, 156–8
Othello, 145–7

outpatient, 85
overview, 37, 163

paragraphs,
  in essays, 133
  identifying, 107
  plan for, 108, 141, 143
  relevance, 145–9
  structure, 103–6, 141, 143, 147
patients, 80–90
percentages, 65–7, 68–71
periodicals, 52
plan
  article, 113–4
  essay, 121–141
  outline, 128, 132
  paragraph, 104–8
plug, how to wire, 109
Politics essays, 129–130, 132, 147–153, 189–191, 193–4, 196–7, 224–5
poverty, 14–17, 33–40, 123–7, 210–1, 214
preface, 61
presentation of information, 203
Prestel, 51, 103–4
procedure, (in reports) 117–8, 205
profile, 170
project, xiv,
  sources for, 103
pronunciation, 181
proof reading, 189–192
publication date, 58
publisher, 60
punctuation, 184–8

qualifications of school
  leavers 67–9
questionnaire, 118, 202–3
questions, essay (see 'essay
  questions')
questions,
  ask, 126
  of data, 64
  in reading, 4–5, 14, 18
quotation marks, 187
quotations, layout of 187

read, 4–5, 19
  in detail, 6, 17–23
  for pleasure, 6

reading,
  critical, 6, 23, 60
  eye movements, 25, 123
  strategy, 17
  techniques, 5–6
  See also 'scan', 'skim', 'SQ3R'
recall, 4–5, 19, 30, 48
recommendations, 119, 207
reference books, 53
reference, terms of, 117–8, 205
rehearsal, 162–3
remembering, 159–167
report, 80, 117–120, 205–7
research,
  skills, 50
  question, 64–80
retelling, 147
review, xi,
  notes, 47–9, 162–3
  in reading, 4–5, 19, 47–8
revision,
  group, 173
  period, 171–3
  timetable, 171
rhyme, 164
rhythm, 164
rote learning, 167
Rowntree, Seebohm, 14–17, 33–9,
  45
Royal Society of Arts (RSA), xvi

scanning, 4–7
school leavers
  occupations, 65
  O level grades, 69
  qualifications, 67
Self Checks, xi
semi-colons, 188
sexes, equality, 64
shopping list, 101–2
skill,
  learning as a, 165
  writing, 101
skim reading, 6–17
  passage, 8–10
  chapter, 13–17
Social Trends, 67, 69, 84–5, 89
Sociology, 14–16, 37–9, 154–5
  essays, 123–7, 144, 154–5, 194–6
source
  of data, 66, 68, 70, 72, 74

  Government, 74
  of information, 30
speech
  Norman Fowler, 81
  parts of, 181
  marks, 187
spelling, 181–2
spider, (See 'notes, branching')
sprays (See 'notes, branching')
SQ3R, 4–5, 13–4, 18, 30, 65
statistics, 62–88, 207, 64–90
studying,
  dos and don'ts, 96–7
  problems, 91
  suggestions, 92–4
subject
  choice, 71
  in essay questions, 124–5, 127–8
subtitle, 60
survey, 118, 202–4
  critical, 61
  in reading, 4–5
syllabus, xii–xvi, 173

table, 67, 71, 84–5, 89
Tamil, 25
tape recorder, 188, 203
terms of reference, 118, 205
Thatcher, Margaret, 80
time,
  in exams, 176–7
  finding, 94–6
  organise, 94–6, 171
title, book, 60
tone, 116–7
topic sentences, 7, 104–6, 142–4,
  156–7
Townsend, Peter, 39, 44

understanding, 121, 159, 165
unemployment, 78–80

view, point of, 23
vocabulary, 182
void, in exams, 178

waiting lists, 80–2, 88–9
women,
  earnings, 76
  occupations, 72–4, 76

women (*cont'd.*)
  subject choice, 69
  unemployment, 78–80
  working, 72–80
word processor, 106, 109
words,
  history, 182
  meanings, 181
  roots, 182
  significant, 125–8

writing
  article, 110–4
  journalistic, 10
  linking, 12
  paragraphs, 103–114
  poor, 11
  skill, 101
  structure, 7

Youth Training Scheme (YTS), 65